PROFESSIONAL EXPERIENCE & THE INVESTIGATIVE IMAGINATION

This book explains how creative writing can be used successfully in the context of professional education. It argues that there is a role for this imaginative style of work in an area that has traditionally favoured a more distanced approach to reporting on professional experience.

This volume is based on many practical examples drawn from several years' experience of running courses for social workers, nurses, teachers, managers and higher education staff, in which participants explore their professional practice through imaginative forms of writing. These are either 'fictional stories' – leading to discussions of the story's implications for practice – or 'patchwork texts' – in which situations are explored through a variety of linked pieces of writing in different forms or written from different points of view. The participants' experience of the work is presented through a discussion of interviews and evaluative documents, and the book includes a set of distance-learning materials for those wishing to undertake such work for themselves or to establish similar courses.

The book makes available a new and more broadly based approach to the process of professional reflection, and has general relevance for debates about increasing access to higher education qualifications.

Richard Winter is Professor of Education at Anglia Polytechnic University, where **Alyson Buck** is Senior Lecturer in Mental Health and **Paula Sobiechowska** is Senior Lecturer in Social Work.

PROFESSIONAL EXPERIENCE & THE INVESTIGATIVE IMAGINATION

The ART of reflective writing

*Richard Winter and Alyson Buck and
Paula Sobiechowska*

London and New York

First published 1999
by Routledge
11 New Fetter Lane, London EC4P 4EE

Simultaneously published in the USA and Canada
by Routledge
29 West 35th Street, New York, NY 10001

Routledge is an imprint of the Taylor & Francis Group

Typeset in Baskerville by Routledge

Printed and bound in Great Britain by
Biddles Ltd, Guildford and King's Lynn

British Library Cataloguing in Publication Data
A catalogue record for this book is available from
the British Library

Library of Congress Cataloging-in-Publication Data
Winter, Richard
Professional experience and the investigative imagination: the art of reflective
writing / by Richard Winter, Alyson Buck, Paula Sobiechowska.
p. cm.
Includes bibliographical references and index.
(alk.paper)
1. Professional education. 2. Practicums. 3. Creative writing–Study and
teaching. I. Buck, Alyson. II. Sobiechowska, Paula. III. Title.
LC1072.P73 W55 1999   99-12916
378'.013–dc21   CIP

ISBN 0–415–19542–X (hbk)
ISBN 0–415–19543–8 (pbk)

To all the professional practitioners whose stories and reflective writing have provided such inspiration over the years but whose work could not be included in this book simply because there wasn't enough space

CONTENTS

CONTENTS

PREFACE

The writing of this book has been a combination of, and alternation between, individual and collective work on the part of the three authors.

The initial idea for story-writing workshops as a basis for professional reflection first occurred to one of us (Richard Winter) outside a restaurant in Greenwich one evening in 1985. From then on he introduced story-writing into a number of professional inquiry courses, and initiated the Reflective Writing course at the University in 1993. He was responsible for the writing of Chapters 1, 2, 3, 4, 7 and the Epilogue.

Paula Sobiechowska and Alyson Buck were among the earliest participants in the reflective writing course, and the course soon involved all three of us in a close working partnership as joint tutors, planning the sequence of activities, choosing illustrative material, offering guidance to individual participants on the latter stages of their work, and assessing the final assignments. In 1995 Paula decided to undertake a systematic evaluation of the course, and the main part of Chapter 5 consists of extracts from her M.A. dissertation which reports her study. Chapter 6 was initiated and written by Alyson, reporting the successive personal phases of her involvement with the work.

However, each chapter has been discussed by all of us, and the final version has almost always involved rewording and restructuring as well as additions to and omissions from the original draft. The overall structure of the book has also been reworked several times as a result of our joint discussions.

So the text as a whole represents a statement to which all three of us are committed, even though different chapters were initially drafted by one or other of us, and thus retain the style and emphasis of the individual author. Thus sometimes we write in the singular ('my argument') and sometimes in the plural ('our book'), and we hope that this preserves a sense of the balance between individual and collective work, without creating confusion. Even more importantly, of course, the book presents material written by participants in a course which has become a jointly shared project, particularly with regard to Chapters 3 and 4; and much of the most important writing which follows is not so much 'our' work at all, but that of the course participants, to whom we would like to take this opportunity of expressing both our admiration and our indebtedness.

Richard Winter
Alyson Buck
Paula Sobiechowska

Address for correspondence:
Anglia Polytechnic University
School of Community Health and Social Studies
East Road
Cambridge CB1 1PT
E-mail: r.j.winter@anglia.ac.uk

ACKNOWLEDGEMENTS

The writing of this book was largely made possible by the award of a Fellowship by the Leverhulme Trust to Richard Winter during the academic years 1997–9, thereby providing funds for secretarial assistance and the most precious gift of all: time.

Particular thanks to Gillie Bolton for illuminating conversations about her long experience with creative writing courses. A number of her thoughts have been incorporated into specific activities of the Reflective Writing course, and are further acknowledged in Chapter 4.

Sincere thanks to the following for kindly finding time to read and make helpful comments on early drafts of individual chapters: David Ball, Gillie Bolton, Dawn Hillier, Gill Kent, Vivien Nice, Gill Plummer, Stephen Rowland, and in particular, Susan Hart.

And many thanks to Helen Fairlie of Routledge for her always helpful combination of challenge and encouragement throughout the development of the book.

Thanks also to Nelly Radionovas, who did much of the early work of typing manuscripts and transcribing tape recordings.

Many of our nursing and social work colleagues in the University have provided general support and encouragement, which has been much appreciated.

Permission to reprint copyright work is acknowledged as follows:

Extracts from V. S. Naipaul's *Finding The Centre* are reprinted by permission of Gillon Aitken Associates Ltd.

'Starting where we are' (© 1985 V. S. Naipaul) by Valerie Hannagan, from *Taking Reality by Surprise: Writing for Pleasure and Publication*, edited by Susan Sellers, first published by The Women's Press Ltd, 1991, 34 Great Sutton Street, London EC1V 0DX, is used by permission of The Women's Press Ltd.

The extract from *Old Glory* by Jonathan Raban, first published in 1981 in Great Britain by Harvill, © Jonathan Raban 1981, is reproduced by permission of The Harvill Press.

Extracts from Penelope Lively's story 'A Christmas card to one and all', in

ACKNOWLEDGEMENTS

Beyond the Blue Mountains, published by Viking/Penguin, 1997, are reprinted by permission of Penguin Books Ltd and David Higham Associates.

The extract from *Wild Mind* by Natalie Goldberg, published in the USA by Bantam in 1990 and in the UK by Rider in 1991, is reprinted by permission of Bantam Books, a division of Random House Inc., USA and Random House UK Ltd.

Extract from *Out of Mind* by J. P. Bernlef, London, Faber & Faber, 1988.

Extracts from 'Reflective writing on practice: professional support for the dying', by Brenda Landgrebe and Richard Winter, *Educational Action Research*, vol. 2, no. 1, 1994, are reprinted by permission of the editors.

Extracts from the article 'Interviewers, interviewees and the exercise of power: fictional-critical writing as a method for educational research', by Richard Winter, *British Educational Research Journal*, vol. 17, no. 1, 1991, are reprinted by permission of Carfax Publishing Limited, P.O. Box 25, Abingdon, Oxfordshire OX14 3UE.

Extracts from *Learning From Experience*, 1989, by Richard Winter, are reprinted by permission of Falmer Press.

LIST OF STORIES AND PATCHWORK TEXTS

Note: The names of all people referred to in either the stories or the patchwork texts are of course fictitious.

Stories

Chapter 1

Chapter 2

Chapter 4

1

REFLECTING ON EXPERIENCE AND THE IMAGINATIVE CONSTRUCTION OF MEANING

Writing and sharing 'fictions'

Prologue

The general argument of this book is that the role of the creative, 'artistic' imagination has been regrettably neglected in courses of professional education. It is based on several years' experience of courses for professional practitioners, where participants explore and represent their professional practice through 'artistic', 'imaginative' forms of writing, in particular, 'fiction'. We usually think of the term 'fiction' as referring to events that didn't actually happen, characters who don't actually exist, i.e. a sort of 'fantasy' – as opposed to the 'facts' or 'theory' of 'non-fiction'. And that is indeed part of what this book is about – exploring experience by *imagining* 'stories'. But the word 'fiction' also has a broader meaning, derived from its Latin origin, 'fingere' – meaning 'to shape, to fashion, to mould', and it is this meaning which is more central to our argument. So writing 'fictions', in the title above, refers generally to the process of exploring and reflecting on the meanings of experience by representing it in forms of writing which have been shaped by the writer's imagination. By 'imagination' we don't just mean general mental agility and resourcefulness; we mean specifically the creative faculty which shapes the raw material of experience into *artistic* form.

Of course, the artistic imagination uses many different media (paint, music, dance, sculpture, and so on) and so our general argument could, in principle, be expanded and adapted to suggest the value of all these media in exploring the meanings of our professional experience. But we focus on just one medium – writing. We celebrate the learning potential of the writing process, but suggest that the largely analytical forms of writing in which we are usually asked to explore and represent our understanding of experience are too limited: they do not draw on artistic and imaginative capacities which we all possess, so that many people are prevented from doing justice to the power and subtlety of their

1

thinking. Hence, our argument is not simply that the artistic imagination could play a larger role in professional learning, but that it *should* do so.

Most of the book is centred on examples of imaginative work by a range of professional practitioners (nurses, social workers, schoolteachers, managers, university lecturers, counsellors) exploring their practice by means of stories, poems, satires, fictionalised descriptions, etc. We begin with these examples almost immediately, but this brief prologue provides a preliminary statement, a general summary and a 'menu' for what is to follow.

In an important respect, this book is a challenge – a challenge to current conceptions of the role of imaginative literature in society and in education. The world of literary art is conventionally seen as the specialist realm of famous novelists, dramatists and poets, in which the rest of us think of ourselves as merely spectators. But let us remember that the term 'artistry' is regularly applied to common features of our everyday performances. There is, we say, an 'art' to parenting, to packing a suitcase, to driving a car, to organising a party, and – of course – to the skilful practices of nursing, social work, teaching, management, and so on. The 'artistry' of reflective practice, says Donald Schön, refers to that close link between expert action and understanding which occurs whenever we deal sensitively and effectively with 'situations of uncertainty, insta-bility, uniqueness, and value-conflict' (Schön 1983: p. 50). In other words, 'artistry' is required on all those many occasions when there is no simple general rule, no single 'right way' of doing things. And yet, in spite of Schön's repeated references to the artistry of skilful professional performance, he nowhere suggests that artistic means of expression might be valuable or appropriate as a way of representing practitioners' understanding of their work.

But if many (or even most) people regularly demonstrate a capacity for artistry in their actions, why should we not assume that they can use artistic means for expressing their understandings of those actions? And indeed, our work suggests that professional practitioners do indeed have a capacity for repre-senting and exploring their professional lives in the artistic medium of fiction, which they themselves find both surprising and impressive. The examples presented in this and the following chapters are intended to show the scope and nature of their work and to indicate its professional value. In this way our argu-ment is fundamentally about widening access to advanced qualifications: it introduces formats for representing professional understanding which enable practitioners to draw on the full range of their cultural resources and the full range of their capacities (including imaginative empathy), rather than requiring them always to present their understandings within the restricted but normally dominant modes of 'description' and 'analysis'.

In our work over the past six years, we have developed two approaches to the use of imaginative writing as a medium for reflection: first, the writing and sharing of short fictional stories; and second, the production of what we term 'patchwork texts', in which different forms of writing are 'shaped', 'fashioned' and assembled to explore the relationship between a variety of perspectives.

Both approaches involve the sharing of short pieces of writing, so that writers can learn from several readers how their writing may be interpreted in different ways, and incorporate this learning as a 'critical commentary' on their original text. (Hence earlier versions of the ideas presented in this book used the term 'fictional-critical writing' to describe the overall process – see Winter 1986; 1989; 1991; Bolton 1994). In their different ways, both stories and patchwork texts take advantage of the 'openness' of artistic representations of meaning; they shape experience into meanings which are purposeful and yet ambiguous and inevitably incomplete, and they represent experience in such a way that the form itself suggests that interpretations are open to question and critique. In this sense, then, they both use the methods of 'fiction' (shaping experience through artistic form) to represent the 'uncertainty, instability, uniqueness and value-conflict' which, as Schön says, is characteristic of professional work. These two approaches to the use of fiction as a method for professional reflection are introduced separately in the next two sections of this chapter.

The plan of the rest of the book is as follows. Chapter 2 begins with an introduction to the nature of 'stories', describes the story-writing workshops, and presents a collection of stories written by professional practitioners concerning an aspect of their work experience, together with discussions of each story's professional significance. Chapter 3 gives, first, further explanation of the concept of the 'patchwork text'; second, a description of the University 'Reflective Writing Course' in which the patchwork text is the basic format for participants' writing; and third, a number of examples of the work produced in this format. Chapter 4 consists of 'distance learning' course materials, which enable readers, if they wish, to work through, step by step, the same process as the participants in the reflective writing course whose work is presented in Chapter 3. Groups of practitioners could use this chapter, together with the rest of the book, as the basis for a sequence of professional development workshops; and tutors responsible for professional education courses (whether in universities or in the workplace) could use it (or adapt it) as the basis for their own courses. Chapter 5 describes and discusses the impact of the 'fictional' approach to reflection, based on interviews with a number of participants and on their own written evaluations. Chapter 6 is a detailed case study of one participant's involvement, first as a student and then as a tutor; it then describes the impact of this method of working on her subsequent practice and on her personal response to a bereavement. Chapter 7, which may be of particular interest to staff responsible for professional education and training and also to staff involved in teaching 'literature', provides a detailed theoretical elaboration of the argument outlined above, concerning the relationship between the educational processes of 'reflection' and the creative aesthetic work of the imagination in producing 'fictional' representations of experience; tracing the argument to its philosophical roots and drawing out its political and cultural implications. Finally, the brief Epilogue presents a couple of examples to reinforce the parallel between the cultural role of the artist and that of the reflective practitioner.

The book as a whole is intended to provide sufficient examples and explanations to enable practitioners and professional educators to try out for themselves an innovatory approach to professional development, using what we take to be the widespread (but curiously ignored) human capacity for understanding experience through imaginative representation.

Sharing stories

Let us take a look through this window of the university building and see what is going on. At one end of the room is the usual whiteboard and overhead projector, and a litter of furniture is pushed to the edges to create a space for three separate circles of five or six chairs. The people occupying the chairs may be social workers, or nurses, or teachers, or health visitors, or school teachers, or university lecturers, or managers, or counsellors, or doctors. And what they are doing – with great concentration – is reading and discussing the 'stories' concerning their professional work which they have written since the previous session, a week ago, when the idea was introduced and the task explained.

At the moment this group is reading a story by Christine Dale, a social worker. It is neatly typed on two sides of A4, about 800 words, and is called 'Great expectations', and can be summed up as follows:

> A client has a dream in which a social worker arrives bathed in light, a fairy godmother figure, called Pandora. The client's children are Red Riding Hood, Cinderella and Jack (of beanstalk fame), and in complaining to the social worker of her difficulties with them, she comically turns the three fairy stories of children's heroic initiative upside down to provide symptoms of 'problem' behaviour! ('Jack will not do as he's told. … He's dug up the few flowers that we had and planted this bloody great plant in the back yard.') The fairy godmother social worker opens her bag and brings out magical gifts for the children – a coach and six white horses. The children step into it and wave to their mother. At this point the client is awakened from her dream by a knocking on the door : 'It's probably that bloody social worker again.' (The End).

Now the group have finished reading and start to discuss what they think the story is saying, while Christine listens and makes notes. Clearly, it is about the unrealistic expectations to which the social work profession is subjected. As though they could suddenly wave a wand and change clients' lives! And anyway, what would happen if such dreams could be realised, since the client seems to have an excessively negative view of her children, and seems even to want them to vanish! Furthermore, the fairy godmother social worker is called Pandora, and her ability to produce limitless gifts from her capacious bag (like Mary Poppins) is actually very worrying, because when Pandora's box was opened, all the evils of humankind were let loose, leaving us only 'hope'. So this seems to be a story about the dangers of unrealistic expectations on both sides: social workers' powers are limited, and that is as it should be: professionals and clients are both liable to be misled by their 'dreams'. There is a lot of careful poring over the text to see what it actually says, and much serious discussion of the nature of the professional role – as it is and as it is idealised – as well as considerable laughter.

The two sessions on story-writing came at the beginning of a course where the participants' main task was the compilation of a 'journal' of reflections on their professional work. The purpose of the story sessions was to broaden their sense of what might be important themes to look for in their own interpretations of events. The suggestion, the previous week, that they should write a fictional story based on their professional life had initially been greeted, as usual, with anxiety. They associated 'writing' with, on the one hand, producing a professional case report, or on the other, an academic essay or perhaps making descriptive entries in a diary. The notion of a 'story' offered a somewhat worrying form of liberation from these familiar formats and often evoked distant but still powerful memories of not being 'good at' a school subject with the curious title 'English'. Writing 'stories', they had assumed, was either for children or for 'specialists' – Jane Austen, perhaps, or Graham Greene, or Barbara Cartland.

Once upon a time (so the story goes) everyone used to be a story-teller. Every traveller, from nearby or afar, was expected to have a tale to tell; personal experience was recreated and represented, shaped, framed and structured into performances for collective entertainment. And not only travellers: there was pleasure to be gained from celebrating the familiar – anecdotes concerning local events and characters and myths embodying timeless patterns of experience. So stories were exchanged – round the fire, in the shade of a tree, in the village inn and in the workshop – to pass the time on a journey (Chaucer's *Canterbury Tales*) or even while waiting for an outbreak of plague to abate (Boccaccio's *Decameron*). But, this story continues, that happy time is now past. The popular and universal art of story-telling has been extinguished by the passive habits of reading professionally published novels and watching the products of the film and TV industry. This is a popular myth of cultural decline, feeding the pleasures of nostalgia as we shake our heads lamenting lost arts, skills and forms of social relationship.

But there is another, contrasting story – that the art of the story is alive and well. In the offices and canteens of workplaces, in the staffrooms of schools, colleges and universities; in pubs and parks, on beaches and round dinner tables; stories are told of the bizarre/comical/extraordinary/'typical'/ depressing/delightful behaviour of acquaintances, relatives, colleagues, bosses, customers, students, clients and patients. The specialisation of life in modern societies means that we are all travellers in realms unknown to some of our neighbours, while the mass media remind us endlessly of the themes which provide a framework of general significance both for public events and for individual experience: technological progress and social suffering, oppression and resistance, catastrophe and hope, glamour and sleaze, the investigation of wrongdoing and incompetence, and (above all) issues of justice and injustice. Moreover, our ancient ability to tell stories orally is now enhanced by our familiarity with the written narrative. And whereas the oral narrative has to have a simplicity and directness to be immediately understood there and then by the listener, the structure of the written text can be more complex and allusive, because it can be re-read, pondered at length, and analysed in the light of alternative interpretations.

A 'high tech' version of this latter story is also gaining ground, in which stories are shared by e-mail or the internet. At the press of a key or the click of a mouse my story is transmitted to any number of readers, over any distance; and – within minutes – my printer is reeling off their various responses for me to ponder.

Hence the feasibility and the value of writing and sharing stories in a course aiming to develop a 'reflective' understanding of professional experience. The first time I tried out the idea, I shared students' initial anxiety. Now, years later, I can respond to their worries by saying, confidently: 'You will be amazed at how "interesting" you will find other people's stories and how interesting they will find yours. You will also be taken aback at the "quality" of the writing, although that will not be the point at issue because you will be discussing "non-judgementally" what the story seems to mean, what effect it has on you, its professional significance.'

Although the initial hesitancy is real, the responses afterwards are immediately enthusiastic. Here are the evaluative comments written by the group we have just been observing:

- An excellent medium for exploring issues and dilemmas … for freeing up one's own thoughts and feelings, as well as gaining understanding of common problems.
- The session drew out implicit feelings and values and made them explicit; acknowledged and identified professional feelings that could impede good professional practice; created an awareness of real issues that may have been dormant; a therapeutic experience.
- It was interesting to see the different interpretations that could be made from one piece of work – an interesting exercise in the need for awareness and openness to other options.
- Enjoyable and creative – interesting to hear others' stories and their perspectives on our own story.
- All the creativity we hold within us – and so rare to get the chance to use it in the systems we are caught up in!
- I have in the past not considered writing to be a skill that I possess, certainly not this type of writing. Nevertheless, I felt freed up to write in a way I found to be very enjoyable, and to my surprise it evoked reactions I did not expect. A powerful tool I may well introduce to others.

But so far we have only seen a single example of a practitioner's 'story', and there is a danger that this could leave a misleadingly narrow impression of the sort of work that is produced. One of the reasons for both the success of story-writing sessions, and also for the initial anxiety about them, is a sense of uncertainty about what might be meant by 'a story', and one of the points which is noted immediately in the group discussions is the enormous variety of forms that people use. Because a story is not simply a narrative, and a fictional story is not simply a narrative of 'imaginary' events which did not actually occur, but (as we have already noted) a portrayal of events, people and scenes which has been consciously shaped and structured by the writer. And if there is a process of shaping, there is a purpose which guides the shaping. Thus a story, in the work described in this book, means a piece of writing where the raw material of memory and imagination has been purposefully fashioned, moulded, selected, combined and edited, to give it (or bring out) a sense of its significance.

There are many ways in which this can be done, many ways in which we know already how it might be done, from our prior understanding of the structure of written texts. This variety, and our awareness of this variety, is important, because it explains why the instruction to write 'a story' or 'a fiction' is, after an initial worry, experienced as a freedom rather than a constraint. So to remind ourselves of some of the many ways in which 'a story' can be constructed, let us look at the variety of forms which members of this one group used, quite spontaneously, to shape their professional experience, to convey their sense of its significance; or, in other words, quite simply, to 'make a point'. In this way we will, I hope, get a broader sense of the the imaginative, creative, shaping process which the rest of the book will explore in detail.

1   We have already seen Christine Dale's method: the conventional format of the dream as a way of contrasting reality with imaginary possibilities. She also builds her story round other stories that are already familiar – the three nursery tales, and the myth of Pandora, so that several sets of meanings are made to interweave.

2   In 'Sam', by Esther Wilkins, a health visitor, fitting in some necessary shopping at the end of an exhausting day, finds a former client on the checkout who wishes to tell her about the progress of her little boy, Sam. Sam had been a sickly child and had been much indulged because he was 'special' although he and his mother also wanted him to be 'like the other boys'. Now, his mother complains, he is extremely 'naughty', but is this because he is 'special', or – on the contrary – because he is 'like the other boys'? However, the story is also about *boundaries* in the role of the community-based professional: does the narrator, the health visitor, have to continue to be 'special', even at the supermarket checkout?

   (Esther sets the account of a former client as a memory or flashback within the framework of an incident in the present, so that the two elements of the story are used to throw light on each other.)

3   'Timmy the tiniest coach', by Pam Jennings, is written in the style of the
     popular children's stories about 'Thomas the tank engine'. It tells of Timmy
     the railway coach, who every day has to go either with Harold the
     Hightown engine or with Lennie the Lakeside engine, who 'were always
     arguing about who was going to pull him because he wasn't a bit heavy and
     told them stories and sang funny songs along the way to make the journey
     go quicker'. Timmy never knows which engine he will have to go with each
     day, and he also wants to spend some time in the shed on his own, but the
     stationmaster is unsympathetic. In the end he refuses to move and gets his
     way, thanks to the intervention of the 'Chief Station Officer' who has a few
     words with the engine drivers and the stationmaster. The author, a social
     worker concerned with child protection, is suggesting that the needs and
     wishes of the child need to be taken into account in making care arrange-
     ments; and it is deeply worrying that Timmy has to resort to outright
     defiance and that the Chief Officer has to be brought in to the case.
        (Pam's method is that of allegory – the apparent setting is fanciful (a chil-
     dren's story in this case) but each detail can be read off as referring to
     another, wholly serious reality.)

4   In 'Ignorance', by Naomi Ball, events in a maternity ward are narrated by a
     social worker who has just had her first child and is waiting anxiously to
     start to experience 'maternal' feelings. A teenage girl with learning difficul-
     ties comes over to her to complain that when her baby is born it will be
     taken away by 'The Social'. When she leaves to go downstairs for a cigarette
     the middle-class women in the neighbouring beds suggest complacently that
     'people like that' ought to be sterilised. The narrator is dismayed at their
     ignorant prejudice, but then the teenager returns to introduce her parents to
     her newfound 'friend' and reaches over to pick up the narrator's baby son,
     and as she does so the story ends: 'I [the narrator/social worker] could feel
     my throat tighten and my back tense'. The maternal response has arrived at
     last, but provoked by the very prejudices (against the disadvantaged
     teenager) which she has just been criticising. The contrast between personal
     feelings and professional values – a universal dilemma?
        (A sequence of events and conversations is contrived here so that the final
     punchline draws them all together and brings out the theme which links
     what had previously seemed to be unconnected feelings and relationships.)

Here, then, are some of the manifold ways in which we know how to shape
our experience by means of a written text conceived as a 'story'. It is not
intended to be a comprehensive listing, just a note of the very different methods
used by members of one typical group (further examples are given in Chapter 2).
It is also presented as evidence that the art of writing stories is indeed (as
suggested earlier) alive and well, and widespread, and thus available to be used
as a tool for professional reflection.

Constructing a 'patchwork text'

A story always moves towards an ending. Even though the ending is often ambiguous ('open-ended'), it still represents some sort of temporary closure on a train of thought; the ending is, after all, very often the focus of the shaping process at work. So the question is: how do we 're-open' the ending of a story, in order to continue the reflective exploration that the story has started? This leads to an important practical question: how can we put together a course of professional reflection in which the process of shaping experience through fiction is continued over a period of several weeks? And our answer is: by constructing a 'patchwork text'.

A patchwork text may start from, or include, a story, but it includes a variety of different forms of writing, each of which provides a further perspective on the others. What defines a patchwork as an artistic medium is that its overall pattern is gradually assembled from smaller pieces, each of which has its own individual pattern. Thus, just as a patchwork fabric is a texture built from a variety of textures, and a design built up from a variety of sub-designs, a patchwork text is a fiction which is shaped at two levels, or twice over. Each piece is shaped in itself, but then there is the shaping of the overall meaning, as contrasting pieces of writing are put together, creating unity from the subtle parallels or stark contrasts between them. In the construction of a patchwork fabric this unified design is often planned from the outset, but sometimes each new segment is improvised, as in 'crazy patchwork' (Parker 1991: p. 34) where the unity and balance of the overall texture and design emerge gradually and even retrospectively. It is this latter process which is mirrored in the patchwork texts produced for our reflective writing courses.

By way of introducing a further perspective on the concept of the patchwork text, here, to begin with, is a pleasant scene. A narrator is telling us a story – sitting there in front of us and holding our attention – creating for us through her words the people and events she is recounting. We hang on her words, and she transports us, portraying for us the world she describes with such skill (in selecting and presenting vivid and evocative details) that it seems to become a reality – she makes us feel that we are actually there. But then, to spoil this pleasant scene, a worry arises: is there not an element of falsity at work here? Because this is, after all, only her view of the story; its reality is a creation, not a description. So if we the readers come to accept this story as reality, we are deceived; and if the story-teller is convinced by her own skill into thinking that her story is the only story, then she also is deceived. Then, to confuse matters further, here come the philosophers, telling us that there is no such thing as an accurate representation anyway; that all descriptions and narrations are selective – based on value judgements which can never be absolutely justified and which will be shared by some people but never by everyone. So, the argument runs, our narrator should not deceive us (and herself) by creating the illusion that this story is *the* story, but should make it clear (through the form of the narration) that there are many possible stories, that no story is ever the only story. Consequently, we should not think of narrators as encompassing an 'overall' perspective within a single authoritative 'voice', and narrators should not think of themselves in this way. Instead, a narrative should recognise that it is merely assembling a variety of voices and perspectives into a 'multi-voiced' text, presenting contrasting points of view through the eyes and voices of different characters, as though they were contributing to a sort of documentary, or as though they were actors in a drama.

Of course, the long tradition of the directly persuasive, single-voiced 'realistic' narrative is still very much with us. But the less familiar concept of the multi-voiced text (what we have called the patchwork text) has the merit of drawing attention directly to that essential process of fiction which makes it so appropriate a method for exploring the meanings of experience: collecting different aspects and interpretations of events and examining the relationships between them. Indeed, the argument for the value of the patchwork text could be made more strongly and more generally: its flexibility, together with its essential characteristic of seeking a provisional unity within varied material, make it in many ways a more 'natural' format for the presentation of complex understandings than the sustained analytical essay which has come to play such a dominant role in educational assessment processes. More precisely, whereas the analytical essay focuses exclusively on cognitive and logical skills (and thus favours the special talents of a minority) the patchwork text enables students also to draw on their imaginative, empathetic, affective and aesthetic modes of understanding, and thus takes more account of current theories of the variegated structure and distribution of human capacities (Gardner 1983). Perhaps, therefore, the patchwork text may be, in quite general terms, a more appropriate format for representing the complexity of understanding in a society which hopes to provide 'higher education' as an opportunity for the *majority* of its citizens.

So, how do participants in the reflective writing courses set about constructing a patchwork text? What happens is this. The course participants form small working groups of four or five members, which remain constant throughout the course. Each week everyone brings along several copies of a short piece of writing – a description, an account of an incident, a story, a poem, a dialogue (remembered or imagined), etc. To begin with, interpretations of the meaning of the piece are exchanged by the readers; but then further questions are raised. How might these events be portrayed from a different point of view? Or, what might be thought of as, perhaps, 'missing' from this piece of writing? Consequently, what is the next piece of writing going to be, which might explore this missing dimension? In this way the group sharing process suggests to the participants how they might continue their writing and their reflections. The assignment submitted at the end of the course is a selection from the various pieces of writing, arranged in a sequence which may or may not be the order in which they were written, together with a final commentary which analyses the unifying theme(s) underlying the different pieces.

Here, as illustrations, are summaries of two contrasting patchwork texts produced within the reflective writing courses. The texts usually consist of five or six pieces of writing, each about a page or two long, sometimes with short linking commentaries (further examples, including longer extracts and complete texts, are presented in Chapter 3).

Assessment: 'Dream or reality?' by Liz Morris

Liz Morris is a nursing sister with responsibility for the care of all the patients in one ward of a hospital.

The first piece in Liz's patchwork is called 'Dream or reality: the stroke'. John awakes in a strange environment and wonders where he is. He realises he is in hospital but he does not understand why and has no memory of how he got there. He tries to shout for help, but no words come. He tries to get out of bed to go home to find his wife, but finds that one of his legs will not function.

> when the nurses reached him his numb leg was trapped in the cot side and he was half hanging out of the bed. They untangled him and hurled him back up the bed. 'You mustn't do that, Trevor,' they told him, 'You'll hurt yourself.' And then they went. John was left alone.

He goes to sleep hoping to wake and find it was all a dream. When he wakes up and finds his wife there he thinks it was indeed a dream. But why is his wife weeping? 'He reached out to comfort her but his arm would not move. [She] reached out to stroke his hand and he too began to cry'.

The next piece is called 'Dream or reality: 5.30'. A nurse awakes and sees her alarm clock showing 5.30. The beginning of another hectic day. A dizzying round of endless work is described 'with two staff off sick and no help available'. Suddenly:

> she noticed one of the patients climbing over the cot sides. 'Oh no,' she thought, 'Not geriatric gymnastics, not now!' Quickly she called for help and deftly put him back to bed. 'You mustn't do that, Trevor,' she said, wincing slightly as she recalled he preferred to be called John. Still that wasn't important right now, she had other priorities.

Exhausted, she falls asleep and then wakes to find her alarm clock showing 5.30. Thinking that the day has not yet begun she is relieved at the thought that it had all been a dream. But then she realises that the time is 5.30 in the afternoon, and that it has not been a dream.

Then there is a 'Commentary' in which Liz draws attention to the acute shortage of resources in hospitals: nurses are overstretched and cannot offer the care they know they ought to provide, so that the emotional needs of patients like John go unrecognised. Medical care has become 'a consumer-led industry' with managers always 'on the look out for increased productivity from less staff'.

Indeed, an important report on health service management has just been compiled by the chief executive of Sainsburys, a nationwide chain of *foodstores*!

This leads on to the fourth piece of writing: 'The Sainsbury's Guide to Good Management: a recipe for success?'

Take	A few tired harrassed nurses
Add	Large quantities of patients (the difficult demanding variety are best)
Mix well	
Now, in another pot	
Take	One political party with fresh, new and unpalatable ideas
Remove	All evidence of cash flow
Blend well	
Gradually	Chill public perception of the service
And	Allow all negative emotions to be displayed attractively throughout the national press
Finally	Mix all these ingredients together and simmer gently, never allowing them to come to the boil
Sit back	
Relax	
Enjoy	

In the final piece of her patchwork, Liz analyses the implications of the previous pieces of writing and provides an overall commentary on the problems of managing a hospital ward. She also notes that, although the individual pieces convey rather negative messages, she actually believes that the situation contains an 'exciting' opportunity for nurses to respond actively and positively. The crucial challenge is how to balance optimism and pessimism.

It is interesting that Liz finds that the 'dream/reality' theme which evokes very directly the patient's vulnerability in the first piece has a resonance for the wider situation, and uses it for her general title. Medical practice, and management decision-making are both forms of 'assessment': are they perhaps both currently based on 'dreams' and delusions, such as the supposed parallel between nursing and the production and marketing of food? Both this example and the next show how the fictional process of the patchwork text combines imaginary scenes and events with factual analytical writing. But we should not forget that this is true of fiction in general, and very obviously so in some cases, e.g. the whole of the science fiction genre, the many passages of historical analysis in the novels of George Eliot, and (to take a modern example) the extended accounts of the physics of ice and snow formations in Peter Hoeg's novel *Miss Smilla's Feeling For Snow*.

'Viewpoints on behaviour therapy' by Matthew Stewart

Matthew Stewart is a forensic nurse working in a special hospital for patients whose mental health problems render them dangerous to others and/or who have committed violent offences. 'Behaviour therapy' is a controversial form of treatment based on theories of 'conditioning' in the training of animals.

Matthew's first piece has the punning title 'Personal effects'. In the first section the abstract, 'kindly' voice of 'behaviour therapy' speaks:

> I can change your behaviour, make you a better person, loved (or at least tolerated) by Society. I can mould your behaviour like a potter working his clay. ... Of course it may take time and a little bit of hard work, but a myriad of our animal cousins have pulled levers, escaped from boxes, negotiated mazes and salivated into jars to demonstrate the validity of my claims. Give it a try. There's nothing to lose, is there?

In the second section a patient replies:

> I don't want to change. I don't give a damn if I'm loved or tolerated. ... Who are you to decide what I should or should not do? Who are you to steal from me a part of *my* individuality, to steal that which helps make me me. I don't want to give it a try; there's plenty to lose, not least my very identity.

The second piece is an imaginary interview which brings out the powerful prejudices and emotions of the 'average citizen'. Although the self-righteous anger is shocking, there is no mistaking its insidious appeal:

> When I think of some of the things they've done it makes my blood boil.
>
> I know what I'd do with them. ... lock them up for good as far away from civilisation as we can find. Otherwise they just get let out and the next thing you know another self-respecting citizen drops dead with some nutter's knife in his back. The Victorians weren't daft: lock them away in a nice big building with high walls and let normal people get on with their lives with one less worry on their minds ...
>
> *Would you be in favour then of some form of treatment based on punishment?*
>
> Well that seems to me a much more logical approach. For a start that's the way the world works: you do something wrong, you face the consequences. ... Whereas you guys set up an environment which bears no resemblance to reality. In fact it turns the real world on its head. Instead of sending someone to prison and punishing them you take

them off to your little holiday camp and say, 'Here's twelve quid a week; take care how you spend it'.

What about the research that suggests that punishment is not effective?

Bollocks.

Next comes an imaginary interview with 'a psychologist':

What do you think of behaviour therapy?

Well, when I was studying I didn't believe in its use at all; but since working here and seeing how effectively it works in a lot of cases I think it certainly must have a place.

Do you really get consent or do you just bribe people with a suitable reward?

It's the same thing really. We offer a reward and the client chooses to either have his reward, by not displaying a targeted behaviour, or chooses to forfeit that reward and instead display the behaviour. Voilà: consent.

The next 'interview', with 'a liberal and enlightened citizen', picks up the moral ambiguity just revealed by the psychological rationale:

It's a difficult one. I mean, where do you stop? … You're changing the way someone acts, thinks even, against their will. … The fact that, in some cases, it works is not really the issue. If someone displayed a problem behaviour, picking their nose for instance, a simple and *very* effective approach to eradicate the problem would be double amputation somewhere above the wrists. Effectiveness, therefore, I trust you agree, is not necessarily a justification.

The next piece presents the point of view of 'a nurse', who recognises the potential value of the treatment but expresses reservations. It can easily be overused, leading to treatment programmes which ignore the 'possible causes of challenging behaviour'. Some forms of behaviour offend some sections of society but don't necessarily affect a person's ability to function. So 'who decides what we use it for? Who plays God, if you like'.

Having thus displayed a variety of perspectives on the issue, with all their sometimes frightening ambiguities, crudities and contradictions, Matthew's final piece is his own analysis, drawing on some of the current literature on the subject and arguing that treatment policy must 'steer a course between the polarised views of the persons from the earlier passages'. (This final image seems particularly appropriate, since Matthew's patchwork text has used the format of a series of imaginary interviews to draw up a sort of moral, cultural and intellectual chart of this difficult topic.)

* * *

So, we have had a brief preliminary glimpse at the two sorts of work that this book will describe – the use of a single story and the use of patchwork texts where imaginary scenarios are continued, analysed and contrasted with other scenarios. But there is already a substantial tradition of work under the label of 'reflective writing', with which many readers may be familiar. So how do the ideas presented here relate to this tradition? To answer this question, and thus to complete our introduction, let us briefly consider how the two approaches we have just outlined relate to, differ from, and expand upon other more familiar forms of writing frequently used to promote 'reflection' on professional experience.

Writing fictions as a contribution to 'methods' for reflection

The publication of Schön's *The Reflective Practitioner* in 1983 was followed by several other highly influential books also emphasising the personal, experiential, explorative and – above all – the reflective nature of professional understanding; in particular: Boud *et al.* 1985; Brookfield 1990; Mezirow *et al.* 1990; Schön 1987; Tripp 1993. But although these texts (and others influenced by them) frequently invoke the term 'artistic' along with their basic terminology of critical reflection and reinterpretation of experience, they do not include the artistic, imaginative shaping of experience through the writing of fiction among their basic repertoire of activities. Our argument, in contrast, is that the operation of the artistic imagination through the writing of fiction can be understood, precisely, as a mode of critical reflection upon, and reinterpretation of, experience. This section will therefore review briefly the basic activities proposed in the seminal texts listed above in order to consider how the process of writing and sharing fiction would complement and enrich them.

Keeping a journal

Journals, in one form or another, are advocated as a general process for capturing the details of experience. When Walker (1985) elaborates what he calls the 'diversity' of forms of 'writing as an aid to reflection', he gives the following list: 'journals, diaries, record books, portfolios, verbatims, sociological diaries, dossiers, and logs' (p. 52) (see also Cameron and Mitchell 1993: 'Reflective peer journals: developing authentic nurses'). However, what is common to all these formats, with the possible exception of the 'sociological diary', is the absence of an explicit awareness of the process of *shaping* experience through selection and interpretation. Each journal entry is of course selected and shaped, but the fragmentary and chronological structure of the journal as a format means that it does not, in itself, help us become aware of exactly how we have selected and shaped – nor, therefore, of the alternative selections and shapings that might be worth considering. In contrast, if one's reflective writing is conceived as a form of fictional shaping, then entries in a journal are considered as a set of possible components of a patchwork text, constructed consciously to raise issues by placing discordant elements side by side and thereby pointing directly to ambiguities and alternatives in need of clarification.

Writing in order to structure experience

Walker's mention of a 'sociological' diary suggests, implicitly at least, a recognition that reflection needs a guiding structure. Other examples of this from the 'reflective practitioner' texts are: the analysis of parallel experiences and options (Boxer 1985), the analysis of metaphors as a way of linking specific experiences to general cultural themes (Deshler 1990), and the use of repertory grids to make explicit one's assumptions and values (Candy 1990; Gould 1996). Heron presents the process in general terms as: description followed by conceptualisation, considering alternatives and seeking theoretical explanations (Heron 1985: pp. 136–7). More precisely, instructions are often given for writing a 'critical incident', which moves from 'what happened' through personal analysis (What did I feel? What was I trying to achieve?) and analysis of alternatives (What other choices did I have?) to analysis of learning (Bulman 1994: p. 136). Broadly similar instructions are given by David Tripp, with the addition of a final phase in which one is asked to 'classify' the incident in terms of theoretical categories (Tripp 1993: p. 27).

The limitation of these approaches is that the basic method seems to be a form of unassisted self-questioning, a purely 'rational' mode of introspection with no procedures for tapping into one's imaginative resources. And, unlike the process of writing a story and collecting different readings of it, or building up a patchwork text from a series of contrasts and reflection on those contrasts, these methods do not involve consciously shaping the original representation of the experience. It is therefore not clear how the initial description will provoke the recognition of alternative interpretations. Our argument here, in other words, is that although we agree wholeheartedly with the objectives proposed here, we think that the methods they propose are 'difficult', and that if, instead, writing fiction is the starting point for the work, it is more likely that writers will easily come across a line of thought that they did not initially have in mind.

Sharing interpretations of experience

The general notion that reflection is facilitated by sharing accounts of experiences is emphasised in Main's (1985) account of cooperative learning strategies and Candy et al.'s (1985) description of 'learning conversations'. More specifically, both Brookfield's and Tripp's approaches to critical incident analysis recognise the limitations of introspection. Tripp emphasises that incidents must be written with an audience in mind, since the knowledge that one is writing for others creates 'the discipline of anticipating what others would need to know, how they might react, what they might criticise' (Tripp 1993: p. 44). For Brookfield, the point of reflecting upon critical incidents is to expose one's assumptions, and he asks practitioners to describe an incident to a group of colleagues, who then suggest what assumptions (about 'good practice') are embedded in the writer's presentation (Brookfield 1990).

Again, we would argue that where the accounts being shared are presented as 'fictional' stories, a specific freedom is provided for readers to bring their own interpretations to bear on the text; the openness with which a story conveys its meaning anticipates and welcomes alternative readings in a way that an analytical description does not. As Bruner says:

> Fiction places events in a wider 'horizon' of possibilities. ... Skilful narrative.... highlights subjective states, attenuating circumstances, alternative possibilities. ... To make a *story* good, it would seem, you must make it somewhat uncertain, somehow open to variant readings.
>
> (Bruner 1990: pp. 53–4)

The fictional format thus provides an immediate creative opportunity for the reader, and it also provides protection for the writer. The ambiguity of a story means that there is uncertainty as to where the writer stands in relation to the text. Discussion about the meaning of the text does not, therefore, put the writer 'in the dock', whereas writing a descriptive account of one's practice and then awaiting others' views as to its underlying assumptions (as Brookfield proposes) is potentially highly threatening. The same potential emotional danger is present in the process of videotaping role-plays for interpretation by a group of peers (Moffat 1996). In contrast, the relative safety of sharing a fictional story (as opposed to a descriptive account) has been specifically noted by participants in our fiction-based workshops and reflective writing courses, often with surprise and relief.

Autobiography

In some respects, autobiography as a format can have the same limitation as the journal, namely that it lacks a clear principle for structuring experience. It might thus be treated as an opportunity for 'recalling' events, i.e. providing 'data' which then require analysing. But then, where would one look for the themes to use as a basis for this analysis, so that it could gain a different perspective from the one already embodied in the descriptive recall? An external researcher can do so quite easily, of course, but this reduces writers of autobiographies to mere providers of data, instead of being theorists of their own lives (Grumet 1990: p. 324).

Moreover, insofar as reflection is, in part, a process of collaborative learning, rather than an entirely private process, the use of autobiographical writing is also beset by the danger of emotional risk already noted above. Powell (1985) gives only minimal recognition to the problem, identifying the need for 'a climate of trust' (p. 49). Peter Abbs, in contrast, presents the difficulties clearly:

> In certain students' autobiographies, we detect a nervous evasiveness, an unwillingness to step into dangerous territory, a complex detour around some massively silent obstacle. This must be accepted and respected.
>
> (Abbs 1974: p. 9)

Or, as Madeleine Grumet puts it, 'Every telling is a partial prevarication' (Grumet 1987: p. 322).

The question, then, for autobiographical writing, is: how does one balance the need for emotional safety against the educational purpose of going beyond one's starting points? A fictional story also may well be, in many ways, a partial prevarication, which is why readers' interpretations can often tell writers something they themselves had not 'noticed'. But a fictional story does not necessarily need to be written with self-protection in mind – as Abbs implies is often the case with autobiography. On the contrary, its status as a product of imagination means that writing a fiction sets us free – to range over the possibilities implicit in our experience, secure in the knowledge that no-one will be able to 'pin down' any particular motive, opinion or action as that of the author.

Finally, it is important to note that the various approaches listed above can be combined with the fiction-based approach described in this book. A brief indication of how such a combination might work, based on our own experiences, is provided at the end of Chapter 4.

Conclusion

This brings us to the end of our introductory outline. We have presented our basic argument – that current forms of writing in courses intended to foster the reflective analysis of experience have ignored the great educational potential locked in our creative capacity for writing fictions – either in the form of stories or more complex patchwork texts. We have given a preliminary indication of what practitioners' fictions are like, and of their value as explorations of professional practices and understandings. And we have indicated how such forms of writing would both enrich and facilitate the writing activities conventionally undertaken. Clearly, we have raised a host of questions and so far given only the sketchiest of answers to a very few of them. What is the general rationale for writing and sharing fictions as a mode of reflection on professional practice? What is the relationship between educational processes, imaginative creation, and the interpretation of imaginative representations of experience? What is the relation between 'fictional' accounts and 'factual' accounts of experience, between the particular and the general, and (most importantly) between 'imagination', 'reflection' and the development of professional knowledge? These questions are examined in detail in Chapter 7. But on the whole our book is organised to enable the work produced by the course participants to speak for itself; so the next two chapters present a wealth of examples – first (in Chapter 2) of stories and then (in Chapter 3) of patchwork texts. We hope that these examples will begin at least to provide support for the arguments and claims that have been put forward so far.

2

THE IMAGINATION OF MEANING

Writing and interpreting stories in a professional context

Introduction

Stories

Stories are what human beings are good at. We lead our lives steeped in stories. The shelves of bookshops are filled with classics and bestsellers, cinemas and video shops promote the latest feature films, and TV provides us with endless soaps and sitcoms, punctuated by advertisements which are also often in the form of carefully angled mini-stories. We structure experience in story form. 'So what's the story?' says the investigating detective to the police officer who discovered the body. Meaning: 'Give me your interpretation of the detail, the sequence and the pattern of what happened'. News broadcasts present events in terms of stories – some new (crimes, scandals and catastrophes), some long-running serials ('The Middle East', 'Drugs', 'Interest rates') and some simply 'good stories': 'Firecrew called out to a fire at their own fire station', 'Twins reunited after sixty years' ('human interest' equals the 'fictional' qualities of pattern, drama and irony). So, we know that everyone can appreciate stories; this chapter sets out to show that most people also know how to write them, and the value of doing so.

If we were asked why we read novels and watch films, plays, drama series and soaps, our first reply might be that it is just for 'entertainment'; but if teachers are asked why they encourage young children to read and write stories, they explain that stories are a form of learning, a way of exploring and ordering experience (Whitehead 1980: p. 49; Graves 1984: p. 88). Stories are different from other forms of narrative – diaries, histories, and autobiographies, for example – in that a story does not simply recount events, and that our interest in a story is not simply that we want to know 'what happens next'. A story is a selection of events (some real, some imaginary, many halfway between the two) which have been organised into a pattern which has a kind of general significance, and thus, in some sense, makes a 'statement'. If the entertainment value of stories lay merely in our desire to know what happens it would be difficult to explain why people often go to see the same play or film several times, and enjoy re-reading favourite novels. It would also be difficult to explain the universal appeal of the TV crime thriller, because we always know in advance that the regular stars will survive whatever danger they may temporarily find themselves in. Instead, one might suggest that each episode expresses a statement about the perpetual threat to moral and political order, about the fragility of virtue in a dangerous world: the permanence of the threat requires the eternal repetition of its overcoming.

If a story can be seen as a statement, then 'thinking up' a set of characters and a plot in which they interact (in a particular context, through a particular series of events, and with a particular outcome) is rather like exploring a 'theory' of that context and such events. The story explores a hypothesis and works towards a conclusion. And the delight in writing a story is that although you have decided on the starting points (the characters, the basic pattern of events) the details often seem to 'write themselves', as though the writing were a sort of experiment, in which the imagination is used to solve the problems posed by the relationships between the fictional characters, and between the characters you have invented and your own experience (Wright 1972: p. 24). In other words, the author's perspective on a situation is embodied in a set of significant actors (the characters of the story) each representing some important aspect of the situation, who thus act out the 'meaning' of the narrative as the 'plot' of their interactions (Lukács 1971: pp. 55–6). Any fiction can be approached in this way. For example, in A. A. Milne's 'Winnie the Pooh' books, each toy/character represents a problematic emotional and moral dimension of childhood and growing up (Piglet = cowardice/bravery; Kanga and Roo = maternal oppression/independence; Rabbit = bossiness; Owl = anxiety about being 'clever', etc.). The stories (as a whole and separately) explore the relationship between these qualities as Christopher Robin comes to terms with them, so that at the end he is emotionally prepared to leave Pooh (his infant self) behind.

A fiction is only partly 'invented'. At another level it embodies the writer's actual experiences and ideas. This is nicely illustrated by Sylvia Ashton-Warner's two books, *Spinster* and *Teacher* (Ashton-Warner 1985a, 1985b). Her novel *Spinster* contains within a fictionalised narrative an account of the author's theories of education, which she had previously tried unsuccessfully to publish directly. Five years later, following the success of the novel, she did publish the non-fiction form of these ideas, in *Teacher*, so that we can clearly see how she used the fictional form as a framework for her theories. For example, the same incidents are presented (in almost exactly the same words) in *Spinster* on pages 14, 197 and 200–1, and in *Teacher* on pages 106, 43 and 36–7. But this example also raises questions about the differences between the fiction and the non-fiction. Why does Ashton-Warner portray herself fictionally as an exiled foreigner and emotionally frustrated spinster, when she was born in New Zealand (where the events take place) and seems to have discussed her teaching regularly over lunch with her husband (Ashton-Warner 1985b: pp. 107–8)? As an answer, we might suggest that this could be her way of representing symbolically the loneliness of her educational crusade and her sense of the erotic component of the teaching process: she is, as it were, wedded to her class of Maori infants. Moreover, to put it this way makes it clear that fiction does not simply contain ideas that an author already knows, but is also a means whereby the implications of incompletely formed ideas can be explored. In fictions, authors play with ideas, images, events, people, and situations from their own lived experience, so that even where (as in Ashton-Warner's case) the fiction is in part a self-description, it is always a self-exploration as well.

There is another sense in which writing is an act of self-exploration, namely as a struggle with the act of writing itself. It is possible to take this process for granted and write a fiction which seems to be simply descriptive of characters and events, but very often an element is included which acts as a sort of concealed confession: 'This is not actual reality; this is me, trying to make sense of reality by writing a story about it'. So, we have films made about film-makers and musicals about the staging of a musical. Shakespeare the playwright makes Hamlet stage a play as one of his attempts to find out what is 'really' going on. And indeed, one of the commonest story patterns is that of an investigation to find 'the truth', so that the events of the story describe the same process as the writer is engaged in through the writing of the story. All hero-investigators (detectives, journalists, lawyers, etc.) are thus indirectly representing their authors, as seekers in search of meaning. For example, in the film *The Third Man* (based on a story by Graham Greene) we mainly remember images of the corruptions of post-war Vienna – crumbling mansions, Orson Welles in the sewers – but the central figure in the narrative is Harry Lime's friend Holly, a writer of thrillers, who – like his creator and like us as we watch the film – is trying to find out the truth, about Harry and about his world. In this sense, stories are often reflexive: part of their meaning concerns the nature of the storying process; they undercut any claim to a single definitive meaning by recognising that the process of constructing meanings (how the story came to be written) is itself part of the story.

Another important point about stories is that they are always open to different interpretations, so that the statements they make are always, to some extent, ambiguous. For example, Richmal Crompton's 'William' stories can be read as somewhat sexist celebrations of 'boys will be boys'. Alternatively they can be interpreted as a critical analysis of the way in which male children, excluded from participation in the adult male world, take refuge in fantasy adult role play, which continually brings them into conflict with the real adult authority of the world from which they have been excluded. Fictions, then, select characters, events and situations in such a way as to bring out the ambiguities and contradictions of experience. Like myths, they are 'engendered by the inherent disparity of the world' (Lévi-Strauss 1981: p. 603) – by, for example, the inherent oppositions between power and weakness, youth and age, heroes and villains, or professionals, clients and bureaucrats. But the oppositions are never simple: power has its vulnerability, and weakness its sources of strength; the hero may go to heaven, but 'the devil has all the best tunes'. In this way, since the statements made by a story are always ambiguous, it is perhaps more accurate to think of them as posing questions. Is this character admirable or not? Is this situation regrettable or not? The answer is always: 'yes and no'. In this respect, stories vary: some are less ambiguous than others. But no story is entirely without ambiguity, and so no story fails entirely to pose the reader a question (Belsey 1980: pp. 90–3). At its simplest, the ambiguity of a story is created by the fact that the reader may sympathise more or less with each of its various characters, and – similarly – in order to create the characters, the author must (in different ways) identify with each one. Consequently, the ambiguities of a fiction may be thought of as representing (in some sense) the ambiguities in the author's and the reader's personal awareness. The questions posed by the text are questions about the writer's and the reader's own experiences and values.

The richness of a story, then, is that its meanings are always implicit, so that it immediately suggests a discussion about its various possible meanings. Having written a story which consciously explores an aspect of their experience, writers can then learn by hearing the various interpretations of different readers, which may reveal aspects of the story and of their own original experience of which they had only been dimly aware. There are no right or wrong answers here, except that the interpretation of any single detail needs to take into account other details and the pattern of the story as a whole. Writers are not told by readers what their story 'really' means, as though they were being subjected to a psychological analysis; neither do writers tell readers what the 'real point' of the story is, i.e. what the writer had 'intended': rather, the story is a neutral ground, where different worlds of experience can intersect and interact. Of course, the fictional form allows unconscious meanings to surface temporarily in odd details and patterns, both in what the writer has included and in how the reader responds. But the fictional form also allows disclosure to be controlled: the discussion of a story can only be about the implications of the text itself, not on what it 'reveals' about the writer, since the relationship between the writer as a person and their fictional text is always unclear, even to the writer. And interpretations are not simply found in the text but also brought to the text from the reader's experience. Hence the fictional form creates emotional safety for both writers and readers: although stories raise questions and previously unconscious themes, the discussion of a story does not provide final answers or a diagnosis, but opens up further lines of reflective thought.

Many of these points will be illustrated in the following stories, which were written by participants as part of a process of reflecting on their professional experience. The professions represented are: nursing, nurse education, community nursing, social work, schoolteaching, counselling and theatre management. They have been selected on the basis that each illustrates a different way of using the conventions and methods of story-writing to achieve that generalised but ambiguous significance already referred to. Other approaches to writing stories have already been presented in Chapter 1; however, there is no suggestion that even these many examples exhaust all the possibilities: a story is simply a way of shaping events to bring out one's sense of their meaning, and there are as many ways of writing a story as there are ways of finding significance in one's experience.

The story-writing workshops

The stories were written in the context of various different university courses for professional practitioners. The main focus of these courses is to support participants in some form of reflection on their professional work – developing an action-research project, for example, or writing a practice journal, or analysing a series of cases. The idea of supporting this work by writing and sharing a fictional story is introduced through a pair of workshops. In the first session the general idea is presented – using the ideas outlined in the previous paragraphs – and one or two examples of stories written by practitioners are discussed, with an emphasis on what sort of statements they might be making about professional issues. This is the point at which participants need to be reassured, both that their own stories will be just as 'good' as the examples being discussed and that the fictional format offers 'emotional safety' in the process of disclosure: it is emphasised that writers will not be interrogated either about their text or about the practice it describes, but will spend most of the time 'eavesdropping' on the readers' exchange of interpretations, only coming in at the end (and only then if they so desire) to make whatever comments they wish. Two or three weeks later there is the second workshop, to which each participant brings four or five copies of their story. The class divides into small groups in which stories are distributed and discussed in turn, with about twenty minutes being available for each one. To allay anxieties, it is emphasised that discussion should not be evaluative, but should concentrate on questions such as: What point do you think the story is making? Why do you think the story ended where it did? What overall impression do you get from reading this? Which passages or phrases in the story stand out for you as being particularly interesting? Finally, the whole class discusses the overall process. The general feelings expressed are usually enjoyment, surprise at the richness of the ideas which have emerged, relief that initial anxieties (about their stories and about the dangers of unanticipated disclosure) have not been realised even when the theme of the story has activated quite profound emotions, and pleasure at the supportiveness of the group process (further details and discussion of the participants' experience are presented in Chapter 5).

* * *

Some of the professional implications of the stories which follow are indicated in brief commentaries after each story, based on the writer's own notes on the discussions which took place within the story-sharing workshop or on discussions of the story when it was presented as an example for a subsequent group. In some cases the commentaries include extracts from the writer's own written account of the implications of the story and of the writing-sharing process, and in one case (Muriel Lace's 'The journey') the commentary is followed by extracts from a tape recording, organised by the writer herself, of the discussion of her story. Sometimes the commentary also links the example with one or two of the general ideas about stories presented above, and the last three stories pose the question of what we mean by 'a story', making a link with the next chapter on patchwork texts.

Finally: although the remainder of the chapter can be read as an argument about the nature of story-writing for professional reflection, it is also a sort of anthology of short stories, each creating a separate world of its own. So it is probably best not to try reading them all at one sitting! Also, it might be worthwhile pausing to consider your own responses to each story before reading the subsequent commentary.

* * *

EXAMPLE 1: A STORY AS A STATEMENT: REPETITION AND REVERSAL

'Brave' by Brenda Landgrebe

'Now I want you to be very brave,' said Mum. 'Doctor Brown thinks it's taking you a bit longer than usual to get over your sore throat so he wants you to go to hospital for some TESTS.' (Billy just knew that word had big letters by the way Mum said it.) 'You probably won't like it, but I'll be with you and I'll help you because I love you.'

Mum had looked worried and Billy had seen her eyes go swimmy like when someone is going to cry, so he had not said anything and had been brave about going to hospital for TESTS, and when his own eyes went swimmy too he waited until Mum went downstairs before he let the tears spill over and run down his face.

'Now I want you to be very brave,' said Dad the next day at the hospital. 'The doctors want to do some more TESTS, just to make sure of some things. It will mean more needles and you won't like it much but I'll be here and I'll help you because I love you.' Funny, Dad's eyes had looked swimmy too, so Billy had been brave, well quite brave anyway. He said nothing and waited until Dad had gone to telephone Mum after the extra TESTS before he let the tears fall down his face.

'Now I want you to be very brave,' said Mum. 'The doctor says there's something wrong with your blood and you have to have some TREAT-MENT to put it right. He is going to put a thin tube in here,' she touched him, 'so that you can have DRUGS without having needles all the time.' (Funny, thought Billy, some words just had to have big letters.) 'You won't like it much but I'll be here to help you because I love you.'

Mum had looked really worried and her eyes were glistening again so Billy had said nothing and he had been brave, well quite brave anyway, and waited until Mum had gone home to get tea for Dad and baby Claire before he let his own tears spill over and wet his face.

'Now we want you to be very brave,' said Dad as he held up the mirror. 'We thought the TREATMENT might make your hair come out remember? Well now you have to get used to seeing yourself. You probably won't like it much at first but we will be here' (he looked at Mum as he spoke) 'and we will help you because we love you.'

Both Mum and Dad had wet eyes and were smiling, only the smiles were tight and thin as though they were hard to make, so Billy said nothing and was very brave, well quite brave anyway, and waited until Mum and Dad had left the room before he let the tears spill over from his own eyes and run down his face.

'Now we want you to be very brave,' said Mum. 'It's going to be strange going back to school but your teacher thinks it is best if you tell the class and let them ask questions about your TREATMENT and your wig. It probably won't be very nice at first but we will both be here to help you' (she glanced at Dad) 'because we love you.'

Both Mum and Dad's eyes had been shining the whole time, his class had been talking to him and they seemed not to be able to say much, so Billy had been very brave, well quite brave anyway, and he waited until Mum and Dad had gone home and he could sneak away to the classroom, away from the curious eyes of his classmates, before he let his own tears spill over and run down his face.

'We want you to be very brave,' said Dad some months later in the hospital. 'Your blood has gone wrong again and the TREATMENT has not helped this time, so we are going to take you home and look after you there where we' (he held Mum's hand) 'and baby Claire can be near you all the time. You will be in bed or downstairs on the sofa as you are not very strong and you probably won't like that very much but we will be there to help you because we love you.'

Billy thought Dad's voice sounded strange and Mum made a little noise in her throat and turned away. Dad moved to give Mum a hug so Billy could not see their eyes but he thought they might be crying so he did not say anything and he was very brave, well quite brave anyway, and turned his own head away from them to wipe the tears from his face onto his pillow.

... Billy opened his eyes and looked at them, Mum and Dad were kneeling by the side of his bed and they were crying. Without any sound at all, tears were spilling out of their eyes and running down their faces. The top of Mum's blouse was wet and Dad held a big handkerchief to his chin. Dad's other hand and arm was around Mum's shoulders and she was holding baby Claire whose little face was screwed up, her lips pushed forward in a pout as she sobbed in sympathy with her parents.

Billy's own eyes became quite swimmy as he looked at them but the tears did not spill this time. He did not feel frightened any more just very calm and very grown up. He knew he had something to say at last.

He held out his hands to his parents and as they leaned closer to him, baby Claire between them, he said: 'You probably won't like this very much and I wish I could be here to help you because I love you. Now I want you to be very brave ... '

Commentary

Brenda Landgrebe is a nurse educator whose particular role is to offer bereavement counselling. Prior to the course she claimed to have had little experience of organising her thoughts through writing: 'I'm a great talker: I communicate through talking and touch, but I've never actually tried to communicate through writing; I'm not a great letter writer, or anything like that'. When asked about the process of her writing, she said she simply started writing the first paragraph, and wrote the whole piece quickly, spontaneously almost, and without, initially, any conscious plan that the work would be structured by its remarkable repetition format and by its final dramatic reversal of the refrain, which would make the central point of the story.

For Brenda, then, the form of 'Brave' just 'came naturally', which in some ways is surprising, since the story is very obviously contrived, consciously artful in its use of the rhetorical device of the repeated refrain. However, Egan (1988) reminds us of the long oral tradition of composition, including not only folk ballads but Homer's epics, based precisely upon repetition and the use of refrains. This might suggest that embodying a general insight into one's experience through the aesthetic structuring of a story is a very ancient cultural skill, and therefore more widespread, perhaps, than one might assume and almost certainly more widespread than writing essays. Walter Benjamin, in his essay 'The storyteller' (Benjamin 1973b) argues that the crucial popular art of storytelling is dying out. But if Brenda found that the form of 'Brave' came 'naturally', perhaps Benjamin's pessimism is exaggerated.

'Brave' was written to put forward an idea that was quite explicit for the author before she started writing: she wished to 'jolt' adult carers into an appreciation of the unrecognised contribution made by dying children to the support and comfort of their families. Nevertheless, discussion of the story always throws up a variety of questions. Are the parents in the story being honest with Billy? If not, is the issue one of honesty/hypocrisy, or one of courage? Is the writer suggesting that the behaviour of the parents is actually making things more difficult for Billy? If so, how should/could they behave differently? Clearly, Billy is the hero, but do we feel critical or sympathetic towards the parents? And in the story, no professional counselling help is described; why? Is the writer merely suggesting that all that is required is that the parents should be less protective towards Billy. What role might a professional play in this situation?

* * *

EXAMPLE 2: A STORY AS AN EXPRESSION OF SYMPATHY/EMPATHY WITH THE 'OTHER' OF A PROFESSIONAL ENCOUNTER

'The games lesson' by Nick Boddington

The bell rings and almost immediately there is the sound of desks and chairs being moved upstairs, the sound of children talking, shouting, running, doors banging, but in the classroom all is still and quiet. All around, children are quietly reading. 'Go on', the boy thinks, 'forget to send us to the next lesson, or at least send us so late that the lesson has to be cancelled.' Everyone is silently reading. The boy's name is Paul but everyone calls him by his surname, the girls are called by their first names. He wonders why? Paul has been nervous since the night before. Tuesday and Thursday are always black spots within the week. The ringing of the bell has triggered a sick sinking feeling of dread, conditioned like one of Pavlov's dogs to the ringing of the bell for this particular lesson change. The rest of the day is alright, no problems, no special anxieties. But from leaving home in the morning he is aware that he must go through the last two periods before he can go home again. He still feels a sense of anger that the next lesson is compulsory, a sense of bewilderment that some of his classmates enjoy the ordeal.

'Sir, do you want me to collect the books in?' a boy calls from the back. Yes, you would want to be there on time, alright for you, you won't look a fool, you can cope. 'For homework you can finish reading this chapter, so you will need the books for tonight,' the teacher replies. Paul takes out his homework diary and writes 'no homework set' in the entry for Tuesday. A 'reading' homework is always 'no homework set'. 'Stand. Chairs under. You may go.' There is no stampede for the door, everyone leaves in an ordered way. If you don't get called back. The stampede begins in the corridor. One boy is holding back looking for his bag, another like you, not very good. He looks sick and panic-stricken. A group are running away up the corridor, laughing. The boy starts looking in the desks but the teacher sees him. 'What are you doing? Is that your desk? No? Well leave them alone then. You've lost your bag? Well I can't help that, I've another class waiting to come in, off you go, you can look for it after school. Well if you need it for the next lesson you will just have to explain, won't you. Now off you go.'

Everyone seems very big in the corridor, and all laughing and shouting. It seems odd to the boy that they can switch off from lessons, many with no homework done, a telling off inevitable, and still laugh and joke in the corridor before the next lesson. Paul still feels sick. The boy who has lost his bag hangs back reluctant to leave.

The girls break away from the boys and head towards their changing room but the boys are forced to queue outside theirs. A class is still getting changed. Suddenly the door opens and a class of three-quarter-dressed boys comes flying out, shirts untucked, wet hair everywhere, bags thrown over shoulders or round necks. Some are laughing, some look relieved; the children passing by on their way to other lessons take no notice.

'Right you lot in, you've got two minutes to change, you will need football boots and take your plimsolls with you.' Oh God, thinks Paul, not a 1500 metres to end the lesson please. The boy who has lost his kit stands with the other children who have brought notes. Paul, whilst changing, watches as note after note is read.

When the boy with no kit is reached the teacher looks down at him. 'What do you mean you've lost your kit?' He doesn't shout, but his voice is clear, the rest of the boys go quiet, changing now in silence. 'When did you last have it? Last lesson? How could you lose it in a lesson?' The boys that have hidden the bag are looking nervous. 'If you forgot your kit say so. Someone took it? What do you mean someone took it? Why?' The boys look more nervous. 'Alright you'll play in your normal clothes. Strip to the waist and bare feet' He moves on. The boys look relieved and start laughing 'Strip to the waist and bare feet' means that the problem has been dealt with, the teacher has dismissed the child and won't think any more about him. Now they are safe, the shirtless boy can be a standing joke for the whole lesson.

Paul has finished changing, and runs outside to join the others. The rule of this game is simple: try not to be noticed for as much of the lesson as possible. He watches as the shirtless boy leaves the changing room and starts to shiver in the cool afternoon.

'Right you lot, south field.' Everyone moves away like one person to run down the path to one of the school fields. Paul passes the gym windows and sees the girls getting out the trampolines. They run down the path beside the main school building past silent classroom after silent classroom. In the tennis courts a sixth former has just finished a game of tennis with another of the PE staff. Paul wonders how you ever get to know a teacher that well that you play tennis with them, on your own.

The footballs are already waiting on the pitches. Paul does up his football laces again. 'Right, you, you, you and you: you're team captains.' (Well they would be, wouldn't they; they play for one of the school teams.) 'Set up your sides, one game on this pitch one on that. Well get on with it.'

The teacher has the boys in a group around him but Paul has learnt where to stand to not be noticed. The captains pick their teams. They argue about splitting the best players, they argue about not splitting the worst. The boy feels no embarrassment. He hides behind the refuge that this is all stupid and that he has no interest if they pick him or not. He also knows he is fooling himself.

'Oh, alright, you're with us, go out on the wing.' Great, that should keep him from being noticed. The rest of the team's organisation doesn't involve him so he starts to run out to the farthest part of the pitch. It seems huge.

He turns back when he reaches the line. The goal keepers are in position but the rest of the teams are still in a large mass arguing. 'Get on with it,' the teacher shouts. They break apart and with no real sense of purpose move out across the field. One of the two captains kicks off.

Now what do I do, he thinks. Do I run along the wing parallel to the ball or stand still? God he's watching me, I'd better run around. He runs up the pitch fifteen yards, sideways fifteen yards, sideways fifteen yards, runs backwards fifteen yards, and then back to where he started from. Quick look: no, he is now looking at the other match not me, I can stand still for a minute.

The game has now moved away down the pitch. Paul feels isolated. He looks around. Another boy like a mirror image of himself is standing on the opposite side of the pitch. He too looks unsure what to do. Paul looks behind to see a goalkeeper standing, leaning up against a goal post. Paul is unsure whose side the goalkeeper is on. Is it his or theirs? He is at the end of his first year but has never touched the football in a game. He thinks he ought to know which way to kick the ball if it should come his way but the chances are so slim he is not really concerned.

The game has split into four. A crowd of boys are running in ways Paul doesn't understand, shouting, swearing, calling but never moving more than a quarter of the pitch away from one of the goals. The goalkeeper at the other end is now sitting down with his back to the post in the goal, the boy standing opposite and himself are both on the halfway line. I wonder whose side he is on, he thinks. He looks like he should be on mine.

It has begun to drizzle and the wind has picked up. It is becoming a cold and miserable afternoon, but oddly Paul doesn't mind. The lesson is going well. He has not been singled out, all he is required to do is stand and run in a square if he is looked at. At least it is not the nightmare of gymnastics. The group doesn't laugh any more. They had at first but after a term it had worn off. Now no one expects him to jump the box. They were now all indifferent to his efforts.

Paul looks round, a quick 'teacher check'. No, it's alright, he is no longer even on the field. It's odd, he thinks, why do matches on the telly need a referee? These games don't seem to require any supervision at all. Like the games in the playground, no one fouls. There, an unknown number of players play around an uncounted number, the conversations of the non-players are like islands in a storm. The rules are never laid down, but are always understood. No one cheats.

The game has not really left the penalty area of one goal, the other goalkeeper now looks asleep and Paul and his mirror image stand at opposite sides of the half-way line.

It does not look like Paul will hit the ball today. Like Charlie Brown, should the ball actually come his way he would be terrified. He has no desire to hit the ball. Just standing in the drizzle is fine, if the whole hour passes like this it will have been a good lesson. He is relieved that Charlie Brown is on the television. If there is a programme like that, can he be the only one who feels like this? But self-righteousness seems like thin armour when faced with his teacher. He watches the bus moving down the road beside the field. With luck the next bus will be the one he catches home. School is not a friendly place, he holds it in no affection, it is a place to escape from. It will be better when he is older. It must be, the third and fourth years look as if they own the place, they never seem to have any concerns and worries. He has seen them in the corridor and heard the way they talk about the teachers.

'1500 metre start!' The voice carries over the field. 'Change your shoes when you get to the start.' The run is hateful. He is consistently last. There are two distinct races, one group race to be the first home, one group race to avoid the indignity of being last. A new game is played. It is called 'act enthusiastic'. Don't be the last to the start. He might not make everyone start together but this time he does. 'Alright, you, you, you and you: a head start of half a lap. Get going.' Paul sets off, no longer embarrassed at being singled out for a head start. He wonders why the teacher bothers? If the race was important to Paul would it not be more tactful to leave him with the main group so that he is the slowest of equals and not singled out at the start as being hopeless? Is it important to win, he wonders. No it can't be; if it was, winning after a head start would hardly be winning. Is it to make us fit? If it is, it obviously can't be working, I feel like I want to die. Are we the hares in a greyhound race, are we the targets for the pack to chase? Perhaps the lesson is only for the others to get fit? In the assembly on the last day of term when the trophies were given out the head teacher said that sport was to encourage healthy competition and teamwork.

The game has now changed. The new game is to run the downhill leg of the track, to walk the uphill stretch of it holding your side and looking in agony, but not too much. He remembers his Christmas report: 'C. C. has difficulties in the subject but really does try.' Strange, thinks Paul, I'm sure he doesn't know my name. He has been overtaken by virtually all of the pack, only the boy in his school clothes is still behind. He can see the school ahead as he runs up the track. The bells must have gone, children are pouring out of the doors and heading for the gates in the distance across the playground. He will miss his bus. The last lap lasts forever, but the teacher does not expect a big finish and Paul will not disappoint him.

'Alright,' the teacher says as he crosses the line, 'Good race.'

He is not last, the boy in his school trousers is still running. Was it a good race? What is a good race? The lesson is over, that's good. Why does he lie and tell me it is a good race? It isn't, it's an awful race. The group of boys who have hidden the uniformed boy's bag are laughing as the last runner arrives, panting and red faced. He has run the race in bare feet.

'Right, shower, change and home, you lot; the bell's gone.'

This had been a good lesson.

Outside the changing room a group of boys in strange uniforms are waiting, a visiting 'away team'. Paul wonders how they can find the enthusiasm for the game tonight in drizzle after school. As you get older it must get easier, you must grow into it.

He is wrong.

Commentary

At the time of writing this piece, Nick Boddington had recently moved from being a secondary (high) school teacher to a role as drugs education coordinator. He is specifically concerned, therefore, with the educational task of fostering a sense of (in his words) 'personal responsibility, self-esteem and positive decision-making' on the part of children in schools. His story expresses a sense of the difficulties of this task by seeing school life through the eyes of a pupil, and thereby enabling the reader to see how the culture of the school fosters exactly the opposite qualities from those required, namely fear, withdrawal, and a sense of helplessness. In particular, we see how the pressure of organising large groups of children through a compulsory curriculum reduces the school's capacity to respond to the needs and anxieties of individual pupils, who are thus reduced to survival strategies which make a mockery of the supposed educational purpose of the activities. The generalisability of Paul's experience of this particular after-noon is emphasised by the image of the race, towards the end of the story, which echoes the well known parallel with the educational process as a whole: the term 'curriculum' comes from the Latin word for a chariot-racing course.

Paul himself does not generalise his experience. He is resigned rather than desperate, considering that, all in all this has been 'a good lesson', and he has hope for the future: the older pupils seem to feel 'at home' in the school, and the sixth-formers seem to have achieved a personal relationship with the staff. But the writer questions Paul's optimism with the final words: 'He is wrong'. So we are left with a number of questions. Is the final comment too bleak? Is school really as bad as this? Only for pupils experiencing difficulties, perhaps? But what proportion of pupils would feel like Paul? Paul is afraid of games lessons: are there other pupils for whom maths, writing, art, science, etc. hold similar terrors? Are there some pupils for whom the whole educational 'race' ('curriculum') feels like this? What can hard-pressed individual teachers do to counteract Paul's experience of alienation? How can the requirements of 'order' and 'discipline' be matched with the requirements of 'care'?

The original readers of Nick's story (who were also schoolteachers) commented, first, that the school activities lack relevance for the child, so that school is thus above all a painful experience; and second, that the teachers seem to consolidate the child's feelings of inadequacy. But one member of the group observed, 'I think the picture you painted is a little too black.' Nick himself, writing about what he felt he had learned by writing and sharing the story, raised the point that where so much school activity is compulsory, a half-hour lesson on 'life skills' within a fragmented timetable could only 'pantomime' a concern for the development of pupils' autonomy. 'Do I (as a teacher) see individuals or a class, a group? Do I sometimes respond negatively to individuals in order to "hold down" the group? How do I honestly judge a "good" lesson? Do I play the same games as the children?'

Nick's final observation, that perhaps he can see ways in which he – as a teacher – may engage in the same survival strategies as his pupils, shows how a story which is initially written as an expression of a professional practitioner's *sympathy* (with the perspective of pupils, students, clients, etc.) can begin to reveal a more direct form of identification, i.e. *empathy*. It also illustrates the value of the ambiguity of a story's relation to the factual experiences from which it was derived: what starts out as a piece of imaginative identification with another turns out to be, at the same time, a form of self-exploration.

* * *

EXAMPLE 3:
EMPATHY/STEREOTYPING/IDENTIFICATION

'Mary' by Jeannette Yems

Mary took a long look at herself in the mirror. Not a bad figure for a woman of nearly 40, shame about the legs, she had always hated her legs. She felt good about herself today, her hair was dark and shiny and the red outfit suited her.

People didn't wear black these days, but she felt somehow disloyal. It was six months now since Steve had died suddenly. Who would have thought he would die first? But he did and, as people kept telling her, she must get on with her life, pull herself together. Part of this 'getting on with her life' included 'the group'. Today was her fourth visit and they were a pleasant gathering, although a strange mixture of people. 'Some of them could be quite good companions,' Mary thought, 'if only they had half a brain.' Mary knew she was an intellectual snob, but could see no reason why people of differing backgrounds and abilities should be lumped together because they had a common problem. 'I suppose bereavement has no social boundaries,' she thought.

'The group' had been suggested by her doctor, and she was still a reluctant attender. She would like to have been allowed to wallow in her grief at times, but she had to be strong for the boys, her brother, her parents and friends. In fairness they had all been very good to her, but were over protective. It was only her sons who kept her sane, they loved her and cared about her but didn't fuss. She was well aware they had lost their father and friend, and they all shared their grief together. There were times when she became quite frantic, wondering how she could possibly manage without Steve's support and all the practical help he gave her, but in her calmer moments she recalled how independent she had once been, and must be again. She had been quite horrified when her parents offered to move in, and she knew her rejection of the idea had hurt them. She felt she had spent her whole life hurting them. She remembered their pain when she had left home at 19, at the unlikely liaison with Steve, and eventual marriage. They had been quite supportive once they got to know him.

Life had not been easy for her and Steve, but they had been very happy together, and the birth of the boys had been a real blessing on their relationship. She had felt all her life she had had to 'prove' herself and here she was now facing another major hurdle. 'I'm not sure this one is surmountable,' she said to herself.

Mary's thoughts were interrupted by the door bell and she glanced out of the window at the taxi. 'Good,' she thought, 'It's Mike.'

'I'm getting quite skilled at this now,' he said as he manoeuvred Mary's wheelchair over the front step. 'I don't know how Steve managed this.'

'His next project was to be a ramp,' thought Mary, 'I suppose I should arrange to get one fitted now.'

Commentary

Jeannette Yems is a counsellor, as were the other students with whom she shared her story. Her own observations on the complex set of 'statements' in her story are given as follows.

> My own story was read by fellow students and a work colleague, and each gave a different interpretation. It demonstrated for me that I do have a need for intellectual stimulation, and this was evident in the criticism my character levelled at the members of the 'group'. This is an issue for me at work where two teams have integrated. For months I was the only experienced worker, and I was quite happy to help advise and support colleagues, but have little tolerance with people intellectually unsuited for the job.
>
> Linked with that, the theme running through the story is that because the main character is a disabled person one should not assume that she is intellectually dull or that she has no right to want to look good and feel good about herself. In my work with older people I am constantly battling with other workers in the department who are judging people on their age and not their individual needs. I was not conscious of this when I wrote the story but the theme is very strong.
>
> Another issue raised by the readers was my own ill health and the discovery recently of a second condition which I am fighting hard not to allow to 'disable' me. One reader said that the main character seemed very lonely, I too feel lonely with my illness although I am well

supported. I had been totally unaware that I was portraying this aspect of myself when I had written the story.

One issue we all agreed on was the issue relating to 'assumptions'. Each reader had formed an opinion of a rather distant, somewhat lonely lady, dealing with her bereavement in a way which seemed to exclude others. The reader's opinion of the lady is formed and reinforced throughout the story until the end when the whole perspective is changed by the knowledge that she is a long term disabled person. As counsellors, one basic rule is not to judge or make assumptions about a person, but each reader owned to having done just that. One question this raises is why did I choose to write in this way? Possibly to have the most impact, to make the reader aware that they were making assumptions, to leave them in no doubt. Had I intended to lead the reader to make these assumptions? To emphasise strongly how easily we make assumptions? And how wrong we can be about people's motives, attitudes and views if they do not coincide with our own.

Mary alludes to her parents' anxieties when she chose to leave home at 19 years. The implications for a disabled youngster leaving home can be very different from an able-bodied youngster, but there can also be many similarities. We must look at what the person presents as their difficulties and not relate it to our own experiences.

I feel the story demonstrates that we as counsellors need to look at someone as a 'whole' person and to work with what they present to us and not what we choose to interpret from their words and actions. To stay with the person, to look at the situation from their perspective and not our own.

Further note

But this is not so easily done, as Jeannette's story and commentary make clear. In attempting to write about the importance of seeing clients from 'their perspective and not our own', Jeannette invented a client whose qualities and situation she to some extent shares. So Jeannette can see herself in the client (as does Nick Boddington in the previous story). Jeannette's final observation was that the exercise brought home to her the value of 'subjective knowledge', and we can see here the significance of her statement. We cannot, indeed, escape our subjectivity – we can only try to expand its scope, to 'encompass' our clients as being 'like' us, rather than, just because they are clients (or students, etc.), as 'different'.

* * *

EXAMPLE 4: CONTRASTS (I): THEORY AND PRACTICE

'Mixed emotions' by Andy Shattock

Jane walked home from work with a smile on her face, a glint in her eye, a jaunt in her step and her head held high. She felt good, no, more than that, she felt on top of the world. It was days like this that made her realise why she enjoyed being a nurse so much. As she walked she thought back over the events of the day.

She reflected how, on arrival on duty that morning the first person she noticed was Tom, a small and very fragile elderly figure sitting bolt upright in bed in the middle of the busiest part of the ward. His frightened eyes followed every movement, bewildered by the hustle and bustle, and his head turned to every sudden sound within the cacophony of activity of the ward.

'Be careful of him,' the health care assistant had said. 'He's a difficult patient.' Jane remembered feeling surprised at this comment as all she saw was a very frightened little old man. She visualised his frightened face as she went up to him. She remembered how he cowered away from her as she first made eye contact. She recollected how he seemed surprised when she knelt down and looked up at him, and how Tom seemed to relax a little when he realised that she was talking to him rather than doing something to him. Jane was pleased that she had moved his bed to a quieter part of the ward. She felt good that, through gentle encouragement and thoughtful words, Tom had slowly relaxed and sunk back into the pillows behind him. She had noticed how by initially just gently touching his fragile hand the tension and fear in his wrinkled face had given way to the hint of a smile. She had felt pleased when, without further encouragement from her, the wizened fingers had curled themselves around her hand and hung on tight. Jane had felt good when told, 'You've done wonders there' by the Ward Sister as she flew past.

Jane had felt proud and smiled a knowing smile when the health care assistant had expressed surprise at such a nice man Tom was now that he wasn't being so difficult.

But Jane had felt best of all when Tom had said 'Thank you nurse, you are wonderful' and held his arms open and gave her a hug.

Jane bounced up to the door of her flat and opened the door. Lying on the mat was a rather official brown envelope. She suddenly remembered that the results of her essay for her course were due out today. She recollected how she had struggled to write a critical analysis of the nature of experiential learning. Not feeling quite so ebullient now, Jane tentatively tore open the envelope.

Dear Miss Smith,
　We regret to inform you …

The glint in her eye was replaced by a sudden moistness.

Her head was no longer held high as she sat down on the stairs and buried it in her hands. She felt empty, no, more than that, she felt as though the whole world was falling in around her. It was moments like this which made her wonder if she would ever make it as a nurse. As she sobbed quietly to herself, the thoughts and the feelings generated by the events on the ward were lost for ever.

Commentary

Often, a story is created by bringing different worlds of meaning into collision, which immediately creates drama, contradiction, irony and an implicit overall critique: the story forges a unity which reveals the limitations of its separate elements.

Andy Shattock is a nurse educator and his story points to the gap between practical sensitivity, as a key quality of effective professional experience, and the critical analysis of that experience required by academic courses of professional education. One level of irony is presented by the contrast between the basis for Jane's success (eye-contact, gentle talk, touch, hug) and the form of her failure: an 'essay' of 'critical analysis'. A further irony is added by the fact that the critical analysis was supposed to be of 'experiential' learning. We are left with several sorts of questions. First, what is wrong with the format of academic assessments, such that they fail to match up with what seems to be a very high level of professional skill? What form of assessment would be more appropriate? How would one demonstrate a grasp of experiential learning as a personal accomplishment, rather than as a theoretical concept? But second, if, indeed, Jane cannot 'analyse' adequately what it is that makes her successful, will she be able to maintain and develop her skill? Does she need to do so? For example, would she be equally successful with a very different sort of patient? Is it enough to be free of professional categorisations ('a difficult patient') and to be able to see only 'a frightened little old man'? Third (and this was a point raised by Andy's fellow students, which had not been part of his own thinking as he wrote the story), if Jane does need help with 'critical analysis', then the sudden and unprepared delivery of results in an official brown envelope makes matters worse, by crudely destroying the confidence derived from her practical success.

So, how can the university manage the communication of assessment results so that students' practical successes on the ward are not lost for ever in a sudden, damaging loss of morale?

This last point is particularly important. In Andy's story the device of the unprepared-for official letter is necessary to make the dramatic contrast; but by noting the importance of that device in the story we can see how the issue raised by the story might have been addressed, e.g. through careful tutorial guidance to prepare Jane for the result of her assessment. It is the incompleteness of stories that can open up new avenues of thought and possibilities for changes in practice.

* * *

EXAMPLE 5: CONTRASTS (II): PROFESSIONAL AND CLIENT

'If only she knew ... ' by Julia Plunkett

'Why can't you leave me alone? I am rude and a lazy slob so if you don't like it – tough. You just go on and on and don't know how I feel. I can't wait to be out of here so I can do what I like when I like and not have to do things your way. I hate you!!' Her daughter screams hysterically as she pounds up the stairs and slams her bedroom door.

Sally follows her up, throws open her door and screams in her daughter's face a few more home truths then runs from the room sobbing.

'Here we go again,' Sally weeps to herself exhaustedly. Like someone who travels the same road and repeatedly takes the same wrong turning. Why have I made such a mess of motherhood? Nobody told me it would be like this or what to do. So how was I supposed to get it right? What did I do wrong?

She remembers last week, when it all got too much to bear and she had to do something. Had to talk to someone about it.

Sally

Driving along in the car, Sally wonders what Barbara will be like. Her mind runs wild with images of anything from a new age hippy type to Mrs Marple!

The point is will I be able to relate to her and trust her?

I expect she'll be dripping with

Barbara

Driving along in the car, Barbara wonders what Sally will be like. Will she be old or young, smart or scruffy?

The main thing is will we be able to get on together? Will she like me?

I hope I can cope with the

qualifications which always makes me feel inferior to start with. I'm only your average woman with a family and a part-time job.

I'm pathetic really, what am I doing going to see a complete stranger, exposing myself and allowing her to see what a mess I've made of bringing up my daughter? I feel like a child who's missed out on some important lessons in life and now needs to catch up.

Will she understand? Her life is probably totally together. I wonder if she's married – hope so. Or if she's a mum herself. If she is, I bet her kids love her to death and it's happy families all round.

problem and she won't expect me to solve it for her. I always feel they expect an expert with letters after their name. Well she'll be disappointed! I'm just little old me with a couple of years training as a counsellor. Who do I think I am anyway – setting myself up like some sort of guru? I've got problems too you know. I haven't got it right. How am I supposed to help other people? If only they knew …

Later …

Sally felt relief. She felt she had passed a burden to someone better able to cope with it.

Barbara's the expert. We can sort it out together. She seems to have heard what I have said. Unperturbed but not unmoved. Even though I know she can't know how awful it feels to be drifting apart from your daughter – she's had all the training and read all the books.

Later …

Barbara felt frustrated.

If only I could tell her just how much I really know how she feels. I've been there. I am there. But – got to keep everything professional … I am not her friend. God it's hard to keep up this facade. If I don't she'll vote with her feet anyway. I need to find a way of letting her know that she could be me talking.

Barbara remembers back to last week: 'Why don't you leave me alone and drop dead?' her daughter screamed, 'CALL YOURSELF A COUN-SELLOR?!!'

Commentary

Ah, the marvels of the word-processor! Julia Plunkett's story presents the parallel misrepresentations between counsellor and client in terms of the spatial arrangement of the text on the page, reminding us that our awarenesss of events and situations is not linear (a single argument), but simultaneous and interlocking, dramatic and ironic. Cinema makes the same point through use of the split screen, and counterpoint has been an essential aspect of music for many hundreds of years. How eloquent is the blank space between Barbara's column and Sally's; and the balancing blocks of unified text at the beginning and end – so similar and yet so different.

Julia Plunkett is a counsellor. She wrote afterwards that she wanted her story to be 'spontaneous, not thought about with a deliberate attempt to incorporate certain themes, but for the underlying issues to just be there, waiting to be found'. So, although there clearly is a deliberate theme in the story, having selected her two characters as a 'hypothesis', Julia deliberately wrote the story as an exploration: she expected that more would emerge from the story than she was conscious of having intended. After sharing her story she commented:

> As I wrote my story, there was a sense of frustration and concern about what I felt about being a counsellor and how I felt about not being one hundred per cent honest with a client; and therefore, I felt, there was a lack of authenticity. The feedback by the group, however, conveyed it as an optimistic view: although communication was limited and some things were never said, the best was made of it and the client felt helped; an implicit understanding existed and was conveyed somehow. The awareness, of the counsellor, that [she and her client] were just missing one another is strong, so it becomes important to find ways in the future to change that.

In other words, the counselling process can still work, even where there are unrealistic mutual perceptions and self-doubts on the part of both professional and client. But writing and sharing the story has brought out clearly, for the writer, the need for greater clarity in the relationship. Otherwise, instead of the professional ideal of 'authenticity' there is the danger of a process which relies largely on power: Julia writes, 'In practice there is a danger that the counsellor "knows" and the client accepts the counsellor's interpretations without question as the truth.' It is precisely this danger which her story exposes. And, she observes, the situation of freely exchanging possible interpretations of her story with her colleagues has clear parallels with the ideal of the counselling process itself, when it is not dominated by a power relationship and, consequently, 'the client can begin to make their own interpretations as well as the counsellor'.

* * *

EXAMPLE 6: CONTRASTS (III): THEATRE AND SOCIETY

'Cakes and ale'* by Pamela Henderson

The soft, brown eyes looked down at him kindly. She held out her right hand. He gripped it and, taking his weight, she pulled him upright.

'Come,' she said. 'Walk with me.'

As he moved closer to her his fatigue and frailty vanished, replaced with the strength and vitality that poured out of her. His balance steadied, his frame expanded and his new-found confidence raised his gaze. They moved together, as equals, towards the audience. At the edge of the stage they stopped.

The immediate blackout was followed by a pregnant pause – that precious silence at the end of a fine performance when the world stands still and the audience is united in a complicity of understanding. The applause, when it came, was generous.

Greta, however, sat still, her hands clasped in her lap, her throat tight. Furtively, she wiped some of the tears away from her cheek that spilled down her face and threatened to mark her cream silk shirt. Henry prodded her.

'Clap!' he hissed. 'You can't just sit there snuffling. You ought to be clapping like the rest of us.' He shrugged dismissively, adding as an afterthought, 'It was only a play for God's sake.'

The house lights came up and, realising that the curtain call was over, the audience stopped clapping and switched their attention to leaving the auditorium as quickly as possible and thereby beating their immediate neighbour to the bar. Never one to surrender easily in these circumstances, Henry took Greta by the arm and propelled her towards the nearest exit. Greta smoothed her hair and adjusted her shirt as she went.

'Didn't you like it then, sweetheart?' inquired Henry, dutifully.

'Of course I did,' replied Greta defensively. 'It just wasn't what I was expecting.'

Feeling obliged to continue with his line of questioning, Henry continued: 'So what were you expecting then?'

---

* Shakespeare: 'Dost thou think that because thou art virtuous/There shall be no more cakes and ale?' (*Twelfth Night*, II, 3)

'Well,' she hesitated. 'You know, something more light hearted, something entertaining. Watching that play makes me want to get out there and change things for the better.'

Henry rolled his eyes at the earnest worthiness of it all, momentarily concerned that Greta's new-found social conscience would result in an evening's enforced soul searching, which was not how he planned to spend the next few hours with her.

The December night air was sharp and biting, all the more so after the theatre's comforting warmth. Henry and Greta walked briskly alongside the river towards the bridge that would take them to the station and beyond to the familiarity of home.

Lanterns lit their path, and the noise of traffic and trains was deadened by the gentle lapping of the river beside them. The couple walked closely together, their shared warmth allowing them to enjoy the chilly night.

'I do wish they would make more of an effort to keep this city clean,' said Greta. 'I mean look at all the piles of rubbish everywhere.'

'Mmm,' murmured Henry, half-heartedly. Greta continued, warming to her theme. 'It's just not good enough. Somebody should do something.'

Such was the energy she gave to her speech, she failed to see a particularly large mound of debris in her path. Henry took her hand and helped her over the boxes and newspapers. Greta grunted disdainfully, hoping that dirt had not transferred itself to her new cashmere coat.

As the pair walked on hand in hand towards the bridge they failed to see the pair of weary brown eyes looking up at them out of the receding heap of cardboard. Slowly a weathered hand stretched out, waiting for the helping hand that would never come.

Commentary

Pamela Henderson is manager of a community theatre and she wrote her story as part of a course where she was preparing to undertake an action-research project to develop a theatre membership subscription scheme. The question, therefore, was: what sort of a membership scheme did she want to establish, and – consequently – what sort of a relationship did she envisage between her theatre and the community?

The quotation referred to in the title announces the basic idea – the contrast between the theatre as mere entertainment ('cakes and ale') and the theatre as a form of committed social action ('virtue'). At the beginning, on the stage, virtue is achieved – the needy are given renewed vitality – whereas at the end, in real life, members of the audience who have been moved by the play nevertheless ignore the appeal of the same neediness, and refuse to give the 'helping hand' which they have just applauded. The contrast is emphasised by the final echoes of the opening – the brown eyes, the outstretched hand.

At the centre of the story is Greta's ambiguity: on the one hand the play has made her want to 'get out there and change things for the better', but on the other hand that was not what she had expected, or even, perhaps, wanted; she is concerned about her expensive clothes and, although she is offended by the state of the city, she thinks someone else should do something about it. Although the ending seems pessimistic (help would 'never come') the character of Greta does offer grounds for hope: the play *had* managed to get behind her materialism and self-centredness, if only temporarily. The story is thus poised between pessimism and optimism, and on the various occasions where the story has been presented as an example, there has been heated discussion as to where the balance lies.

There is also the character of Henry: dismissive of soul-searching, social conscience and 'worthiness', he seems to dominate Greta ('he propelled her towards the nearest exit') and is unaffected by the play except as entertainment. The two characters may be seen as representing the writer's 'theory' that the community contains two types of people – those who are susceptible to the theatre's moral and political appeal, and those who are not. Unfortunately, the latter group is more powerful and dominates the former group in ways they are not aware of. So the theatre and Henry are battling for influence over Greta. Quite often, readers of the story see the relationship between Henry and Greta as being important as an expression of gender politics – would the story not feel quite different if it had focused on the differing reactions to the play of two women friends? Does community theatre, then, perhaps make a stronger appeal to women, as generally more community-minded? Should a theatre membership scheme perhaps, therefore, target women especially in the first instance?

* * *

EXAMPLE 7: A GHOST STORY

'The visit' by Jane Arnett

It had been a busy day. The District Nurse had just finished the afternoon visits. In the office she glanced at the fax machine. 'Oh no!' she thought as she quickly scanned the fax: 'VISIT TODAY PLEASE'.

She felt irritated; a new patient this late on a Friday, she really needed to be home on time tonight. 'Mrs Toby, End Cottage, Windy Lane; Leg Dressing, Referred by patient'. Why hadn't liaison bleeped her earlier? She looked in the files to see if she had any previous notes. She had only been working on this 'patch' for a week. She found a set of old notes, Mrs Toby had been discharged a year ago: a healed leg ulcer, so she could use the old notes. DAMN! Someone had written R.I.P. on them by mistake. Couldn't use them now.

She got into her car and scanned the map. It was raining again. After a couple of wrong turns she finally found Windy Lane; needless to say it was an unmade road. She drove on, trying to avoid the muddy ruts and holes. The houses became further apart and the house names were difficult to see through the rain spattered car window. She drove on. Just as she was about to give up, there it was. She knew it was the one by the neglected state of the garden and paintwork. She walked towards the house. Was that a face at the window? It looked vaguely familiar. The front door was ajar and she entered slowly shouting an introduction as she went. A quiet voice replied; well at least the old lady wasn't deaf!

The nurse entered the room, which was surprisingly tidy. The old lady was clean and neatly dressed and around her lower leg was a bandage. She explained that she had fallen down a step that morning. The nurse was irritated; why didn't she phone earlier? The nurse filled in the assessment quickly; most of the information was in the referral anyway. She unwrapped the bandage, there was a nasty looking laceration underneath.

She cleaned and dressed the wound and made a mental note to see the local doctor about some antibiotics. She told Mrs Toby that she would get another visit the next day and, as she turned to leave, the old lady put her hand on her arm. 'I have something for you,' she said. She got up and opened a drawer and handed the nurse a small package. 'My husband wanted you to have this,' she said. 'You looked after him on the Stroke Unit just before he died.'

The nurse then recalled where she had seen Mrs Toby before. It had been a long time ago but she remembered how close the couple had been. She unwrapped the package and inside was a beautiful miniature jug. 'You told us that you collected jugs.' It's amazing what small details people remember in times of great stress. 'You were so kind to him, he was very grateful.'

The nurse felt a lump in her throat. How much of that shy compassionate young student nurse remained?

She thanked Mrs Toby for the jug and left. She thought she saw the old lady wave as she drove away. When she got back to the surgery she made out a list of dressings that Mrs Toby would need over the weekend, then she asked the receptionist to have them delivered to the house. 'You must have the wrong name and address here,' the receptionist said. 'Mrs Toby died six months ago in a house fire. Shame really; she never got over the death of her husband, poor thing.'

The nurse shivered; she reached into her bag and her fingers closed around the jug ...

Commentary

The ghost story expresses levels of awareness which have been repressed; it brings to mind important matters which have been forgotten, should not have been forgotten, and therefore return to haunt us. The ghost is a projection of moral authority, of conscience, reminding us that there is more to our lives than we are currently admitting. The ghost story is thus a powerful and economical genre, because its fundamental structure already points strongly towards the need for reflection or action in a neglected area.

Jane Arnett is a district nurse. She notes that she was at first convinced that she could not write a story, not 'ever' having written one before, that it was originally three times its present length before she removed a mass of detailed description, and that in the end she was surprised and pleased with the result. Thus, even though this is a first attempt, Jane shows a sure grasp of a highly structured set of conventions: the difficult journey through wind and rain, the lonely desolate house, etc.

So, what are the important matters that the (un-named) district nurse in the story is reminded of by the ghost of Mrs Toby? There are two short sentences in the middle of the story which carry the whole message (so we can see how important it is for the balance of the piece that Jane reduced its original length):

> The nurse felt a lump in her throat. How much of that shy compassionate young student nurse remained?

By this point in the story there have been so many (apparently quite justified) references to the nurse's hurry, brisk efficiency, and (above all) 'irritation', that the term 'compassionate' comes as something of a shock, reminding us, like the nurse herself, of what we had not realised, until now, has been missing. The supernatural jug, then, is a reciprocal gift, recognising the quality of the nurse's former professional relationships with patients, a quality now buried beneath the busy routines of practice. Like all ghost stories, 'The visit' leaves us not only with the question, 'What can we do with this reminder?' but also with the injunction: 'We *ought* to do something'. If Mrs Toby had not turned out to be 'from the Other Side' her message would not have had the same authority. In one sense the point could have been made in a story simply about receiving a gift from the wife of a former patient. But the ghost element makes the point stronger, and Jane notes that it was the ending and ghost story format which was the origin of the story. So she is not simply regretting the loss of her professional idealism, but implicity reminding herself and her readers that it must be recaptured.

* * *

EXAMPLE 8: A STORY AS A METAPHOR FOR PRACTICE (I): AN EXOTIC MYTH

'The sorceress' by Choo Tan

She stood at the edge of the cliff looking out towards the horizon with her piercing green eyes. The glare of the sun forced her to raise her right arm to shade her eyes. In the distance, she could just see a speck circling slowly towards her against the backdrop of a cloudless sky. As it circled closer, she could see that it was a majestic eagle gliding on the warm thermals rising off the desert floor.

'What do you see, Belgara?' asked the old woman.

Belgara turned with a surprised look on her face but gathered her composure and said, 'An eagle, flying free.' She then turned and gathered her staff and leather pouch that she had carelessly discarded on the ground earlier. 'How did you know I was here? I did not hear or see you come up the path.'

'I wanted to say good-bye, and I knew you would come here. This has always been your favourite place to think when you had things on your mind,' answered the old woman.

'Yes, I always felt at peace here, and I could always think my problems through. Did you know that I managed to understand the Elven Scrolls whilst sitting and contemplating on that rock over there?' Belgara said as she pointed to an egg-shaped boulder. 'I also feel that I am closer to the gods when I'm here,' she continued as she turned her head to face the old woman. She wanted to say more but decided not to and looked up at the eagle again.

The old woman turned and walked towards the boulder and sat down. 'You have done well, Belgara. You have grown into a fine young woman and your skills have developed beyond my expectations,' said the old woman. 'I always knew that this day would come when you would leave and find your own way in the world.'

'Yes, Old One, I feel that I cannot stay here any longer. Something is calling me away and I have to answer its call. But. ... Why not come with

47

me? You have no one here. I will look after you. There is a whole new world out there. Think of all the adventures that we will have!' said Belgara excitedly, her green eyes shining.

'No, Belgara, my place is here and my time is almost over. This is your time. You have learnt to accept who and what you are. You have faced your dark side and embraced it. Your are whole … it is time for you to go forward,' the old woman said as she hugged her cloak closer around her even though it was quite warm up on the cliff.

'Are you all right, Old One?' asked Belgara anxiously.

'Do not worry about me, Belgara. Can't an old woman rest her weary bones without you young ones hovering around like gnats asking if one is all right? Do not be deceived by age, Belgara!' sniffed the old woman irritably.

Belgara smiled affectionately at the old woman as she knelt next to her and said, 'You were the only one who did not impose your will on me. You let me explore my skills and powers without interfering even though I could see you cringing at some of my mistakes. What I could not understand was, when I was tempted by the dark side, you still did not step in, when I thought you would. Why? That was the most frightening experience I have had to face.'

'Would you have listened if I had stepped in?'

Belgara shook her head slowly as it dawned on her that she would have done exactly the opposite to what the old woman said at that time of her life. She understood now that she had to find her way herself by understanding her own weaknesses and strengths. Belgara knew now that her powers lay with herself. She turned to the old woman to tell her her newfound knowledge, but she was not there. She looked around her and ran down the path but could not see the old woman anywhere.

Belgara felt hot tears welling in her eyes as she whispered, 'Good-bye, Old One.' She stood looking down the path which led to the village for a while longer hoping to catch a glimpse of the old woman but she knew that the woman had not gone there. Belgara slowly turned away and faced the horizon again. Her world is out there now, she has to move on. Her lips moved noiselessly, there was a shimmering in the air where she had stood.

The magnificent golden eagle shook out its feathers before it took off into the air heading towards the far horizon, excitement in its heart.

Commentary

One way in which a story can explore an aspect of practice is by translating the situation into a quite different context, so that the meaning has to be read not merely as a potential generalisation (as in the first three stories above) but also symbolically. Choo Tan is a trainee counsellor and this story about the sorceress and Belgara standing at the edge of the cliff looking out at the horizon, and a gliding eagle, was intended to symbolise a counsellor saying farewell to a client at the end of a course of therapy, thinking of the broad scope of the client's future life which she will now be able to live as a free agent. This, then is a highly optimistic vision of the counselling process, focusing on the need to resolve the problem of the client's dependance on the counsellor in order to achieve a successful end to therapy, and the mythic setting allows ideas to be presented in their theoretical form (e.g. the discussion of the client's acceptance of her 'dark side') with a poetic dignity and power, whereas if the setting were realistic this might have seemed somewhat heavy and academic.

But the mythic, symbolic format does not mean that there are no questions or ambiguities. On the contrary. One of the readers surprised Choo by suggesting that the choice of a mythical style made the story's optimism seem rather unrealistic, as though the writer were not wholly convinced. Another thought that the story had a feminist feel, particularly in its emphasis on strength and self-reliance. A third reader suggested that the story was not only about the successful end of a counselling therapy but also about the end of the counsellor's own training. According to this reading the sorceress is the course tutor and Belgara is the trainee counsellor. (The story was written in a workshop for students nearing the end of a counselling diploma.) Another reader focused on the egotism of Belgara in wishing to take the sorceress with her, while another saw her wish as a feeling of guilt in leaving the sorceress behind. The plausibility of this reading comes from the fact that the writer has made the sorceress a frail old woman, and this opens up the question as to why the counsellor (or the tutor) is seen as 'weary': is this an implicit recognition that the exercise of the profession is (or is going to be) draining and exhausting? However, Choo points out that in her culture old age implies wisdom rather than weariness, so this is not an interpretation she had intended. This wisdom, she notes, is not the wisdom of the counsellor as a person but the wisdom which may be attained by the client through the counselling relationship. By the end of the story the old woman has disappeared, mysteriously. Why? Is the departure of the client (or student) a sort of death for the counsellor (or tutor)? Is the story, then, asking: how do professionals manage the emotional side of a professional relationship when the client/student 'flies away'?

* * *

EXAMPLE 9: A STORY AS A METAPHOR FOR PRACTICE (II): A MUNDANE ALLEGORY

'The journey' by Muriel Lace

Stephen gazed out of the window. The earlier glimpse of hazy sun had disappeared completely as the early autumn afternoon became still and the sky took on a greyish tint. He sighed and turned again to the pile of work on his desk. This report was needed for a meeting the following day and, although it was shaping up well, it was taking longer than he had anticipated.

The time ticked by and the mug of steaming coffee which he had only sipped twice turned cold and uninviting. Stephen twirled the pen between his fingers, a frown making two deep lines between his dark hazel eyes as he re-read the completed report for the second time. Finished – at last! A smile appeared at the corner of his mouth and a hand pushed back his straight, thick hair.

Stephen looked at the clock. Six-thirty, not really late. It had been his arriving home late every evening the previous week, which had been the cause of the row with Jill. Why could she not understand that he worked hard for them both? Her harsh words still rang in his ears and that resounding bang of the front door this morning, as she had left with a packed suitcase. Even now, he could feel that heavy thud in his heart. There had been nothing further he had been able to say to her, to persuade her to stay.

Stephen shook his head as if to shake the thoughts away. He really could do without the hassle. It would be better on his own.

Grabbing up his coat and briefcase, Stephen left the office. Stepping into the street, he was surprised at the dense fog and that the street lights' usual bright glow was now no more than a faint yellowish haze in the darkness. It felt strange. Even the noise of the traffic and the usual bustling people seemed muffled and distant. The regular cry of the paper seller guided him to the corner of the side street where he had parked his car. Stephen dug deep in his pocket for the car keys as he walked slowly and uncertainly towards his accustomed parking place. His footsteps had a remote echo along the now deserted path. *He was on his own.*

There was a certain feeling of relief to be sliding into the seat of his car – sort of contained and safe, shutting out the fog which had felt cold and damp. It was still there, but now on the outside giving something of a strange, eerie sensation. The car sparked into life, and Stephen turned the radio on, allowing a sense of normality to flow over him.

Stephen carefully eased the car out of the darker side street, guided by the main street glow ahead and into the busy flow of traffic heading for the out-of-town routes. The way was so familiar that Stephen seldom used his full concentration on his driving, often singing to the music or deep in thought about his day's work and how best to manage his time the following day. But tonight was different. As the wipers worked to clear the droplets of moisture, Stephen peered through the windscreen at the yellowish glimmer of street and shop lights, seeking to recognise the stage of his journey by known landmarks.

As he reached the outskirts of the town, there was a diminishing and thinning of other traffic going in his homeward direction. The street lights ended abruptly and Stephen felt a momentary panic, as the darkness closed in around him. His car's headlights did not pick out the road ahead but seemingly reflected off the fog, giving a whitish glare which hurt his eyes, as he searched ahead for some sign that he was still travelling forward in the right direction. With immense relief he caught sight of two, faint, red gleams some distance ahead. Stephen focused on these, knowing them to be the rear fog lights of the car ahead, and speeded up to be closer, despite feeling slightly unsure of the quicker pace. Being nearer brought Stephen the sensation of safety and support, as well as feeling he was being enabled to travel through the blinding gloom, which had the sense of cutting him off from the surrounding world and from reality.

This other traveller eased Stephen's journey and he realised that it would have been much more difficult without something visible to hold on to. He felt greatly relieved by this support and the passing thought that *he was not on his own*.

Nevertheless, how glad he would be to reach his journey's end. As the miles slowly passed by, the fog appeared to take on a more swirling effect, giving a few momentary glimpses of clearer visibility. Stephen hoped therein contained some promise of an easing of the conditions and as a few more miles ticked by, the clearer patches became more frequent and more lengthy. At these times, Stephen could see not only the car ahead but the red gleams of the rear lights belonging to the car preceding that. So the *other traveller had not been on their own either*. The support had been there for them too.

The conditions being very much better, Stephen found his old confidence returning. He could manage now without watching the car ahead and shortly after, Stephen veered towards the slip road which led him in the direction of his home. He remembered how earlier in the day, he had been determined to cope on his own without Jill. Now he felt different.

Perhaps, she was right. There were more important things in life than his work! Life too was a journey. He did not want to be on his own.

Stephen pulled into the driveway of his home. A light was on and, as he approached, the front door opened bathing him in a shaft of golden light. Stephen stepped inside and disappeared from view.

Commentary

Muriel Lace is a counsellor. Her story also presents an aspect of practice in the form of a general metaphor, but this time the metaphor is taken from everyday experience – a car journey through fog. She wrote a full account of the process and provided a transcript of the discussion, which she had tape-recorded. Extracts from her account and the transcript are reproduced below.

> To write a fictional story with a counselling content seemed a rather vague request since it conjured up so many possibilities of theories or presenting problems. Just where was I to begin? Journeying home after counselling clients one evening, I ran into some foggy weather and in the driving through these murky conditions, I felt there seemed some parallel to my concept of the counselling process.
>
> Often, clients enter counselling when they find they are unable to view their way ahead with clarity, looking to the counselling relationship for support and to enable them to tolerate and manoeuvre through their difficulties as I had to in the fog. It seemed the rear lights of the car ahead supported me in a similar manner to a counsellor, who, like the driver in front, usually remains personally unknown to the client other than in that professional role. The driver of the car ahead of me was also helped by the rear lights of another car, in the way supervision too provides a level of support for the counsellor.
>
> I attempted to write the story on two levels, the surface problem and the underlying level indicating my own impression of the counselling relationship and process. It was my intention and endeavour that these two levels should occur and develop simultaneously. Clients repeatedly feel themselves very isolated and on their own with their problem and, through the support of the counselling relationship and process, realisation dawns that they are not alone. Often their perspective or view of their situation alters as they work through the layers of their problem.
>
> The ambiguous ending of the story was intended to reflect something of a non-directive conclusion, the readers, as also with the clients, being open to choose their own interpretation and take from the story/counselling what they themselves wished.

Transcript of group discussion

Members present: Steve, Shelly, Sandra, Beverly.

BEVERLY He starts off on his own, he wants to be on his own and then he decides he was better off with Jill. When he was on his own he turned the radio on to feel a sense of normality.

SHELLY It's like a parallel with the counselling process, finding your way through the fog, being able to hold on to the light. The importance of someone being there at the right time, like the car being there in the fog, at the right time, the right place. It's like a knock-on effect: as the fog clears you realise that you're not alone, getting back, through the counselling, in touch with people as well. This line of cars through the fog, they all felt lost and alone but, in fact, they weren't.

STEVE I feel there's a tension between 'being on your own' and 'not being on your own'. It sort of feels there's lots of places he would be better on his own; he was on his own; he was not on his own; the other traveller not being on their own; he didn't want to be on his own. It feels like a constant pull in both directions and even at the end it's ambiguous, because there's a sort of feeling that maybe she's there and he's not on his own and even if she's there maybe he's still on his own. Just because she's there doesn't mean, he's not alone. So I feel there's that pull all the time between being on your own and not being on your own.

BEVERLY It's OK on your own, but turning on the radio was allowing a sense of normality. Then it didn't feel normal to be on his own. I think it's very confusing.

STEVE But is that the sense of normality, is it reality? In reality, he is on his own. Switching the radio on may give you a sense of normality, but that may not be the real thing, which is actually – he is on his own. And similarly, when he's in the car, he's on his own; even though there's a car in front, he's still on his own.

SHELLY It's a paradox.

STEVE There's lots of things going on here – a doubling up.

SHELLY I thought to begin with, he was on his way to a counselling session using the car as the vehicle.

BEVERLY 'Nevertheless, how glad he would be to reach his journey's end' – what is a journey's end – a car journey?

SHELLY A car journey, life's journey, journey through the problem or trauma – or perhaps, it's never-ending.

BEVERLY Does it ever end? What is the difference between alone and loneliness?

STEVE You can be alone without being lonely.

SANDRA Everyone is alone and this picks it up, about the support ...

STEVE What strikes me about the support is that it's not really intentional. He gets support from the fact that there's a car in front of him that he can latch on to, but that car isn't there for that reason. So, it's not actually intentional, it's just a fact, if you like, that there happens to be another car and he can follow that car.

SANDRA You're drawn to the bit about the other traveller – 'so the other traveller had not been on their own either. The support had been there for them too'; and I feel he is not on his own.

SHELLY I was thinking about the counselling and it's like prostituted friendship. Maybe there's something of that in there as well.

STEVE It's made me think just now of Wilber and the existential stage. Where you may have to come to terms with the fact that you are on your own and there's reality there, and it's almost like he's breaking through it into that level. Or is he? Or perhaps he doesn't want to go into that level. Maybe it's too painful to really have that realisation. I almost felt the ending, if it implied that the wife was there, was almost a cop-out in a way. It was like a happy ending. He was going back to where he was feeling he had got his nice little unit there.

BEVERLY I felt quite flat when I finished reading it. I don't know why that was though. Confused and flat.

SHELLY I didn't. I almost got like this heavenly vision of him being bathed in this shaft of golden light – enlightenment or whatever.

BEVERLY So that relates to the counselling setting. When you come out of the counselling room bathed in this – with all the answers.

SHELLY An illusion.

SANDRA I felt that he was alone when he walked into the house. I don't think the partner was there.

BEVERLY Well, at the beginning it was said the partner had packed her bags and left.

SANDRA Maybe. I'm not a romantic!

SHELLY Mind you, being in the fog is very frightening and if you are driving in fog maybe that's why he had this whole change of heart from wanting to be on his own before, and now being on his own but not being on his own.

STEVE To come back to my existential thing. On page 2, end of paragraph 2, there's 'the sensation of safety and support which had the sense of cutting him off from the surrounding world and from reality'. Somehow or another, the safety and support actually cuts him off from the reality, almost as though in some way it's actually preventing him from seeing what the real situation is, which is almost holding him in an illusion. As if it's an illusion of safety and support!

BEVERLY Could he be going on a journey as if on automatic pilot and not noticing or feeling?

STEVE I thought that quite worrying from a counselling concept: that somehow or other if we are providing safety and support, that it has the effect of cutting someone off from the surrounding world and from reality.

Finally, Muriel comments:

> By using the feedback from the fictional story and reflecting this into [my thinking about a current client, 'Kirsty'] I gained an insight and understanding, not only about my client but about myself as well. It seemed that for me 'The journey' represented the idealistic progress through the counselling process, but I have come to realise that to be a fiction – almost an illusion. Not all clients make that progress and some may never come out of the fog. Realising that not all clients that come to me for counselling will find 'enlightenment' through the counselling relationship and process seems an important lesson for me to learn. *I cannot be ideal.* There is no magic cure for Kirsty and yet she hangs firmly to the belief that one day she will be able to, once again, go out without her wheelchair. Have I too clung to this belief, and is it an illusion for both of us?

* * *

EXAMPLE 10: WHAT IS A STORY? (I): 'REFLEXIVITY': A STORY ABOUT WRITING A STORY

'A difficult assignment' by Hilary Engward

FICTION: literary works invented by the imagination (*Collins English Dictionary*); an invented story or explanation (ditto); (or: work invented to reduce one to a literal/literary state of 'can't do it')

'Write a piece of fiction,' he said easily.
'Oh yeah,' I thought, 'Easy is one thing this isn't going to be.'
'I've got to write a piece of fiction,' I said to my Other Half.
'Fiction,' he said, 'What for? Can you do it? I couldn't.'
Not what I wanted to hear. Not the 'What for?' – that seemed irrelevant. But the 'couldn't do' sounded horribly familiar.
'H. has got to write a piece of fiction,' the Other Half said to his colleague. The colleague said he couldn't, hadn't done since his school

days – which is more recently than me, and (some consolation) more recently than the Other Half. The 'couldn't do' rang another familiar bell.

'I've got to write a piece of fiction,' I said to the prospective mother-in-law (otherwise known as the Outlaw).

'What on?' (the dreaded question) 'Why don't you write about Mars; that's current. Or,' she continued, 'Sue's good at creative writing, or at least she used to be, she once did … '

'Whoopee doo', I thought, 'I'll get her to do it then; at least someone can do it!'

* * *

All weekend it bugged me, and the fact that it bugged me bugged me even more. Finally frustration kicked in, closely followed by helplessness and despair. (A slight over-exaggeration, but this is fiction, after all.) 'That's it,' I announced, 'I am going to create', and stomped off in a rather dramatic fashion, eager to nip such feelings of inadequacy in their infancy.

'What exactly are you going to create?' the Other Half rudely interrupted.

Not what I wanted to hear.

'Oh I don't know. – Anything; after all I can knock up academic type waffle easily enough; this can't be that difficult, can it?'

I thought of all the good books I'd read and romanticised myself as the next Charlotte or Emily Brontë, and then philosophised myself as the new, up-and-coming Jostein Gaarder … and realised this *was* going to be 'that' difficult.

'I just can't do it.' I flopped onto the settee next to the Other Half feeling dejected, and attempted to look lost and forlorn, just in case a cuddle or positive words were about to be offered.

'No such thing as "can't",' he said.

Horribly familiar, those words. I imagined myself saying something similar to stressed students who just 'can't' write an essay on … and suddenly felt, well, rather empathetic.

Commentary

Is this 'a story'? It seems to be 'factual' rather than 'imagined', so if it is a 'fiction', it is a fiction in the less familiar sense of the word 'shaped'. And indeed it is very dramatically shaped in the obvious sense that the whole impact is delayed until the last line, and this also means that a very typical element of a conventional story is also present – a feeling of suspense: is the difficult assignment going to get written or isn't it? is this going to turn out to be a story – a completed piece of writing – or is it going to remain a series of fragments? So this piece reminds us of another idea mentioned in the introduction to the chapter: that one dimension of a story may concern the very process of attempting to write it. (This 'reflexive' [self-analytical] aspect of fiction is explored more fully in the following chapter on patchwork texts.)

Hilary Engward is a nurse educator, and she wrote the story at a time when she was worried about the difficulties her students were experiencing in courses she was teaching. So her title neatly refers to the significance of this piece of writing: by finding herself unexpectedly faced with 'a difficult assignment' (writing a story) she is suddenly able to identify in a new way with her students. The title is thus ambiguous, a sort of pun, but we only realise this when we read the last line – when the significance of the title is suddenly revealed. Hilary said, 'I knew those students needed something, but I didn't know what it was.' By thinking about writing her story, she decided what she thought it was: emotional support on the part of tutors and others to combat the despairing resistance which builds up in response to students' sense of the difficulty of an academic course. Finding an assignment difficult is not merely a matter of intellectual capacity, but a defensive emotional response when a task is experienced as unfamiliar. Hilary noted that as soon as this analogy between her own situation and that of her students occurred to her, 'It seemed obvious what to do; I didn't have to ponder about it any more; writing the story just seemed natural, comfortable.'

But what sort of emotional support is it that students need? The details of the story offer some interesting thoughts. Although it ends with 'empathy' (cf. the stories by Nick Boddington and Jeannette Yems), that is not 'the whole story'. Certainly, the role of 'trusted others' is important throughout: the Other Half, the mother-in-law, even the Other Half's 'colleague' are turned to for support, but mere sympathy and advice don't work. What does work is a 'moment of insight', and this comes from 'bracing' rather than 'positive' words from the Other Half. And not a new piece of advice either, but a reminder of the relevance of an already familar idea. We can thus see how the reflexivity of this piece creates another sort of metaphorical story to set alongside the two previous stories: the process of writing the story is a metaphor for what the story is 'about'. And this in turn reminds us of Julia Plunkett's comment ('If only she knew', above) that the sharing of stories enacts the ideal mode of sharing of information between professional and client.

* * *

EXAMPLE 11: WHAT IS A STORY? (II): VOICES FOR A 'DOCUMENTARY'

'The judgement' by Steven Childs

Who are these people? What do they know about me, or my children? It feels like my whole life has been laid open, questioned, judged. I know that things have gone wrong but why won't they believe me? ...

We have heard the evidence from the social worker, the mother, the father and the guardian-ad-litem ... [*]

Three days we've been in this cold room. I feel scared. The questions they asked confused me. What did my barrister want me to say? We talked about it last week, we went over the questions she would ask. I made such a mess of it, everyone was looking at me. He was looking at me with those dark piercing eyes. I could feel them burning into my head every time I opened my mouth. I tried not to look at him, but I couldn't help it. Calls himself a father! All he ever did was drink and beat me up. It's because of him I got into such a mess. I hate him for putting me through this. Do they believe him? He says I'm lying. I'm not ...

... the mother's evidence, although honest, was not based on the reality of the situation ...

That's not true! I did everything the social worker asked of me. I went to his meetings, I saw the children every week. The kids told me they wanted to come home. They have to give them back to me, I'm their mother, what would I do without them? I can't stand this, I wish they would get to the point, why are they repeating everything that's been said? They're just trying to make me look bad. Come on, tell me what you have decided ...

... that the child is suffering or is likely to suffer significant harm ...

They are saying I harmed the children. I told them the truth about my drinking. There was enough food. ... the police exaggerated it, they always do. The neighbours never gave me a chance, social never helped me, they all had it in for me. I never hurt my kids, they love me, you ask them. ... I feel tired, I'm not going to let them see I'm upset. I'm not going to cry ...

... It is clear to this Court that the mother loves her children ...

They do believe me. They're going to give me a second chance. My barrister said we will tell them you are willing to go for a residential assessment, we accept the threshold criteria has been met, whatever that means,

---

[*] *Guardian-ad-litem*: an experienced, qualified social worker appointed by the court specifically to uphold the interests of the child during the proceedings of a child protection case.

just me and the kids together, being watched, but that's OK, I can do that, then I can show them. I could collect the children tonight, take them home. I know, we'll have their favourite tea, fish fingers and chips, then me and Ally will take them down to my sister's, we can all go down to the park together, we can be a family again, like it used to be …

… it is our belief that the father was not telling the truth, we believe the mother's account over that of the father …

See, they said they don't believe him, they believe me, they must be giving me another chance. They're right, he was a rotten father. Where has he been for the past six months? He said he wanted to care for them and then he disappears, what sort of father does that? He lied, I'm glad they saw through that, trying to make me look like I had the problems. He's staring at me again, serves him right, I don't care what he threatens to do, he can't do no worse than what's happened during the past year …

… The Guardian concludes that these three children will need above average levels of parenting …

What do they mean, above average? When will I know when I have been above average? I thought I was doing all right, no one said if I was an average parent or not, how will they decide that? Do I have to take some sort of test? Will it be like being back at school again? I did terrible at school, I didn't pass any exams, I've no qualifications, I didn't even do child care, although I was OK in home economics …

… It is therefore this Court's decision to grant Care Orders to the local authority, and for the children to be placed for adoption …

I don't understand … I thought … I'm their mother, you can't give them to someone else. What will I say to them? This can't be right. What gives them the right to take my children from me? I gave birth to them, I had them, they're mine … why won't anyone look at me? I've got to get out of here, it's so cold. I'm so cold …

Commentary

Steven Childs is a social worker. In this story a judge is making his final summing up, granting a Care Order to the local authority and placing children for adoption. Interspersed with the official judicial phrases we are given the thoughts of the mother as she misinterprets what is being said and thinks up to the last minute that she will be able to keep her children. The mother's thoughts reveal her lack of understanding of the issues and her continued absorption with her own needs, so that although we feel anger at her disempowerment by the official process we can also see the rationale for the judge's decision.

Steven's story has elements of a drama and of a documentary. The two voices (that of the judge and the mother) are presented alternately, without any comment from a narrator. This story, then, has something in common with the patchwork texts in the next chapter: instead of the single voice of the narrator, we have the pure contrast between the voice of the judge and the voice of the mother. But the contrasts between the two voices are carefully contrived to create a powerful emotional impact, so even though there is no narrator there is a strong sense of a statement being made – about the disempowerment, helplessness and suffering of those who do not understand the rationale of the system in which they are caught. However, the 'documentary' format enables us to appreciate that there is a perspective other than sympathy for the mother. Without a narrator we, the readers, are distanced, just as the narrator has distanced himself by abstaining from comment. A story in this format very obviously presents its statement in the form of a question, a dilemma: there are two sides here, and it is not easy to know with which to sympathise.

But to say that Steven's story has the format of a documentary is not to say that he was conscious of knowing that format and using it. Story formats seem to be like an 'unconscious' cultural heritage – a richness in our means of expression of which we seem to be almost unaware. Thus, like the writers of most of the stories in this collection, Steven found himself, in his words, 'suddenly freed up' to write in a way which he had not done before, and in a way which 'to my surprise evoked reactions which I did not expect'.

* * *

EXAMPLE 12: WHAT IS A STORY? (III): A PATCHWORK OF QUOTATIONS

' "And the word was made flesh and dwelt amongst us" '
by Tricia Hill

A distant voice cried 'Help' and a rectangular sheet of parchment in a peaceful shade of green was created. Upon it were inscribed many meaningful words including the words 'concern', 'child' and 'Justine'.

The paper passed through many hands, and telephone calls were made on the basis of its contents. Details were entered onto a computer where they would remain stored, safe, for many years. A final hand inscribed 'NFA' (No Further Action) and the paper was joined by several others, white in colour, and neatly typed upon them were details of the information provided. The small sheaf of paper was put to one side, soon to be lost beneath many other similar bundles of paper, all bearing similar words.

Sometime later another piece of green paper was inscribed with 'Justine' and 'concern' but this time including the word 'offence'. This paper was enjoined with the first. Again the original sheaf, passing from hand to hand, this time being encased in a protective covering, denoting its fragility and vulnerability. A visit was made, records made and added to what was now called a file.

'The school should deal with this.'

'Refer it to Child and Family Consultation Service (CAFS).'

'Youth Justice are involved, let them deal with it.'

'It's not within our remit, give it to Childcare.'

'It doesn't meet our criteria.'

'It's low priority.'

'It's not our responsibility.'

'Hold it on duty.'

A voice cried, 'Help' and a piece of pink paper was generated and inscribed with many words including the words 'harm' and 'Justine'. It was added to the ever-growing sheaf of papers in their protective cover.

'It's already open with CAFS.'

'Who's going to take this?'

'I'm at capacity, ask someone else.'

'We haven't got the resources.'

And the papers were passed from hand to hand, each brow furrowing in concern. This concern being quickly replaced by the next sheaf of papers passing through their hands.

In a dark room somewhere, Justine cried, 'Help.'

Commentary

Like the author of the previous story, Tricia Hill is a social worker, and the themes of the two stories are clearly related. But the form of Tricia's story is very different. Here the fragmentary phrases which make up much of the piece are so small that it seems more like a mosaic than a patchwork. As a result, this is a story which not only has no narrator but has no characters either! It is not like a documentary (in which each voice is heard quite clearly) but like a TV advertisement, consisting of a rapid kaleidoscope of shifting images deftly edited, which gives it a sort of abstract quality (this aspect of modern forms of fiction is discussed in more detail in the introduction to Chapter 3). Moreover, in this story the abstract quality of its format matches exactly its theme – de-personalisation. There is no subjectivity at all here, because a bureaucratic system of 'documentation' has taken over the human 'word'.

At the heart of the story is the ironic contrast between the neglect of 'Justine' and the almost 'loving' care with which the files are created and their 'fragility and vulnerability' protected. Justine herself is 'a distant voice … in a dark room somewhere', but the documentaton of her case is a thing of multi-coloured beauty, consisting of 'parchment in a *peaceful* shade of green' and white and pink, 'neatly typed'. This is not so much 'child protection' as 'document protection'.

The title has biblical echoes, but the meaning of the story is the exact opposite of the biblical phrase: instead of the word (of God) being made flesh, humanity has been converted into 'mere' words (records, sheafs of papers, files). Thus one reader thought that the biblical echo might be interpreted as suggesting that there is something blasphemous about this bureaucratisation of a human life. Tricia had not specifically intended this, but readily agreed that this meaning was 'there'. Similarly, she was surprised when another reader focused on the fact that as the system members passed on the files their brows furrowed in 'concern' and suggested that the story thus demonstrates that they are not just perpetrators of the depersonalising system but, like Justine herself, are its victims. In the end, then, there is (as usual in a story, as we have often noted) a recognition of an ambiguity: the staff manning a depersonalising care system *are* actually caring and concerned.

In other words there is something seriously incomplete about this presentation of a system in which abstract documentation is the only form of coherent life, with human voices reduced to helpless fragments; it provokes the question: what strategies might there be for care staff to 're-personalise' their work? This is a question which needs to be answered: at one level the title is still intact: the word does still exist as a moral ideal for humanity and does still dwell amongst us. This story, then, is only the start of a train of thought; it needs a continuation. And this leads us directly to the purpose and value of the patchwork texts presented in the following chapter.

* * *

The striking thing about these stories is their variety. Without consciously studying the various ways in which experience may be shaped into a fiction, and stimulated only by discussion of one or two examples, professional practitioners find some version of a genre or some personal format which expresses a complex set of ideas with a degree of aplomb which is interesting to others and satisfying for themselves. In almost every case these are people who have not written fiction since they were at primary school, but – once they have grasped the basic idea – they find that the actual writing flows 'naturally', 'spontaneously'. Only Jane Arnett ('The visit') reports that she revised her story substantially after the first draft, and that was a decision she took before sharing it with anyone else. This suggests that writing fiction is experienced as 'permission' to draw on resources for expression which most people are surprised to find they possess and which they were initially fairly sure they did not possess. There is thus an emancipatory potential in this type of work, which will be discussed at length in Chapter 7.

Meanwhile, we need to consider the limitations of simply 'writing a story' as a mode of professional reflection, and it is these limitations which will be addressed in Chapter 3.

3

THE 'PATCHWORK TEXT'

Shaping meaning through the exploration of diversity

Introduction

One obvious feature of the stories in the previous chapter is that they are all very short (much shorter than the average length for a conventional published short story), as are almost all the stories which have been written by participants in our various workshops and courses over the years. The conciseness of the stories has various advantages: it makes the task of story-writing less daunting and the sharing of the stories easier, and it also means that the stories are very 'pointed', offering clear themes for discussion. But this brevity also suggests a problem: how can such brief and self-contained pieces of writing (no matter how powerful and rich in ambiguous meanings) form the basis for a process of reflection which is sustained over the several weeks of a reflective writing course, or over a substantial period of professional work?

Moreover, a story always has a clear sense of an ending. It is the ending of a story which (retrospectively) shapes its various elements into a pattern, and thus reveals the overall meaning. Indeed, a story is often conceived at the moment when the writer has the idea for the ending; and what makes a story work is the sense that it is 'rounded off' by an ending which is felt to be satisfying. Thus there is a tension between this aspect of the story format and an important aspect of reflection on professional experience: a short story moves purposefully towards its ending, whereas the process of reflection strives to be open-ended for as long as possible, starting from a known point but exploring outwards, seeking alternative points of view and different experiences as points of comparison and contrast.

There is a second potential tension between the story format and 'reflection'. A story presents itself as a finished product: it fashions the raw material of the writer's ideas and experiences into an artistic shape, so that it presents a statement and suggests a point of view; but in doing so it disguises both the shaping process and the original material from which it was derived. In the introduction to the previous chapter we noted that some stories do contain oblique references to the process of their own making, but Hilary Engward's story (story 10, 'A difficult assignment') is most unusual in focusing directly on how the story itself came to be written. An account of a sustained process of reflection, in contrast, often starts from a personal interpretation of events and explores 'inwards', seeking to make explicit the origins of this interpretation in ideologies and in the writer's own experiences and values.

Of course, sharing interpretations of a story always reveals its personal basis, its limitations, and – therefore – alternative possibilities; the apparent closure of the ending is always incomplete and the statement made by a story is always an ambiguous statement – more like a question than a proposition. But if writing fiction is to be the basis for a process of reflection that is to be sustained, we need a format where questioning and exploring beyond one's initial set of ideas is made explicit and is built into the writing process itself, as well as into the discussion of the writing.

Now, in theory, one could perhaps have encouraged writers to expand and develop their original short stories into longer, more elaborate narratives, but that would have seemed uncomfortable, for at least two reasons. First, most writers felt very pleased with their stories as they were, so that the suggestion that they should substantially change what they have written would have felt unwelcome and even intrusive. Second, the discussion of the significance of the stories always leads in a variety of different directions, as we saw in the previous chapter, so that further work would tend towards 'multiplying' the story, rather than simply extending it.

Thus, in order to sustain the reflective process, a format is needed which is flexible enough to allow different ways of writing to be combined, a format which allows the writer to move easily between description, imaginative creation and analytical commentary. The format of the text needs to be one which can be built up gradually over a period of time, even while its final form remains uncertain, a text which can allow the focus to shift, in response to the discussion of each successive piece of writing. It needs to avoid the rigid linear logic of the essay and to retain as much as possible of the freedom which derives from the ambiguity and implicitness of the fictional mode. Hence, although writing a story about one's professional work is an important and central part of the reflective writing course, the overall format for participants' writing is not simply 'a story', but a 'multi-voiced' text, a 'patchwork text'.

The format of the patchwork text, as illustrated in the examples which follow, developed gradually as the course was repeated in successive years. It is an attempt to enable participants to draw on the whole range of work they produce over a period of about ten weeks. A patchwork text always includes a story (in the general sense illustrated by the examples in the previous chapter), but the story is used as a starting point for other pieces of writing (some of them stories, some not), which 'open up' endings, continue themes, explore contrasts, and consider experiential and intellectual origins and alternatives. Most of this chapter, like the previous one, consists of illustrative examples, but we begin with some introductory explanations, first on the format of the patchwork text, and second on the context in which the texts were written.

The patchwork text

The defining characterisic of a patchwork is that it is obviously not entirely produced by one person: it is assembled from the work of others. Similarly, the patchwork text is constructed so that it presents the voices of others as well as the voice of the author. It assembles a plurality of voices concerning an event but without explicitly claiming to include those voices within the single authoritative voice of the author. It thus expresses a recognition that any given voice (presenting an interpretation of events) is informed by other, prior voices (expressing different views of those events). Everyone constructs their own reality from the voices they have heard and, since no single text can include all possible voices, the reality constructed by any author/narrator/observer must be presented as both incomplete and questionable. In this sense, the patchwork text differs from a story in which the voices of the characters are carefully placed within the author's overall scheme

It has been argued that even in a story, especially in a long novel, the various characters retain a sort of separate vitality which is independent of the author's overall narrative (Bakhtin 1984: p. 6; Lodge 1990: p. 86). (As examples, we might think of all the quirky minor characters in Charles Dickens' novels, who can be so much more interesting than his heroes and heroines.) One explanation of this is that writers identify to some extent with all the different characters they invent, which brings us back to the point that the overall meaning of a work of fiction is always ambiguous (see introduction to the previous chapter). But in the patchwork text this ambiguity is made explicit: the author is but one voice among many and the text remains a collection of fragments, in spite of its efforts to synthesise; it does not set out to present a single compelling vision of 'the truth', but admits that in the end it can never be more than a set of allusions to possible, plural, truths.

The purpose of the patchwork text, then, is to express directly a sort of cognitive 'modesty' on the part of the author, since it makes explicit the uncertainty of our understanding and its inevitably subjective basis. In other words, the basic problem which the patchwork text tries to address is as follows. How can we attempt to represent our understanding in a way which is strong and persuasive (which arouses and sustains the reader's interest) but which also makes clear its limitations? How can we present our explorations of reality in a way which minimises any suggestion that we have reached an objective or final conclusion? And the solution proposed by the patchwork text is as follows: to include, alongside the author's voice and the author's perspective, the voices and perspectives from which it has been derived. Like a story, it is a synthesis, an imaginative shaping of diverse elements into a unity. But its unity is looser and more obviously fragile: it shows that its general analysis is based on a particular range of details and on imaginative identification with others' experience; it makes visible the process whereby its unity is derived from an irreducible diversity, the obstinate diversity of other people's realities.

The concept of a patchwork is a familiar one, and patchwork-making has its origins as a practical folk art, making something new and useful of already available material (Parker 1991: pp. 6–11), sometimes using a template as an organising pattern but sometimes as a free improvisation (Jackson 1985: p. 8; Parker 1991: pp. 34–9). We have therefore borrowed the term as a general name for written texts where the unifying structure is not simply a linear narrative but a series of loosely linked pieces illustrating a theme or gradually building up a set of perspectives. In this sense, patchwork texts are not new. The tradition of text-as-collection goes back at least as far as Chaucer's *Canterbury Tales*, and modern examples are not hard to find. Douglas Coupland's *Generation X* (1992) and Irvine Welsh's *Trainspotting* (1993) both have the form of a linked series of stories illustrating aspects of a way of life, and Ilya Ehrenburg's *The Life of the Automobile* (1929) and Julian Barnes' *A History of the World in 10½ Chapters* (1990) both present general themes by means of an amalgam of stories (historical and imaginary) and analytical reflections. Even more relevant to the work described in this chapter are Primo Levi's two books *The Periodic Table* (1986) and *The Wrench* (1988) in which he organises a series of autobiographical reminiscences and speculations, which he calls 'stories' (Levi 1986: pp. 128, 203) to form a celebration of the moral and spiritual significance of a professional role.

Finally, it is also appropriate that our name for this more-than-narrative format is borrowed from the visual arts. In part this is a reminder that many of the arguments presented above are derived from ideas of collage (in painting) and montage (in photography) which were very influential in the early years of the twentieth century (see Chapter 7: p. 212–13). It is also a reminder that over the last few decades our awareness of written texts has been substantially influenced by our immersion in the visual language and techniques of cinema and TV. For example, we are used to having a statement presented to us in the form of a sequence of images which are simply placed next to one another, either as a rapid succession of fragments – in the style of cinema and TV advertisements – or as in a documentary where the overall statement gradually emerges from a series of interviews and scenes. Sometimes the maker of the documentary includes linking comments, but often there is no explicit commentary, as in the 'fly-on-the-wall' format, where, in the words of documentary maker John Grierson, 'a pattern of thought and feeling' is formed from 'the material of experience' (Hardy 1966: p. 139). A pattern, of course, expresses a theme, and the work of shaping and forming this pattern is what Paul Rotha (a pioneer in the art of the documentary) calls 'analytical editing' (Rotha 1936: p. 134), i.e. managing the speed and rhythm of images to convey mood and feeling (p. 160) and the variety and conflict which make up the theme (p. 163). A perfect description of the shaping process of fiction and, as we shall see, of how patchwork texts are produced.

We are therefore used to films which begin to tell their story by presenting a succession of apparently unrelated scenes or images, so that we are drawn into the film by being posed the question: how are these different matters going to turn out to be linked? And many modern novels use a similar method (e.g. Michael Crichton's *Jurassic Park* (1991), Ben Elton's *Stark* (1989) and *Popcorn* (1996), and Douglas Adams' *A Hitch-hiker's Guide to the Galaxy* (1979) – itself derived from an original TV series. So, we have become accustomed to reading with a sense of 'incompleteness', knowing that the full meaning of this scene or image will be revealed later on, after other scenes and images have been added. We have become used to reading a text almost in the same way as we put together a jigsaw puzzle, because our deep experience of film language has taught us to approach the art of fiction (the shaping of experience into meaning) in terms of the art of the film director – assembling and editing, requiring the viewer to work out connections. For example, we easily read the blank spaces between sections of a printed text as similar to the edited 'jumps' between the scenes of a film, as marking an as yet unknown shift of either time or space or theme, or some combination of all three. We are, in other words, used to being 'interested' in a text because we are, in the short term, puzzled (see the opening pages of Toni Morrison's *Beloved* [1987] and Michael Ondaatje's *The English Patient* [1992]), knowing that later sections of the text will make things clear. Salman Rushdie, in his novel *Midnight's Children*, acknowledges the novelist's general debt to cinematic language by beginning to write in the form of a screenplay: 'Close up of my grandfather's right hand. ... We cut to a long-shot – nobody from Bombay should be without a basic film vocabulary ... ' (Rushdie 1982: pp. 32–3).

In writing and reading patchwork texts we draw on skills and understandings derived from our grasp of film language, which has become an essential aspect of our ability to construct stories. Susan Hart reports a nice piece of research evidence indicating how deeply the language of film has affected our approach to verbal texts: 'Adrian', a ten-year-old boy whose difficulties with writing were causing his teachers much concern, was nevertheless able to construct highly effective science fiction stories using a sophisticated understanding of narrative structure derived from watching TV, e.g. creating suspense by rapid switching between a variety of scenes (Hart 1996: pp. 61–9).

Thus the method of the patchwork text has strong analogies with processes which are familiar to us in the medium of film. However, when these methods are embodied in written texts, as in the examples presented in this chapter, the effect is somewhat unexpected. Patchwork texts do have a linear development, not unlike that of a narrative or an argument or a report, but they have to be read in a slightly different way, because they also have a 'radial' structure, not just moving forwards but working outwards from an initial point, assembling and editing together a variety of contrasting material, surveying a circular horizon of meaning in different directions. In other words, each piece makes its own point as well as contributing to the whole, and the writer's commentaries are just that – commentaries: even when they are placed at the end they don't (necessarily or fully) form a conclusion and sum up everything which has gone before.

Further discussion of the theoretical background to the concept of the patchwork text is presented in Chapter 7 (see pp. 210–13), but in order to illustrate the 'problem' of reading a patchwork text (as a preparation for the texts in this chapter) it is interesting to compare George Eliot's novel *Daniel Deronda* with Julian Barnes' patchwork text *A History of the World in 10½ Chapters*. Both works may be thought of as being explorations of the question: how shall we find general spiritual significance in the relationships of our daily lives? George Eliot tells a single story which focuses on the contrast between two characters. One, Gwendolen Harleth, is a worldly woman who marries for money and social position, and discovers that in doing so she has lost her self-respect as a moral being. The other, Daniel Deronda, discovers that he is a not an English aristocrat but a Jew, and responds by abandoning his former social opportunities and becoming a member of a community devoted to philosophical Zionism. The novel includes a wide variety of characters, but each one has a place in this overall scheme, and as we follow the sequence of moral choices made by the two central characters, we are left in no doubt about the novelist's purpose, which at one level has the clarity of an ethical treatise. In contrast, Julian Barnes' book presents eleven different scenarios, each with some oblique link to the story of Noah's salvation and survival by building the Ark in obedience to God's will. For example, we have a woodworm's critical viewpoint on the story, arguing that Noah's self-righteous religious conviction led him to behave with oppressive injustice; we have the story of a woman who concludes that, due to the insensitivities of human social relationships, a nuclear war is inevitable and tries to escape on a raft with two cats; there is the story of a man who disguised himself as a woman to escape from the *Titanic*, and the conversion to religion of an astronaut after hearing God command him to seek the remains of Noah's Ark, during his landing on the moon. And so on. Each story is written in the voice of a different 'character' except for the 'half-chapter' which is written by Julian Barnes 'in his own voice' (see Barnes 1990: p. 227). This half-chapter is an extended essay on the importance of a loving relationship between two individuals in defining the meaning of human existence, but it is not the final chapter, nor does it explicitly sum up the significance of the others. The final chapter is the story of a man who finds that 'heaven' is a dream where all your egotistical wishes are gratified and that in the end this becomes intolerable. This *may* be read as a general response to the other previous chapters, but (again) this is nowhere made explicit. Thus the ambiguity of Barnes' work is simply that, although each piece is clear (and highy entertaining) in itself, it is not clear exactly how they are related, which requires us, the readers, to make our own emphasis and, indeed, allows us to see different links on different occasions.

The texts which follow do not have quite as much ambiguity as Barnes' book, but they do have something of the same quality, and should not be read, therefore, simply as 'essays' with 'illustrations'. Although they are not – overall – 'stories', the process of their writing is a fictional, artistic shaping; they are allusive rather than analytical, their basis is more an imaginative richness than an argumentative precision, and much of their overall significance is presented implicitly, rather than explicitly.

The 'reflective writing' course

The course in which the patchwork texts are produced is a separate module within the University's overall programme of modular units. It consists of ten weekly meetings which start with participants working in small groups (four or five people) exchanging pieces of writing they have produced during the previous week. The second part of the weekly meeting introduces general aspects of the writing process, e.g. beginnings, endings, links, etc. (The distance learning materials in Chapter 4 provide full details of this aspect of the work.)

The first piece is written in response to a very general set of possible titles (e.g. 'Home', 'A learning experience', 'Coping', 'A misunderstanding', 'The contents of a room/cupboard/handbag', 'Why have I remembered this incident after all these years?'). Thereafter the pieces all need to be in some sense consciously related to the writer's professional experience. The first of these is a 'story', and the process for this is the same as for the work illustrated in the previous chapter; but the next piece to be written after the story is a 'continuation' of some sort. Some initial guidance is provided on what this might mean (e.g. 'Describe these events from the point of view of one of the other characters', 'Rewrite the incident with the centre of power altered', etc.) but it is made clear that the nature of this continuation should arise from the discussion of the professional themes when the pieces of writing are shared. For the next four or five weeks participants continue to write different pieces in any genre or style, but always arising from some aspect of their professional work. In the last two or three weeks of the course they begin to consider what professional themes underlie the variety of their writing and to select and edit together a unified piece, including, at this stage, such introductory, linking or final comments as they think would be helpful for the reader.

The anticipated reader is an important presence in the course for two reasons. First, participants know from the outset that at the end of the course a booklet will be compiled containing all the texts produced by the whole group (which may consist of three or four small working groups), and that copies of this booklet will be distributed to all course participants, on the understanding that it is (initially) treated as confidential. Second, it is emphasised that the purpose of the writing is not simply to construct an acceptable assignment for academic assessment, but to create a piece which might be appropriate for wider publication among colleagues, as the dissemination of 'practice wisdom' derived from personal insight and experience. (A collection of the texts written for the course by Essex social workers was produced and circulated in Essex Social Services Department [Maisch and Winter 1995].) Hence the patchwork text form is intended not only as a method for exploring and formulating professional experience but also as an effective format in which to communicate this experience to colleagues.

The process of sharing one's writing is potentially threatening, and for this reason the working groups are small and remain constant throughout the course; and ground rules are drawn up drawing attention to the need for confidentiality, commitment and supportiveness. As with the story workshops, there is a clear directive that the writer is not there to be interrogated, but to listen to, and make notes on, the variety of responses from readers. Readers are told to avoid evaluative responses, and to focus on the professional issues that the piece of writing raises; on what passages stand out for them, as readers; the significance of beginnings, endings, and titles; and possible directions in which the writing might be continued.

The assessment criteria for the reflective writing course (which are used by participants in constructing their texts, and which thus guided the production of the following examples) were designed to synthesise professional and academic educational objectives, as follows:

(a) Careful, detailed observation of events and situations;
(b) Empathising with the standpoint of other people;
(c) Noticing the various emotional dimensions of events and situations;
(d) Addressing the complexities of issues, events and situations;
(e) Making connections between different events and situations, and between specific details and general principles derived from a range of professional knowledge;
(f) Demonstrating learning, in response to both professional experience and the process of reflecting upon/writing about it.

These criteria were developed through a research project which involved:

1 developing a general theory of the professional role, with particular reference to the professional worker's responsibility for

(a) interpreting a body of knowledge and values in specific cases,
(b) sensitivity to the emotional dimensions of situations,
(c) their own self-awareness, and
(d) their own continuous learning.

2 An investigation into practitioners' views of the personal qualities required by professional work;
3 An investigation into the intellectual qualities required for success in academic work (see Winter and Maisch 1996: ch. 4)

The criteria for the work are thus derived from a model of professional reflection. Our contention (and our experience) is that the patchwork text is a format which enables these reflective criteria to be met in a way which is professionally enlightening for the writer and artistically satisfying for the reader, as well as satisfying the requirements of academic examiners.

* * *

The following examples have been selected, as with the stories for the previous chapter, to illustrate a variety of professional contexts and, above all, a variety of approaches. One example moves backwards and inwards from professional practice to explore autobiographical origins; another consciously uses a variety of written genres to present a clearly defined theme; a third puts together a variety of incidents to explore complex professional role issues. Due to the length of the pieces, only a few examples of complete texts can be given, and some of the examples consist only of sections from a text, illustrating a certain aspect of the process. Most of the texts include passages of analysis, so in order to clarify the presentation, editorial commentary is presented in the form of an 'Introduction' and (in most cases) a 'Final note' for each example.

* * *

EXAMPLE 1: OPENING UP THE ENDING OF 'A STORY'

Introduction

The following extracts from Matt Capener's text 'Through the keyhole' illustrate how the patchwork text opens up the ending of a story. The first section ('Peter … just lucky!') presents the thoughts of a man with learning disabilities recently transferred from a residential institution to his 'own' flat, with professional support, under the recent government policy of 'Community care'. The title and the final line give a specific theme and shape to the piece. But then Matt (a social worker who works with clients like Peter) raises, in his commentary, a question about how far Peter's new-found contentment is cause for professional satisfaction (these commentaries are like the 'stitching', with which Matt 'sews together' the sections of his patchwork). In his next piece Matt goes on to present the story of 'Frank', where the tone and the perspective is much less optimistic, suggesting the limitations of the support Frank is receiving from his 'friend' (the social worker). The term 'friend' is made to take on an ironic edge in this piece, whereas in the first piece Peter does indeed seem 'lucky'.

'Through the keyhole' by Matt Capener

1. Peter ... just lucky!

Peter sat on his new bed, next to his new bedside locker and new comfy chair, looking around the four walls of HIS bedroom. At sixty-two years old he now, at last, had his own room. 'They' had made a real effort to make his room a lovely place ... nice carpets, pictures on the walls and curtains that he could close. 'They' had helped him buy some ornaments and put up some nice corner shelves. He had his own little sink with towels and soaps for the morning. He had a wardrobe full of new clothing. Peter had a keyworker [responsible social worker] now and he seemed really nice. They spent time just talking. Peter enjoyed that. Just talking with someone and having someone who could help him with things. Most of all though, Peter liked his own space, his own bedroom where he could be alone and lock the door if he wanted.

Peter didn't know why things had changed so much. What he'd done to make 'them' decide he could go 'free'. Why 'they' had chosen him instead of some of the others who were still there. Still in the big place. Why 'they' had changed over the years and started to treat him differently.

'Just lucky I suppose,' he thought.

His keyworker Ben knocked on the door and brought in a cup of tea. 'There you go Pete ... A nice cup of tea before you go to sleep. I'm on in the morning so I'll help you get up.'

'Yeah,' Peter replied.

'Okay mate, see you in the morning. Sleep well,' said Ben as he left the room, closing the door behind him.

Peter drank his tea slowly as he sat on the edge of his bed and had some more thoughts. The 'not so lucky' type of thoughts. The type of thoughts that you and I would have and then wake up and say, 'I had a terrible nightmare last night'. The type of thoughts that have violent images attached to them or scenes of inhumane degradation. Peter remembered when he was the 'piss boy'. He had to empty the full up toilet buckets that were left in the ward at night. Splashing against his legs and then being hit for spilling some on the floor. He remembered sleeping in a room with twenty-four other boys and men. The snoring, the noises, the unwanted advances. Peter remembered the funny overalls he had to wear and the nurses talking about him, joking about the way he walked and talked. Peter remembered the years and years of nothingness. Nothing to do. Nowhere to go. No-one to see. He could remember his bathroom that had three baths in it and the toothbrushes that always got mixed up. He knew when to queue up for his tablets which were good for him and when to queue up for his food. Peter could remember going to the 'big place' when he was young but he never knew why. What happened? Why couldn't he live with mum anymore? Peter could remember hours and hours of daytime television. He remembered which staff were 'safe' and which ones beat him. These 'bad thoughts' that Peter had spanned over 43 years.

He was 'just lucky' he thought as he settled down to sleep.

Commentary

This piece concentrated on issues of transition and 'community care'. The current trend towards hospital closure is obviously regarded as good practice and a step forward in service provision. But what does it feel like? Do we really make a difference to the lifestyles of these people or is this merely a geographical shift in many cases? We create residential services that apply the principles of 'normalisation'. We ensure that our 'service users' are valued and involved in the community in which they live. At least we try …

2. Frank

He sat quietly in the pub at lunch-time enjoying half a pint of Guinness. He enjoyed the smoky noisy atmosphere. The pool table balls clattering around, the muffled noises of laughter, chatter and music. Frank didn't come here very often (not as often as he would like anyway) because he always needed someone to bring him.

Frank was a large man. His curved spine meant that he sat in an unusual way in his wheelchair and his long muscular arms could almost reach the floor. He had a very heavy brow and a 'blue' chin, despite being wet shaved every morning. His dark hair was receding at the front and was kept very short (as soon as it got long enough, Frank would pull it out and eat it!). His huge hands dwarfed the half pint pot as he brought it to his lips and drank noisily. He tried to put the glass back down on the table carefully but it never worked out that way. An enormous belch erupted from the pit of his stomach and it felt so funny that he laughed.

'Shhhh. Frank. Say pardon me,' said his friend.

'Prggnd me,' Frank attempted noisily, still chuckling to himself a little.

He really liked it here. The music, the people, watching the traffic go past the window and getting out of the 'home'. He could come here everyday if there was someone to bring him. That would be great.

Frank never really knew why people stared at him so much. He had grown used to it over the years but he still felt a bit uncomfortable. Little kids were the worst. They looked at him for ages, until their embarrassed parents pulled them away. Sometimes Frank would smile back at them but this seemed to make them stare for longer.

His saliva collected on his bottom lip and then slowly dripped into his lap. A large damp patch was evident where the drip had joined the others before it. Frank could not control this and it was always worse when he was drinking or eating. His friend (support worker) usually helped him keep his chin dry but he'd just nipped off to the loo. The stares continued but Frank didn't mind ... too much. He just sipped on his Guinness, spilling some more of it down his trousers. More stares.

His friend came back and they talked for a while. Well, Frank listened, to be accurate. What Frank really wanted was another Guinness. One of those big glasses. He attempted to tell his friend what he wanted but ended up being assisted to the toilet instead. God, that always happened!!

Now it was time to go. These trips to the pub always seemed so short but his friend was due to go home soon. Still, it was nice to get out for a while. Frank would spend the rest of the day in his 'home' watching telly or listening to other people talk. Sometimes about him. He wasn't sure when he would go to the pub next.

That evening, Frank's friend went to the cinema with some mates. After the film, they stopped at the local Chinese take-away and the off-licence for some cans. The next few hours were spent drinking, chatting and laughing. They had a great evening and planned to go out ice-skating this coming Friday. Eventually his mates went home and Frank's friend began to clear up his flat before falling into bed.

'Must take old Franky to the pub again next week, if I get the chance,' he thought, as he tossed the Guinness cans in the bin.

Commentary

It is healthy to examine our work and look at the issues of inclusion by demonstrating the stark differences in the lifestyles of Frank and his keyworker, who lives in the real world.

As stated by Wertheimer: 'We are on a journey from the artificial world we have created for people with learning disabilities towards the real world where we dream of supporting them in ordinary lives in inclusive communities' (Wertheimer 1996: p. 1).

Final note

In other sections of his text, Matt presents other incidents, seen from the view of staff and of clients, and a satirical 'glossary' of phrases with the different meanings they have for those who use them and those who hear them. The analytical commentaries are very brief, providing merely the professional 'context of ideas'. But the detail with which the worlds of Peter and Frank are presented allow us to see the complex nature of their experience, its intense suffering alongside its new-found positive aspects, and we feel the pathos of their gratitude. A powerful critique of professsional 'care' is subtly suggested when the second piece ends with Frank's 'friend' 'tossing the Guinness cans in the bin' – a gesture full of carelessness, which contrasts with the enormity of Frank's needs. On the other hand, the earlier details of Frank's behaviour and persona enable us to appreciate just how enormous are the demands which he places on his carer. We (like Matt) may feel critical of the carer but we are also given a basis for feeling some degree of compassion towards him as well as for Frank. There is a carefully sustained emotional and professional balance, in these two imaginative descriptions which the commentaries take for granted but do not refer to. And why should they, since the points are already made?

* * *

EXAMPLE 2: VARIATIONS ON A THEME

Introduction

This example consists of three sections from a text by Bernadette Saharoy, an operating theatre nurse in a hospital, in which she argues that operating theatre staff need to spend time talking with patients about to undergo a surgical operation. This overall theme was explicitly defined by Bernadette beforehand as the purpose of her writing, and each piece was chosen as a different angle and a different method for writing about it. So this example illustrates one way of constructing a patchwork text, namely as a set of variations on a given theme, rather as a textile patchwork is often based on a template. With the theme clearly present at the outset, e.g. in her title, Bernadette does not include any linking commentary, but allows each piece to make its own contribution to her overall argument (which she makes explicit in a final section, not included here).

The first piece presents the complexity of the patient's life-world, in which the approaching operation is a massive crisis, and the last line suggests how inadequate is the time available within hospital procedures for pre-operative discussion: how can fifteen minutes be sufficient when it seems that what may be needed is an exploration of the role of the patient's religious beliefs at this crucial time? The second piece adds to this argument: by showing the extent of a patient's misunderstanding of what is happening, it demonstrates the need for imaginative understanding on the part of theatre staff and for clear explanation of the different stages of the process. The third piece takes up and develops the arguments of both previous pieces by showing how a busy, technically oriented nurse can easily overlook the patient's emotional needs and that she needs to draw on her imaginative identification with the patient rather than merely present technical information.

'The case for pre-operative visiting of hospital patients by operating theatre staff' by Bernadette Saharoy

1. Contents of a bedside locker

Looking down on the standard bedside ward locker, I saw a display of family photographs. Some were framed, some were just propped up against other items that were standing there. All showed faces, smiling, laughing, people with arms around each other or interlinked in a friendly manner. These people looked close and supportive. Rachel appeared in certain photos, she looked healthy, a warm glow touched her face. The situations these photos showed were far removed from the stark clinical ward surroundings we were part of. I had been asked to visit Rachel on the ward. As a theatre nurse, it was part of my job to talk to patients pre-operatively and to offer any help they needed.

My eyes were drawn back to her locker. A very simple crucifix stood upright against the wall, it looked old and worn. It provided just a hint of the presence of Christianity in her life. Various 'Get Well' cards were scattered on top of the locker. I thought they were all so vaguely designed, equally relevant for a dose of Chicken-pox or even for malignant breast cancer which was Rachel's diagnosis. My mind pondered on those cards; in the shops they were found among greeting cards of all descriptions, birthdays, weddings etc. The buying of these cards in such trivial, bright settings seemed distant from the circumstances they represented. A small pile of books was stacked at the back of the locker: *Coping with Altered Body Image*, *Alternative Medicine*, and a Maeve Binchy novel was placed on the top. A strange combination, I thought at first. A mixture of information seeking (or was it an obligatory display of 'helpful books'?) and fictional escapism. A coping strategy perhaps for this personal crisis. There was a smell of cleanliness and freshness in the air. My thoughts were interrupted by the sound of muffled music, only the beat could be made out through Rachel's headphones. Vivaldi, I thought, 'The Four Seasons'.

The hospital bedside locker contained snippets from this woman's life. She was a Mother, a Sister, and a Daughter, totally encompassed by family love. She possessed an awareness of her religion at a time when she needed it. Acceptance of the true situation seemed to be lacking, a desire to escape was vividly present. A freshness to cover the smell of malignant disease and a sense of the seasons. Was it of new beginnings she thought? I hoped so. I wanted to learn more about Rachel, could I be of some help to her?

But the clock told me the afternoon list started in fifteen minutes: I must leave soon.

2. Through the eyes of a child

Jimmy wasn't keen to put a dress on anyway, to go to the operating theatre, but couldn't understand it at all when the nurse insisted he put it on what appeared to be 'back to front'. His back felt cold as he tried to pull it around him tightly to keep it closed. His Mum always had to pester Jimmy to eat his food at home. He'd promised to be good in hospital and eat everything the nurses gave him, but today the nurses did not give Jimmy any food at all. It was his favourite for lunch as well, corned beef. Jimmy wondered whether it was a punishment for not eating his meals at home. He asked his Mum whether he would not be able to have corned beef after he'd had his tonsils out either. He didn't really understand everything that was happening and wondered when he would be able to eat again.

A nurse began to put a sticky white cream on Jimmy's hands and plasters over the top of it. He told her over and over that he hadn't fallen or cut himself, but she didn't listen to him. Suddenly a man arrived at Jimmy's bedside and lifted him over onto another bed which he then began to push. Jimmy wondered why HIS bed was moving and no one else's was. He felt quite special. Jimmy's Mum and a nurse followed him out of the ward. When they arrived at the operating theatre, everyone had masks on covering most of their faces; it was difficult for Jimmy to hear what they were saying. They had looked at Jimmy's plastic bracelets with his name on: Jimmy had thought he could have told them his name and his address and telephone number, if they had asked him. He was nine years old after all. As he was pushed down the corridor, he peered in through windows. In one room he saw people washing their hands and getting dressed in green clothes. He thought they must have just woken up. He found himself next in a small room, where a man was mixing strange coloured fluids from different sized bottles. They looked like those on his Mum's dressing table at home. A lady in the room clipped a peg onto

Jimmy's finger, and a machine above his head began to bleep. He wondered why it was so far away from his throat. Everyone seemed quiet, he didn't like to ask questions. Jimmy's Mum had told him she would see him soon. He couldn't understand why she was crying, when everyone else in the room was smiling. He noticed a long black tube with a balloon on the end; a funny smell came from it. The man standing by Jimmy's head told him the smell would send him to sleep. Jimmy tried to explain that he wasn't tired but couldn't manage to say the words. He thought to himself that he preferred it back on the ward where his friends were.

3. *Your mother v. my mother (my professional self v. my private self)*

My appointment diary told me Mrs Rivers on E ward had to be seen at 2 p.m. for a pre-operative visit before her hysterectomy operation tomorrow.

I picked up her case notes on entering the ward. Drug history … Present illness … Past illness … Family history: this told me she was 59 years of age, widowed, and lived alone. The bed allocation board informed me where to find her.

Now let's see, introduction, checklists, anaesthetic, recovery, postoperative pain …

As I began with my routine explanation of pre-operative checks, I was interrupted by her rather abrupt question:

'But what will this surgery really mean for me?'

Total abdominal hysterectomy – intravenous infusions, skin clips or stitches, patient-controlled analgesia …

'and surely my womanhood is being taken away from me?'

A very complex issue …

'Yes but think of the discomfort and pain you've had for so many years. Anyway, about your intravenous infusion … '

'Have you any particular worries about tomorrow's surgery?'

Probably nausea, wound healing, chest infections …

'It's my family you see, I'm terrified of never seeing them again, I'm terrified of dying,' she replied with obvious fear in her voice.

Why didn't I think of that? Yes, losing her home and family. Of course, wouldn't my own Mother be just as afraid? And then I surprise myself by saying

'Your fears are the fears of any caring Mother. I'm sure your children would be proud to know that they are your priority, even during this very stressful time in your life.'

The look in her eyes told me that my simple reassurance had been of some help to her. As I turned to leave, she said:

'You see Motherhood means everything to me.'

It was only then that I realised that maybe my explanations of the practicalities of surgery, the drips, fluids and medications, were not the real issue here.

'I've always been the carer you see and have never really been cared for. I'm afraid of being a burden on them.'

As I sat down again to listen, it occurred to me that I must give a part of my private self to people, so that I can become a successful professional carer.

Final note

Bernadette's approach to a patchwork text is to utilise quite consciously a range of different methods of writing. The first piece starts out from description of significant detail, the second from an imaginative identification with the patient, and the third from the contrast between what is spoken and what is thought within an interaction. In a sense, each of these pieces may be thought of as a different way of writing a story. We noted the enormous variety of story formats in the previous chapter, and these three pieces add to the list of possible formats, as it were. But by writing a collection of stories using very different formats, Bernadette also shows how one story can take up and develop the point made in a previous story.

At one level the links between these pieces are clear enough: they are part of the case for pre-operative visits. Other sections of Bernadette's patchwork include a discussion with a manager about the resource implications and a review of some of the literature on the subject. But the imaginative pieces reproduced here have the effect of making Bernadette's text much more than a case for an administrative arrangement. They bring us up against the human reality of surgical operations in a hospital, illustrating the contrast between the patient's life-world and the hospital routine and the emotional demands on nursing staff, and raising the general question of how such poignant interactions can be managed – both by staff and by patients. The particular context of hospital surgery thus becomes a dramatic and extreme example of the tension between humanity and professional boundaries. In this way, Bernadette's text shows how the complex artistic effects of the patchwork format can expand the significance of the work, even when the original idea was to construct a fairly explicit argument.

* * *

EXAMPLE 3: EXPLORING A ROLE (I)

Introduction

Here is an example of a complete patchwork text, illustrating how it assembles different types of writing, different voices and different perspectives, leading up to a final explicit statement. Funghai Nhiwatiwa works as a forensic nurse, i.e. in a residential institution for patients whose level of mental disturbance has led to their having committed criminal offences or being diagnosed as a danger to others.

His first piece presents the tone and feel of the personal experience of pressure, so that we become aware of the significance of the question-mark in the subtitle: how does one cope in such circumstances? The second piece makes explicit the theme of stress, and presents the two sides of the institutionalised relationships which create it: the vulnerability of the staff and (in contrast) the apparently justifiable perspective of patients who feel that their humanity and dignity are systematically undermined by hospital procedures. The third piece ('The interaction') describes a particular incident: a patient who has good reasons for breaking hospital rules is confronted by an inexperienced nurse whose fear of being seen as weak leads her to behave insensitively. We see how the roles of patient and nurse become uneasily tangled with issues of age and gender: a middle-aged man outraged at being rudely addressed by someone who could have been his daughter and a young woman trying to 'make out' amidst the sexist mockery of male colleagues.

In the fourth piece ('Discussion') Funghai broadens out these role issues to address the harshness of the staff culture, including its institutionalised racism, which means that new staff do not receive the support from managers and experienced staff which they clearly need.

'Stress and the stressed: a focus on forensic nursing' by
Funghai Nhiwatiwa

1. Coping?

It is 7:30 in the morning and another long day at work is beginning. How do I do it? Only six hours ago I was saying 'goodnight' as I hurried out of the door, and here I am back again. I sit and listen in a daze as the previous night's report is read, head propped up in fake concentration. My mind drifts on ahead, anticipating how the shift will turn out …

Will it be a so-called 'good shift', full of action, assistance calls echoing on the hospital radio system, burly men bursting through doors ready to 'deck someone'. Or will it be one of the usual 'let's nag the nurse to death' sort of days. The demands are endless: 'Nurse go upstairs and get my trainers', 'Nurse lend us a fag', 'Nurse call my social worker now!', 'Nurse can I have my pass?', ' What time is the shop open, Nurse?'.

My mind comes back briefly to take note of things to be done and gently slips back. Do patients deliberately 'wind me up', or is it really their illness? If it is illness, why do some of them have a smug expression on their faces as if laughing at you, whilst hiding behind the illness? Why do I have to keep a straight face and be professional?, Why not be human and tell people exactly what I feel or think of them? Hang on: how am I different to the patient if I do that? It is probably this lack of self control that led to the patients being admitted in the first place. Maybe the majority of us who manage to stay out, are better at hiding our 'madness', staying in control.

It is now 8:00 a.m., time to wake the patients up and get ready for a 'new day'. It's time to switch off the 'real' me and to switch on the 'professional self'; the caring, patient and empathetic self.

'What time are we going downstairs Nurse?' 'Same as usual, at 8:30 a.m.' 'Can you take me downstairs so that I can have a quick fag?' 'I cannot do that at the moment, wait until there are more people ready to go down so as to justify sending a member of staff down.' 'I won't take long Nurse, please, it's your job.' 'That is not the point, we do not have enough staff to nurse you on a one-to-one basis and hence we have the rule that patients all go downstairs at 8:30 a.m., I cannot discuss this any further.'

'Nurse can you open the shower room for me, what time is it?'

'It's 8:05 a.m.' I can't believe it myself. It's going to be another long day.

2. Whose stress?

In every forensic setting there is a deep rooted source of stress, the origin of which is unknown to its members. Nurses and patients blame each other as a source of stress without really working on resolving the problem.

The nurse's view

It is having to follow the same routine of coming to work, get a lot of physical and verbal abuse, go home and abuse my body with alcohol in the guise of socialising, sleep, and start again. The patient sees me as a human punchbag on whom to take out their anger, frustrations and loss of freedom. The real culprits (the courts, doctors, managers and the government Home Office) are all too powerful for the patient and he knows this. The working environment causes most stress: fear of being attacked for no reason by some 'unrepentant criminal' who happens to dislike you. Most of these fears, although totally unrealistic, are real and should not be underestimated. Constant verbal abuse does take its toll, even on passive, easy-going personalities, reducing one to an irritable wreck. Such attacks on the individual induce feelings of inadequacy and self-doubt. 'Maybe I am not right for the job.' 'Am I such a bad person to deserve such abuse?'

One nurse when discussing stress at work described it as a chisel chipping away at your patience, kindness and coping mechanisms. 'I used to be a nice bloke, full of life, now I am irritable, moody and often depressed at the thought of coming to work.' 'It's not that I hate patients, but some of them get to me, they seem to know what hurts me the most and "push the button". ' 'The worst thing about this is that my colleagues don't help, they think I am weak and inexperienced. Now I am sick all the time, I get the 'flu' often and have to take time off.' 'Sometimes I feel a lot of pressure in my head as if my head is about to explode. Maybe for the patients it did.'

'Some of the patients see me as a source of entertainment, someone to wind up and then laugh at when I lose my cool.' 'They are constantly pushing the limits, especially when the manager is in view; it's like they want me to lose my job.' 'It is very difficult to be professional sometimes, I just want to tell them where to get off, not in so many words.'

The patient's view

Why do you wake me up at 7 in the morning when you can lie in on your day off? Why do you barge into my room without knocking and invade my privacy? You have taken my freedom and now you want to take my dignity away. Don't! I am human.

Why do you force me to bath in the morning when I prefer one at night? Why do you insult me, tell me I smell in front of everyone? It's embarrassing. Why do I have to eat breakfast so early in the morning when I would like it mid-morning? Why am I forced to sit with people I do not like? I have feelings, I am human.

Why do you force your daily activities on me? Just leave me alone, I don't want to do Art, I hate Bingo and despise competing in quizzes. Why do you stop me from smoking when you can shut yourselves in the toilet and smoke? Why deny me one of life's few pleasures in hospital? You can go home, escape the nightmare, if only for a night: I cannot. You can have your comforts, your freedom and your life: what have I got?

Why can't I have intimacy and affection in my life? Why can't I fall in love without being accused of taking advantage? Why do you call me inappropriate and disinhibited when I am only responding to natural human urges? Why do you put labels on me which delay my release? Don't do it, I hurt, I am only human.

Why do you speak to me like a child when all I want is to be treated like a man? Why do you call me psychotic when all I am doing is speaking my 'mother tongue' and expressing my culture? Why do you provoke me with your rudeness when all I want is a little respect?

Why do you inject me with medication which makes me sleepy, stiff and unable to express myself? Why don't you listen to me instead of isolating me in the observation lounge? I don't want much, just want to be treated like a human again.

3. The interaction

Steam from the half-filled bath filled the bathroom, making the temperature of the room deceptively warm for a chilly January morning. Joe staggered into the bathroom, eyes drugged by a sleepless night worrying about the forthcoming tribunal. Will he be let out this time? After all, he is on no oral medication and has been making good progress. His family had noticed a change in him, the distant look in his eyes had gone, replaced by the glow of reality. Making a good impression was all important to the commissioners and presentation was foremost in Joe's mind as he stepped into the hot bath and immediately jumped out, reaching for the cold tap to adjust the temperature.

In the eighteen months Joe had been in hospital he had seen nurses come and go and had always tried to charm them with his music and artistic talent, but lately he felt uneasy. Joe had just settled into the bath when Carol stormed in shouting, 'Get out now, you should have bathed upstairs like everyone else!' She strode across the small room in two strides and reached down and unplugged the bath. Joe sat there staring at the small, chubby form of the new nurse, Carol, thinking she can't be much older than Julie, his daughter. 'I said get out; are you deaf?'. This appeared to trigger a mixture of emotions, anger at having a woman intruding on his privacy. How dare she barge in speaking to him in that manner? His old-fashioned beliefs battled with the institutional rules which seemed to empower nurses to deny patients their basic rights.

Carol watched with increasing anger at what seemed to be blatant insubordination. Joe had been in longer than most patients and should know the rules. His stare was an attempt at threatening her as a member of staff, it was time to make her mark, to set an example. What would the others think if she could not show authority? Two male nurses helped Joe out of the bath and for the first time, Carol felt a rush of blood to her face – Joe was naked.

The door was slightly open as Carol approached the office. A roar of laughter stopped her in her tracks as she reached for the office door. Were they laughing at her, her inexperience at dealing with 'real patients'? She had trained for three long years for this job, but had not prepared herself for this.

4. Discussion

The interaction between Joe and Carol demonstrates a typical nurse/patient relationship which is potentially destructive. Both have hidden agendas which influence their attitude in the interaction. Joe's priority is to create a good impression to aid his discharge from hospital, and his disregard for rules may be justified to some extent by the importance of the event. He may even have had a good excuse for not bathing upstairs.

Patients often feel that staff are very rigid in enforcing the rules, and this may be perceived by some as staff deliberately victimising them. This lack of empathy often leads to confrontations which at times lead to violent behaviour. It is generally accepted that violence is a major source of stress and has increased in recent years (Davis and Boster 1988). Carol's tone of voice when instructing Joe to vacate the bathroom may have influenced Joe's anger reaction. Some staff members are guilty of talking down at patients which inevitably causes anger reactions. The degree of offence taken in such situations, according to experience, is dependent on the patient's age, culture and race. Complaints of racist attitudes by staff towards ethnic minorities may be the result. The fact that there is a high percentage of ethnic minorities in forensic settings may be racist in itself (Faulk 1994).

Carol's reaction is typical of many inexperienced nurses under pressure. There is constant pressure from patients who are demanding and limit-testing, colleagues who are very critical of new staff and managers who at times make you feel useless by constantly highlighting faults. In my experience as a new staff member, colleagues and senior staff caused most stress. Their attitude, which implied that new members are incapable of dealing with patients, caused a lot of stress. Sometime I felt that unless I restrained someone and 'proved myself' I would never gain the respect of more experienced junior staff. Senior staff did not help the situation, with their constant criticism of minor issues. What I also found stressful as a new member of staff was the difficulty of breaking into the closed circle which existed among staff, and patients used my insecurities to create division and confusion. But I knew I had to deal with it, because they need help.

5. Conclusion

It can be said that the best way to manage stress is to prevent it. Stress management is often thought of in terms of three major areas: self management, organisational improvements and support systems. Social support from members of the team is important. One feels alienated without such support. Supervision from managers and senior staff is important for morale, one needs to feel appreciated and valued, which is sometimes lacking in forensic settings. Staff burnout continues to be a problem in forensic settings and is reflected by the high staff turnover in this area. Supervision, support networks and education must be a priority with managers, and ignoring this could prove expensive.

Final note

The final 'Conclusion' sums up very clearly Funghai's specific concern: the need for more support in coping with a highly stressful professional role. But it is also clear that this is only one response to the complex realities that Funghai has portrayed. As we read it, we also continue to hear all the other voices we have heard earlier, combining to create a powerful impression of a climate of aggression, fear, resentment and machismo. A professional relationship of 'care' is threatened by a complex pattern of divisions, among the staff as well as between staff and patients. In this context we may perhaps assume that racism has been an important experience for Funghai, but although he refers to this, the most dramatic incident (section 3) focuses on issues of age and gender. We might see this as an evasion, but we might also see it as a dignified artistic choice, enabling the writer to handle the pain he portrays with greater balance and objectivity. In either case, the text overall is much richer and more complex than the brief concluding statement, which thus takes on an authority it might otherwise lack. In this way Funghai's work illustrates one of the ways in which the patchwork text can be an effective means of professional reflection: by including imaginatively reconstructed scenarios and a diversity of perspectives, it can give subtlety and depth to an otherwise familiar general insight.

* * *

EXAMPLE 4: 'PROFESSIONAL' MEANINGS IN 'PERSONAL' EXPERIENCE

Introduction

All the previous examples are clearly focused from the outset on professional experiences, but for their first piece of writing the participants in the reflective writing course are explicitly told that they can write about 'anything', i.e. about an experience which need have no apparent connection with their professional role. This initial, 'general' piece often proves to be highly illuminating, in unexpected ways, as illustrated in these extracts from the work of Marion Bromfield, a social work training coordinator.

'Difference and change, loss and regeneration' by Marion Bromfield

When I began the work for the 'Reflective Writing for Professional Learning' course, I had no idea of a title or of the themes on which the writing would be focused. I just knew that I wanted to share the experience that I have written about in 'Facing the right way'. Later, ideas for further titles came flooding into my head and slowly I became aware of 'emergent themes' …

Facing the right way

It was raining on the morning we buried him. Not heavy, torrential rain nor a soft meaningless drizzle, but a steady, life-giving rain that I imagined the emerging spring grass and peeping primroses would welcome. But it was chilling for us, and I pulled my coat more tightly around me as we walked through the familiar wrought iron gates and up the gravel drive.

I'd already seen the box they'd made for him. Made of rough but sturdy wood, it now rested on wooden pallets at the far end of the yard. Strong chains had been placed around each end with another piece of chain linking them. They'd put other things in the box too – the worn leather bridle, the yellow head collar and lead rein that Jan had been so excited about when we'd bought it. The cosy stable rug had gone in too – I used to love seeing him snugly wrapped in this on cold winter nights, though I always grumbled at him because he wouldn't stand still while I fastened the straps. Latterly he'd had to have extra blankets underneath because he'd become so thin and shivered easily.

Yesterday I'd been cross when I found out they had put all these things in the box. I suppose it offended my middle class sensibility about rights of ownership. Will had looked uncomprehending when I'd protested mildly that it was me who had bought those things. Now it didn't seem to matter and I was glad I hadn't made a real fuss.

Someone had written, 'Tim, died 18 March 1996, much loved', on the side of the box in uneven childish looking handwriting. Rumour had it that despite his wealth, Will couldn't read or write very well. 'He didn't go to school much, his family being gypsies, you see.'

They seemed to be ready now. The digger lumbered into the yard and we stood well clear as the huge arm swung round, slowly lowered itself down towards the box and a man I didn't know – he seemed to be helping the driver – attached the hook to the centre chain. Slowly the arm rose, lifting the sad load off the ground. I found it hard to believe that those chains would bear such a weight but they showed no sign of breaking as they moved down the yard, the box swaying unsteadily in the chill wind.

There was a gate at the end of the yard and I wondered if it was wide enough to allow the box through. The walls at either side were seven foot high, surely they weren't going to try to swing it over them? But it went through – just – and then we were following the digger across the fields. There were just five of us – Will, still shouting instructions to the driver; Julie walking with head bent; I didn't know her very well and didn't quite know what to say to her; the girls' arms around each other, under one umbrella. I felt alone, apart from them all – Jan hadn't seemed to want me to comfort her and I was glad she had Elizabeth, the big sister that she'd always wanted.

It was quite a long walk – the hole had been dug in the very far corner of the farthest field. I saw that it was underneath a large blackberry bush and smiled for the first time that morning, remembering how Tim had loved blackberries and on our outings would always dart into the hedge to help himself. How carefully Will had thought all this through – a gruff man who the villagers seemed to regard with a mixture of awe, amusement and fascination. He was variously described as 'having a short fuse', 'likely to stitch you up', and 'soft over animals'. Although we had always got on well, I am still a bit scared of him, if the truth were known.

As we walked, I thought of the evening just ten days ago, when Tim had eaten his supper as usual but then stood with his head hanging and I'd known instinctively that something was very wrong. It was eerie and creepy up at the stables at night and I hadn't much liked sitting alone on a bale of straw, waiting for the vet. I had been relieved when I'd heard the crunch of tyres on the gravel, though I knew only too well what he would tell me.

We had reached the blackberry bush by now and the digger was by the side of the grave, its arm poised to lower the box into the deep hole. Suddenly there was a shout, 'He's facing the wrong way'. I felt bewildered: now what was going on? And did I imagine it or did the driver raise his eyebrows heavenwards in a gesture of despair? But Will isn't the sort of person one argues with and the clumsy vehicle deposited its load on the ground, went backwards, then forwards, then backwards again, finally re-positioning itself on the other side of the box.

This time there were no interruptions. The friend with whom we'd had so much fun was slowly lowered into the gaping hole, the digger moved away and I went forward and threw in my damp daffodils. Then we walked back in silence, none of us sharing our thoughts. Glancing at Will, I saw his tears, but felt he would want to be alone.

* * *

I don't have a horse any more but I still visit the field. The stately bay shire with the scars on her legs – what is her story I wonder? – lets me scratch her imperious Roman nose and whinnies softly when I reach up to stroke her massive neck. I like to think that she knows her old friend is not far away but is looking across the field towards his home and towards her. I remember how Tim used to watch the Shetland colts, wild and unbroken, racing around, fighting and kicking each other like unruly children. They never bullied him like they do each other, perhaps instinctively respecting his age and wisdom. Do they feel, that, although, like Hazel, in Richard Adams' novel *Watership Down*, he doesn't 'need his body any more', he's still looking at them with that mixture of resigned disapproval and affection, and are they just a little gentler in their play because of it?

The people who laughed when I told them about the burial – ('what a fuss, and what expense, over a scruffy old pony!') – would be even more scornful if I told them these fanciful thoughts. But I know that I am the richer for this glimpse into the folklore of a culture that is not my own and I wonder what other treasures it hides, perhaps in danger of being lost for ever? I am grateful for the comfort its wisdom has brought me …

… and I am glad that he is facing the right way.

Editorial Note

The next two pieces of writing in Marion's text were called 'When I am an old woman I shall wear purple' (the first line of 'Warning', a poem by Jenny Joseph) and 'At risk?', but unfortu-

nately, due to lack of space they cannot be included here. They both concern an elderly woman, 'Coralie Brown', whose fierce sense of independence in spite of her frailty and terminal illness cause concern to her doctor and her relatives. These pieces raise the question of how professionals in the caring professions are to balance their duty to provide support with respect for a client's dignity as they approach death. The following extracts from Marion's own commentary on all three pieces bring out the implicit professional significance of 'Facing the right way'.

Emergent themes

Re-reading my earlier pieces of writing, it appears to me that two dominant themes emerge: the first concerns an examination of social work values from a personal perspective; the second relates to a search for continuity and stability in the face of loss and change.

The first piece of writing, 'Facing the right way' concerns the concept of 'valuing difference' within a multi-cultural context. It gives an insight into an aspect of Romany culture and folklore. I found the ritual surrounding the burial of Tim not only fascinating but comforting; and I have tried to convey something of how powerful and how full of meaning I found my involvement in the burial to be.

In our hygiene-conscious society, the disposal of the body of a large animal presents a considerable problem, and many horse owners reluctantly allow their deceased animals to go to the local hunt where the carcass is used as food for the hounds. While this arrangement may make practical sense, one needs little imagination to realise that for many people this is a distressing end for a much loved animal. It was only with hindsight that I realised fully how much comfort I derived from knowing, not only that Tim was given a dignified burial, but also that he was facing across the field towards his old home and towards his friends rather than towards the hedge and the road outside. It was this realisation that gave me an insight into the wisdom of Romany folklore.

My second and third pieces of writing attempt to explore the reality of ageing, of deteriorating health and approaching death and what may be the implications of allowing older people choice. They highlight the issue of risk and pose the question of whether the medical and social services should ever intervene against a person's will.

Many professionals would consider that there are clear risk factors in the case of Coralie Brown. She is frail, she does not eat properly and the standards of cleanliness and hygiene in her bungalow leave something to be desired. However, she is mentally alert, her way of life impacts on no-one but herself, and if we are really to respect her dignity and her right to choose then to interfere against her wishes would seem unethical.

90

However, the risk becomes all too apparent in the last paragraph when she falls heavily and we are left wondering whether it will be minutes, hours or even days before anyone finds her. How will we feel if she dies before her help arrives? Are our feelings influenced by the fact that we know that this is what she herself desires? ...

All the pieces of writing contained issues of loss – the loss of a loved pony, Coralie's loss of health and vigour, and her family's awareness that they would soon lose her. Loss and death are of course inevitable, and in the first three pieces of writing, although I did not attempt to deny the sadness of the situation I also tried to convey a sense of acceptance, hope and continuity in the face of change. The feedback from my colleagues indicated that they felt that I had gone some way towards achieving this. One comment was that 'Facing the right way', although sad, did not convey a feeling of raw emotion but of peace and strength. The final paragraphs of the piece contrast the ageing Tim with the boisterous young Shetland colts who nevertheless respect the wisdom of the older horse. The link between the two generations is also expressed in the fantasy and hope that their spirits are still alive to one another.

The feedback also indicated that a similar sense of continuity was present in 'When I am an old woman I shall wear purple' and 'At risk?'. Coralie is weakening rapidly but the ivy will continue to grow, the blackbird will continue to nest and rear his young, while inside the spiders will carry on making their webs, undisturbed by house-proud hands. Coralie has no wish to continue to live a life of pain and discomfort, and death is both accepted and seen as a friend to be welcomed. Group discussions and perusal of my reflective journal reminded me of the pertinence of these themes for myself and my own practice within the rapidly changing world of professional social work: the small Children's Department that I joined twenty-five years ago bears little resemblance to the monolithic structure of today's Social Services Department ...

* * *

EXAMPLE 5: EXPLORING PERSONAL 'ORIGINS' FOR PROFESSIONAL 'SKILLS'

Introduction

This is almost a complete text; just one section has been omitted for reasons of space. Louise Geddes is a social worker who works with children who have disabilities. She was inspired by reading some extracts from V. S. Naipaul's book *Finding The Centre* (presented in the distance learning materials below, pp. 127–9) to produce a text which links together a personal reminiscence and a professional experience into an overall reflection on the basis of the professional/client relationship. Louise uses two different typefaces in her text, one for her own 'reflective' voice and a different one for her imaginatively constructed scenarios. After a brief poetic introduction of her general theme, Louise tells us about an early incident (section 2) where she felt proud of having learned something important. She links this with a story about the need for one's spirit to 'catch up with' one's body, which is a different way of presenting her main theme – exploring the 'origins' of one's current way of being. Section 3 is a brief restatement of this theme in terms of professional theory: self-understanding as the basis for empathy. Section 4 recounts an incident where a social worker enables a client with learning difficulties to make a significant step forward in their general understanding, and, in the final line, reflects that same insight back into her own life as a question: 'How old was I when I discovered that … ?' This is the point when the link between this 'imagined' incident and the earlier reminiscence from Louise's own childhood suddenly springs dramatically into focus, leading to the final reflection on the link between the personal self of the professional worker and her relationships with clients.

'Beginnings' by Louise Geddes

1.

Every person has a beginning.
  At the beginning there must be a start, a heart, a core and the feeling of life.

  The beginning refers to the past.
  It is from where I originate.
  It is my experiences.
  It is my personal self.
  It is that which characterises my present frame of reference.

  Therefore it is this central core in all of us human beings that makes us who and what we are.

  This applies to professional Social Workers and to clients.

  V. S. Naipaul (*Finding the Centre*, 1985) describes his need to return to his incomplete knowledge of his background. Once he clarifies this for himself, he discovers that his writing flows and comes together for him.

2. My beginning

I recall my mother asking me to give her the time on her watch. Her watch was small. I think it was a ladies' Rolex, of which she was very fond. It had an old strap and was in need, I thought at the time, of being thrown out.

We were in what was known as the front lounge at the time, in Africa, South Africa, with, as usual, a bright sunny day.

'Give me the time,' she said.

My response was honest and to the point.

'I cannot read the time.'

I recall my mother falling silent. I think there were other people in the room. They were in the deep recesses of my mind.

A hush descended, all eyes were on me.

Then, from Mom came:

'You cannot tell the time? How old are you?'

'Seven,' I replied.

My mother's response then went into a long telling me off voice as to why can I not tell time. Questioning me how do I know when to wake up? How do I know where to be when? At the end of a now vague, long speech, I remember her saying she will teach me how to tell the time.

Sure enough, a few days later, in fact, the next day, after lunch, this old clock arrived and it was PLONKED in the shade of our oak tree on the grass.

Mom sat with me, explaining about time, its importance, which hand meant what and how the clock worked. I was amazed to see her adjusting the hands with such ease, and realised that this would be a useful tool in the future and that it would play a major part in my life. With this I remember practising for hours under the oak tree, saying time out loud.

When my father came home from work I had to share this experience with him and my sisters and brother.

I recall supper time that evening.

Mom made the comment, 'Well, today Louise, you learned to tell the time, did you not?'

I nodded.

She then said: 'What is the time?'

My response, in a very proud voice was, 'Eight o'clock, bedtime.'

I know I went to bed happy and feeling so proud and good about myself.

Reflecting on my beginnings, it seems to come together for me in a story I recall having read.

Tourists visiting an exotic remote island arranged for local people to be bearers of their luggage, and camping equipment. The locals knew of all the exotic places on the island and the tourists went rushing about the scenic island jungle, enraptured with its exotic sights, taking photographs to capture the moment only to be eager to proceed to the next 'Pandora' experience.

On the second day of their journey they awoke to find that the locals had not started the usual camp routine. Indeed, they were sitting around, resting! On enquiring why this was so, and expressing a wish to tour the other side of the island, the response that took them aback was the following: the locals explained that, with all the rushing of the past few days, they were waiting for their spirits to catch up with their bodies.

3. Professional beginnings

Compton and Galaway (1979) refer to social workers' need to communicate four things to clients: empathy, acceptance, unconditional positive regard and congruence.

Congruence is what the professional brings to the relationship which is consistent and honest, openness and realness; and behaviour and the content of communication with the client must match (be congruent). Social workers need to have an honest knowledge of themselves. Who and what we are. We need to understand ourselves. We need to understand the client and accept them, and reflect this to them by the way in which we communicate with each other.

For me, my childhood background provided the environment of patience and acceptance. This was when I learned and listened the most. My family had patience to enable me to venture to risk learning. This environment needs to be created for clients …

It is so difficult to find the core. Patience is required to do so, as is congruence, warmth and understanding. Sometimes a professional can try too hard to find the core of the client, and one needs to have the patience to allow the client to find their own core when they feel ready. What is important is that the social worker tries to create the environment so as to give the opportunity for the client to convey their feelings and needs.

4. Aware of the beginning

Mary had recently joined the team. A referral had come through a school. His name did not convey anything out of the ordinary. His address indicated that he lived in a new residential development.

As she drove down the road past the new terraced houses, Mary was counting off the numbers on the doors. There it was.

An anxious face greeted Mary. Stephen was at school. Reasons were given. The teacher had not communicated with her. They had moved recently from a flat to the house. He had not been with his mother for two years. Perhaps it was his father's attitude towards him. Or maybe it was that Stephen was not sleeping through the night.

Then Stephen's mother began to calm down and feel more relaxed as she realised that Mary was not blaming her for Stephen's bizarre behaviour, but, that Mary was in fact listening. The past came out slowly. Mary listened. Another appointment was made to meet Stephen, and to support his mother with her request for additional information regarding hearing impairment.

As Mary drove to the house again, she was thinking that Stephen would be there. This time the mother's face that greeted her was smiling.

There he stood. Smaller somehow than Mary had imagined him. He studied her face intensely. His dark face with large brown eyes was serious. He was silent. His eyes followed both Mary and his mother as they engaged in conversation. The house was full of children, it seemed, and there were piles of ironing neatly laid up the stairs.

He was still observing his mother in conversation with Mary. Mary beckoned Stephen to her. With caution he approached.

Mary introduced herself to him in Sign Language. In response, he took his grubby little fingers out of his mouth and handshaped the letter 'S'. His face was more relaxed. He realised that Mary could communicate with him. He was excited about this. By now Stephen's brothers had gathered around. Mary was kneeling on the floor signing to Stephen. Stephen put his fingers into his mouth and his gaze was on Mary.

Pointing to Stephen's mother, Mary asked, 'Who is this?'

With wet fingers and an excited face he handshaped 'M'.

Mary shook her head.

He nodded with his eyes darting from his mother's to Mary's face.

'She is not my mom,' said Mary looking at his mother.

'Does "M" have a name?' she asked Stephen.

His head nodded yes, and he repeated firmly the 'M' handshape.

With a serious face Mary shook her head. With Stephen's now anxious eyes watching her, Mary asked his mother if she had a name as Mary could not call her 'mom'. She was not Mary's mother.

His mother replied that her name was Ann.

Mary pointed her finger at Stephen's mother and said, 'Mom's name is Ann.'

Stephen's eyes were shining and full of excitement at this information. With his grubby wet little fingers he made an 'A' handshape and looked at his mother with a smiling face.

Mary felt moved.

She was observing possibly the first time that Stephen had come to realise that his mother had a name!

Mary then requested Stephen to introduce her to his family. He stood there, delighted, glowing, happy, and with pride.

'A' handshape was for Alex.

'K' handshape was for Kyle.

'L' handshape was for Louis, then he faltered …

He pointed to a young lad about his own age, looked at Mary and shrugged. His mother explained that Guy was her nephew.

Mary handshaped 'G' for Guy and told Stephen that Guy was his cousin. Stephen's eyes and face told their own story. He beamed at his cousin as though acknowledging him for the first time. He threw his head back and laughed with glee.

He was happy and started to jump up and down.

With mixed emotions Mary climbed into her car. Deep in thought as she drove away, she was thinking to herself, 'How old was I when I discovered that Mom had her own name?'

5. Reflections

In order for a caterpillar to metamorphose into a beautiful butterfly, it requires the environment to accommodate to its needs. It requires time to change.

There are many parallels between our clients and ourselves. It is being aware of these parallels that makes the professional difference. There is danger in being unaware. Danger, because then I would not be effective in supporting clients. There is always this personal self behind the professional self that social workers bring to clients.

It is being aware of this personal self that is important or else the self would cause incongruence for the client. However, the boundary needs to be maintained. It is by having balance and being comfortable with oneself that the professional can be congruent with clients.

What are the parallels?

Parallels range from a broad perspective like that of being a human being, to the particular, that of personal self.

I have a beginning, so do my clients.

I have a family, they must too, even if theirs has become fragmented along the way.

Clients have a need for respect, love, warmth, empathy, and understanding, just as I do. Likewise, they feel pain and loss and have their
own sorrows.

Carl Rogers refers to unconditional positive regard. It is accepting
people as they are with all their faults and strengths. Even though
they do wrong, they aren't rejected, only what they have done is unac-
ceptable. He focuses on enabling people to be loved and accepted and
uses positive reinforcement for deeds that are done correctly (Hjelle
and Ziegler 1981: pp. 399–436).

We do this positive reinforcement with our clients through communication. So what, if they do so with their eyes, or with the use of sign
language ...

As long as I can provide the environment, being there with them,
allowing them to express themselves in a non threatening environment, there will be communication.

Like the butterfly, things will happen.

No matter what the disability, it is the communication, the beginning ...

Final note

As with the book by Julian Barnes discussed at the end of the introduction to this
chapter, Louise's text works mainly through oblique, implicit links between its
sections. Although her 'reflective' passages do try to encompass the whole
meaning of her text, they do so through images (the butterfly) and allusions (the
tourists on the exotic island at the end of section 2) as well as general professsional theory. Her final reflection in particular thus has an allusive, fragmentary
quality, so that in some ways its logic is less than wholly conclusive, but perhaps
for that very reason it seems quite a fitting ending: a purely theoretical statement
would have needed to be extremely complex to do justice to the subtlety of the
overall pattern of incidents and ideas. This example, then, illustrates with particular clarity how the assembling of a patchwork text proceeds according to
aesthetic principles of balance, contrast and emotional tension (see Chapter 7:
pp. 200–6) in order to achieve its effectiveness as a piece of 'professional' reflection: the professional exploration is at the same time, and very clearly, a process
of artistic shaping.

* * *

EXAMPLE 6: EXPLORING A ROLE (II)

Introduction

This final example is a complete text, by Jayne Crow, a university lecturer in nurse education. It is placed last because in many ways it brings together a number of the different features illustrated in the earlier examples. Like Bernadette Saharoy's work (example 2) it consciously uses a variety of different ways of writing; like Matt Capener's work (example 1) it opens up a story by adding a further piece – in this case a poem; like Funghai Nhiwatiwa's work (example 3) it assembles bit by bit an exploration of a professional role; and like the work of Marion Bromfield and Louise Geddes (examples 4 and 5) it starts out from a personal memory. This aspect is particularly interesting in that when Jayne wrote this piece, at the beginning of the course, she had no clear idea that it might have any professional relevance at all: its significance only became clear in retrospect (as she points out in her final section) when she re-read it in the light of her subsequent writing about her professional life. This illustrates quite dramatically how assembling a patchwork text can be a genuinely explorative process leading to new insights and new connections between apparently separate experiences. Another interesting aspect of this example is the way in which each section presents a new aspect of the writer's feelings about her role, so that the final section (the 'Epilogue'), reflecting on each section in turn, becomes a sort of retrospective synthesis, albeit a provisional and incomplete analysis, explicitly anticipating further work. In a number of ways, then, this final example illustrates most of the general points which were made about the nature of patchwork texts in the introduction to this chapter.

'Role conflict in higher education' by Jayne Crow

1. Preface

I had woken too early. I had no watch but I knew it was early. There was no sound from the rest of the sleeping house. It wasn't my house. It was big. It had lots of rooms and it was in the country. There were no city sounds, no hum of traffic or slamming of car doors. There were sounds but they were alien rural sounds. I was fifteen and staying here for the weekend with people I hardly knew. I had never done that before and I wondered what I should do now that I was awake. What was the right thing to do?

I lay in bed in the strange room. It had been difficult to get to sleep. The bed had sheets and blankets which were tucked in tightly at the end of the bed with efficient hospital corners. The covers were warm but not giving. They resented having to keep me warm. I was not the person that they wanted to embrace and I did not belong in this bed.

The bedstead itself wasn't against a wall. It stood exposed in the centre of the room. At home there was reassuring flowery wallpaper close to my nose when I first half-opened my eyes in the morning. One false move here and I would end up rolling out of the narrow bed and onto the thin serviceable carpet.

This room was a neglected and unloved room. It was clean and tidy but it had given its heart to the boy of the house who had filled it with clutter and life. When he had gone – grown up and spread his wings – off to university – the room's heart had been broken.

Now as I peered out from the iron bedstead I could see only scant remains of the room's past life. A row of yellowing paperbacks, dog-eared but too tidy in the white painted bookcase. On top, a forlorn glass tube filled with different coloured sand echoed a long-forgotten school trip to the Isle of Wight. A picture of a fighter plane hung from the picture rail in the place where it had been hung all those Christmases ago when an aunt had kindly sent it all the way from Swansea for her little nephew. He would have preferred the money – the aeroplane fad had only lasted a couple of months.

I could see the early morning winter sunlight through the thin cotton curtains. Not much point in buying new curtains for a spare room – it was only used once in a blue moon. The boy didn't come home much these days.

I pulled the blankets up around my chin. It must have been early because the central heating hadn't come on yet. I wondered what the time was and wished I'd brought my watch or, better still, that little folding travel alarm clock of mine. If I'd brought that I could have placed it in the centre of the white lace doily on the white-painted bedside cabinet.

I poked my arm out from the covers into the chilly air and opened the little drawer in the top of the cabinet. Just a roll of sellotape, some slightly rusty nailclippers and a single glove. A disappointing drawer. I had hoped for photographs, picture-card collections, old school reports, but there was no part of the boy here. This was a drawer in a spare room.

Still no noise from the rest of the house. I wondered suddenly if I had made a mistake. Maybe I was late and everyone was up and washed and breakfasted. They hadn't liked to wake me – let me have a lie in. How appallingly embarrassing! I was the last one up! I'd have to explain – everyone would be tolerant and kind: 'After all, she's only young, a typical teenager' (knowing, long-suffering smiles).

I can't stand it and leap out of bed and tip-toe on cold bare feet to the door. The door makes a deafening creak as I open it gingerly. It all seems quiet. Of course it is: everyone asleep, as I knew perfectly well. I tip-toe back to bed and draw the reluctant cover up around me again. Best to wait. Wait for the house to wake and the day to begin.

2. *The contents of my briefcase*

The case is large. More like a small suitcase than a briefcase really. It has a hard business-like shell to withstand the most harsh and careless treatment and a lock to keep the contents safe, though I never use it. Sometimes one of the children plays with the case and locks it and I am always mildly irritated that the lid won't open immediately – at the press of a button.

The case was a present. I wouldn't have chosen it – it is too big, too formal. However now it is mine I am used to it and, despite its great size, I can never fit in all that I need. Inside it is a bit like an office – my office in a box. Many of the things that I carry around are things that I would leave on top of a desk or in the top drawer if I were not always on the move. In fact I never use or look at many of these things and am surprised when I come across them cluttering up one of the useful pouches in the lid – my CV, travel expense claims, map of some obscure rarely visited hospital, lists of student names. But the same strange motivation that made me put them there in the first place ensures that I replace them to be neglected for another couple of months – just in case.

I have two identity cards clipped to the smallest inside pocket of the case. The inane grinning portrait picture makes me wince when I look at it. Is that really me? Is that who people see when they look at me? There must be some mistake. Still I keep them there just in case I need to prove who I am. A different card for each institution. One would not suffice.

Officious little compartments in the lid of the case rebuke me for not filling them with organised clutches of pens, paper-clips, rubber-bands. … Things to make the day go smoothly – of course they remain empty. Those items, when they are there at all, have to be scrabbled for amongst the day papers – they have to take their chance.

My Filofax (what a hateful name) is good-natured however. It could have resented the churlish and ungrateful way in which I let it into my life, all the while clinging to the 'outdated' standard issue diary (the page-per-day ones always made the day seem empty when I knew that they would be full). Now the Filofax is my friend – it keeps order – it shows where I have been and where I may be going. It has phone numbers in the back, of colleagues and friends, to call. I don't have to change them every year. It is comforting to find last year's numbers in last year's writing, still there for me – just lift the phone. The Filofax sometimes even holds a pen for me in one of its handy little loops. Not always, just as a special treat.

The most important item in my case is undoubtedly the photocopying card. The key to success! It will provide proof of letters sent, proof of comments made: 'I enclose a copy of my memo dated … ' But its most crucial feature is its ability to multiply resources! No books in the library? No money to buy? 'Have a photocopy of this article!' I am ever bountiful. It's like the five loaves and two fishes – a minor miracle in itself. How long before 'they' take the card away?

Well I suppose there would still be me and my case.

3. Nurse/teacher

When she came into nurse education her objective was not so much to benefit the students but to improve patient care. As a ward sister her over-riding concern was for her patients – and they really were her patients. They were her responsibility and her over-riding objective was to ensure that they were nursed in the best and most humane way that she knew. She had enjoyed teaching on the ward – but bedside nursing had much greater rewards that fed a need in her to be wanted and appreciated. The main satisfaction for her in teaching students came from seeing them nurse patients more skilfully. Each student that passed through her hands was a means to an end. The 'end' being – better patient care.

But then gradually the feeling grew on her that what she was doing was piecemeal. Just a few students at a time, maybe thirty in a year. How much of a difference did that really make in the wider scheme of things? It was just a drop in the ocean and, with so much ignorance and bad practice about, this was just not an effective approach.

Increasingly the situation became more frustrating. How was her message to be got through? How was she to improve nursing if she could reach so few students? (A passion to increase the degree of humanity shown in nursing burned strong in her and so perhaps we may forgive the arrogance of her aspirations.)

Thus it was that she took the plunge – nurse education was obviously the way forward. *There* was the opportunity to lay the foundations for good practice. *There* was the way to reach hundreds of nurses who together could really make a difference – could really ensure that every patient got the very best care. It was a wrench, of course, for her to leave the ward but, she argued, this way she could make a real impact.

Now it was long ago that she had left the ward and the patients. She had encountered hundreds of students since that time. She had lectured, discussed, tutored, facilitated – all the time drip feeding her message of humanity in nursing. But then gradually the feeling grew on her that the patients, although still there in her mind, were drifting further away and that the students had come more sharply into focus. Increasingly it was their needs and aspirations that had become paramount to her. It was *their* welfare that preoccupied not only her time but also her heart. She listened to their problems, nurturing their development with the same dedication and care she had lavished on her patients. She grieved when they experienced set-backs, encouraged them when they began to show signs of increasing independence and rejoiced when they achieved their goal and left her behind. They were no longer a means to an end, they had become an 'end' in themselves.

4. Sorry

It was clear how much this course meant to you when I first met you at interview. It was your second chance – the education that you had thrown away when you were young.

'I mucked around at school – didn't think it was important. Went a bit wild … you know how it is.'

Yes, I know how it is.

'Then I grew up. I want to prove I can do it. My family are off-hand now and I want to pass this course. I can do it. I'm determined.'

Now here we sit in this cramped book-filled room knowing determination wasn't enough. You perch on the edge of the comfy chair looking down at your rough red nurse's hands, twisting your wedding ring round and round on your finger.

'I'm sorry but I'm afraid that you haven't passed the re-submission of your assignment.'

I don't say 'failed', I know better than that … I'm a professional. You don't look at me.

'I know you must be very upset.'

You sit silently, red-eyed, fighting back the tears. I press on, trying only for damage limitation now.

'There are some very good ideas in the work, I know from our discussions that you have a clear understanding of the issues involved … '

You look up and I can hear your silent question. 'Why didn't I pass then? Why do I never pass?' This time it is me that looks down.

'The problem, as I've said to you before, is that you have difficulty putting your ideas onto paper.... I know what you are trying to say but you sometimes don't manage to make your arguments coherently in writing. ... Do you understand?'

What I want to say is: you haven't got the basic English skills to cope with the course. You have come through the system without gaining the very skill that your intelligence will be judged by; you cannot write things down in the way that is required. You are intelligent, articulate, perceptive, a pleasure to listen to in discussions, a damn good nurse no doubt. But I can't help you.

'Perhaps a course in written English ... to help ... '

Oh so feeble! ... You won't get more time off work to do another course and we both know it. Where would the money come from anyway?

You're devastated. I knew you would be. I should have been firmer when you failed the last module. I should have been harsher and told you straight away that you should give up the course. But I gave you the benefit of the doubt and let you go on. You were determined to continue and I gave in. I didn't seem to have the right to take away your second chance, or maybe I simply didn't have the courage to insist. It doesn't matter now because whichever was the case we now have to pay the price.

Now all the determination and enthusiasm has run through my fingers and we sit solemnly not looking at each other. Oh God, why didn't I shove on a few more marks and push you over the pass line? It would have been so easy. This is where being professional has got me! I have to maintain standards. I have to be objective in these matters. Where would we be if we gave marks for effort? Wouldn't I be devaluing the qualification for those who succeed? Wouldn't their achievement be lessened by offering some credit to you? But you tried so hard.

If only you hadn't tried so hard. How different that would be – so much easier. 'Sorry, you've not passed the re-submission.' Just like that! And I wouldn't be sorry at all. ('Actually you deserved to fail. You didn't listen, you didn't keep appointments, you didn't read the guide-lines. You were arrogant enough to think that you could write the assignment the night before. No, I'm not sorry at all. In fact I'm secretly rather pleased. If you had passed you would have proved you didn't need me, and we can't have that can we?')

But this is much worse. Here we both tried. Hours of tutorials, drafts read, advice given, and still you couldn't jump high enough to get through the hoop. Or maybe I didn't hold the hoop steady enough. We've both failed, but it is your second chance that we've blown.

Now you know that they were right all those years ago at school: you are thick. You were stupid even to try weren't you?

That's what I'm saying as I sit in my cosy book-filled office.

'Sorry, you've not passed the re-submission.'

5. Every number is a student

A student is a customer with a number.
Someone who we have to attract because they are a valuable commodity.
Someone who is followed by money.
Someone who helps us to meet targets and fulfil contracts.
Someone who keeps me in a job.

A student is someone who interrupts me when I'm trying to work.
Someone who asks awkward questions.
Someone who always has reason for not handing work in on time.
Someone who assumes that I have thought of nothing else but their work since last we met.
Someone whose determination takes my breath away.

A student is someone who generates huge amounts of paperwork.
Someone who seems a different person when I meet them in Sainsbury's with their daughter.
Someone whose writing I cannot read.
Someone who nods and agrees when really they'd like to hit me.
Someone who lights up when they suddenly get the point.

A student is someone who will always get hold of the wrong end of the stick.
Someone who makes me see stale old theories in a new and exciting light.
Someone who I fear when I first walk into class.
Someone who, when they leave me at the end of a course, I miss more than I care to admit.

6. Epilogue: An increasingly strange profession: reflections on the role of a nurse/teacher

The untitled piece of writing about the strange room seems to reflect something of the uncertainty and alienation of being in surroundings which are unfamiliar and in some way rather hostile. The discomfort of having one's expectations disappointed runs throughout the work. There is a feeling that the writer does not, in some way, belong in the strange environment, that she is wrong-footed by the circumstances in which she finds herself. There is certainly an atmosphere of uncertainty and ambivalence not least towards the decision about what is appropriate behaviour in that situation.

The 'Contents of my briefcase' piece again shows similar elements of ambivalence, this time towards my own role. The case contains both friendly and hostile elements and there seems to be some sense in which the case and its contents, although owned by me, are partly dictating to me and controlling the way in which I fulfil my role. The need for several identity cards seems to echo the problem of multiple roles. My reaction to the card which enables me to use the photocopying machine surprised me and crystallised what is perhaps a fundamental motivation for me in my role as a teacher – the desire to nurture ability. It became apparent to me as I re-read my writing that I had brought this motivation with me to teaching from my career as a nurse. This is explored in 'Nurse/teacher'.

However this is not the whole story. The role of teacher in a university cannot be and is not, confined to the nurturing of students. It is also concerned with the demands and the needs of the organisation. The teacher has responsibilities to fulfil with regard to maintaining quality and upholding academic standards. The tension between these two aspects of the teacher's role is reflected on in 'Sorry'. Here the teacher finds herself in a situation where she is required by the organisation to play out a scene which is essentially destructive to the student and which undermines what she considers to be her primary function towards that individual. Again there are indications here that she is uncomfortable in this territory. This is not where she should be and this is not what she should be doing. The anxiety surrounding role-conflict is well-documented. When two sets of expectations act simultaneously on the person, that person will struggle to find some resolution and this is a stressful process (Merton 1957). This is similar to the experience of cognitive dissonance as described by Festinger (1957). The power of the teacher over the student and its potentially destructive nature is portrayed as unwelcome and surprisingly unexpected. It is certainly something which sits uneasily with my own view of myself as a teacher.

The power of the teacher and the bureaucratic aspect of the role is a formidable combination which, if it is allowed to overshadow the nurturing role, threatens to change education for the worse. Those of us who find ourselves working in the uncertain and changing arena of higher education today need to consider the tensions in our role and the consequences for ourselves as teachers and for our students as learners.

The tensions apparent within the role of teacher and the increasing uncertainty surrounding that role at a time of rapid change is, I believe, reflected at different levels. As an institution, the university itself has to balance tensions within its role. The realities of the market-driven world have been thrust upon the university and the organisation finds itself in unfamiliar territory. Education is now not only about the nurturing of ability and the development of individual talent. It is also about competition and balancing budgets.

The poem reflects the multi-faceted relationship between student and teacher from the teacher's perspective. The ambivalence and uncertainty of being in the role of teacher with its incumbent responsibilities, rewards and dilemmas. The bureaucratic aspect of the role is interspersed with the personal and nurturing aspect of the role, and in the end, although the conflict remains unresolved, it is perhaps indicative of my own feelings to note that the poem ends on a positive reflection on the relationship.

N.B. As I was re-reading the reflective pieces several other themes occurred to me that could be explored:

What motivates individuals to come into teaching in H.E.?

The nature of teacher/student relationship in H.E.

'Power-over' versus 'Power-to'.

The nature of assessment in H.E.

The individual as part of a large organisation.

The experience of mature students in H.E.

The examples in this chapter are intended to illustrate the 'artistry' with which professional practitioners use the medium of writing to shape experience into significance. In this sense they are fictions, in the less familar meaning of the term which has already been mentioned on several occasions (e.g. Chapter 1: p. 1), as well as containing fictional 'stories' in the conventional sense. A theoretical rationale for the ideas underpinning the general approach illustrated in these last two chapters is presented in some detail in Chapter 7, indicating the relationship between reflection, learning and the artistic imagination, in terms of both psychological and cultural processes. But from a practical point of view, the value of this approach to the process of reflection is that writers find it enjoyable and liberating, readers find it enjoyable and interesting, and the small group discussions which are an integral part of the process of producing the texts occasion intense and illuminating explorations of practice issues. The next chapter therefore contains a detailed account of this process, in the form of a 'distance learning text' which is designed to enable readers to experience for themselves the sort of reflective writing course in which the texts presented in this chapter were written.

4

THE REFLECTIVE WRITING
COURSE

Distance-learning materials

INTRODUCTION

The following materials are based on the sequence of activities and teaching materials which have been used most frequently and successfully in the 'Reflective Writing for Professional Practitioners' course over a number of years.

The format of the tutor-led course requires students to attend the University for a series of meetings, of about three hours each, with approximately a week between each meeting. The assignment written at the end of the course earns academic credit within the University modular degree framework, and is also suitable for various 'professional credit' schemes.

The use of the distance-learning materials allows groups of students to arrange their own informal meetings at which they work through the sequence of activities and illustrative examples, without any further tutorial input. At the end of the process participants should have produced a final text based on the various pieces of writing they have undertaken. These texts will be suitable for circulation among the group and perhaps more widely among interested colleagues. The work is thus valuable as a professional development experience in its own right – as a method of stimulating the sharing of professional insight – as well as a formal course leading to credits within academic and professional award schemes. The examples of patchwork texts included in Chapter 3 were all written during courses following roughly the format presented here.

The materials presented in this chapter and the general process of the course can easily be used in a situation where participants exchange materials via e-mail or an internet website. This option is referred to from time to time, but many of the instructions refer explicitly to a situation where groups of participants are meeting face to face – e.g. the division of the materials into 'sessions' and references to how long should be spent on various activities. Participants using e-mail or website communication will thus need to make their own interpretation of the process at such points, which should not be difficult: it would rapidly become tedious to have two different sets of instructions on every occasion.

The material in this chapter makes frequent reference to the examples and explanations in the earlier chapters, but in addition, further illustrative material is introduced which does not appear elsewhere in the book.

The objectives of the course at the University are given below (they also function as assessment criteria). You may wish to devise your own, but the following list gives an indication of the scope and purpose of the work that the following materials are intended to foster.

- Careful, detailed observation of events and situations;
- Empathising with the standpoint of other people;
- Noticing the various emotional dimensions of events and situations;
- Addressing the complexities of issues, events, and situations;
- Making connections between different events and situations, and between specific details and general principles derived from a range of professional knowledge;
- Demonstrating learning in response to professional experience and the process of reflecting on/writing about it.

If the material is to be used by groups of participants meeting face to face, the number of participants in the group is critical. Three is the minimum number, so that a writer can listen to a discussion of his or her text between different readers. Five is probably the maximum number, so that there is time for each piece of writing to be fully discussed without the sessions becoming too long. If participants are communicating via e-mail or website, then the numbers involved can probably be increased to seven or eight.

The interval between face-to-face meetings should be about a week, to begin with, so that there is time to think about and to produce a short piece of writing, while preserving the impetus of the sequence of meetings. In the latter stages, the interval could be increased to two weeks. Obviously, the use of e-mail or website communication gives much greater flexibility, although each group will still probably wish to arrange some sort of timetable for the interchange of writing and comments.

Two other points which we have found to be important are worth emphasising:

1 It is important that the materials are worked through in sequence, page by page. Don't read the whole package through: there are important points at which it is important that you work out your own responses before turning the page and comparing them with other suggestions.

2 The first exercise – uninterrupted writing – has often been greeted with initial expressions of dismay but has always been found to be most

helpful. Don't leave it out! It provides a real foundation for the rest of the work.

In the material which follows there are general discussions of aspects of the writing process and also specific instructions for carrying out an activity. In general the latter are signalled by bullet points. The illustrative examples are presented in a different typeface.

Tutors using the materials within formally arranged courses will obviously have their own ways of introducing them. The materials at the beginning of session 1, therefore, are presented here as both optional and minimal.

REFLECTIVE WRITING COURSE

SESSION 1

Before meeting with the rest of your group, read the 'Prologue' to Chapter 1, and also the following introductory statement. This will serve to give a general idea of the purpose of the course and its underlying rationale.

1. Reflective writing: an introductory statement

The term 'reflective practitioner' has become widespread as a way of summing up the accomplishments characteristic of skilled professional work. But what is the force of the term 'reflective'? All human beings (over the age of about nine months) make interpretations of events, have opinions about events, possess a range of knowledge about events, and make decisions about what to do in response to events. How is 'reflection' (as a specific and demanding process) something more than this?

To answer this question, let us begin by distinguishing 'reflective' writing from three other types of writing. First: 'bureaucratic' writing – which gives expression to familiar, official lines of thought (policy statements are good examples). This form of writing tends to be rather abstract, rather vague, and thus rather simplistic. Second: 'journalistic' writing, which appeals to those who already agree; it is partisan, it presents opinions forcefully but it doesn't examine the assumptions on which it depends. Third: 'academic' writing, which is depersonalised, focusing on the presentation and organisation of others' thoughts; it thus often lacks a personal voice, a sense of personal relevance and commitment. The point of making these comments (which admittedly are themselves rather simplistic) is merely to sharpen up the point that, in terms of the aims of this course, '*reflective*' writing has the voice which presents the thinking of a writer who is exploring, questioning, and thus – above all – learning. It emphasises, above all, drawing upon the resources for thinking which we have acquired from our prior experience, over a period of time. These resources include unconscious or barely conscious themes and concerns which shape our whole view of the world. Reflection from this point of view is a process of making new links between our many different theoretical resources. It is thus at the same time personal and innovative.

Underlying this general view are a number of general assumptions.

1   Our thinking continuously tends to slip into an 'ideological' form, in which complex matters are made simple in order to create a comfortable sense of order and certainty. Hence, in order to renew and reinvigorate our thinking, we need to recollect our sense of uncertainty, of unresolved and complex dilemmas. Although our questions can be answered, these answers are always only provisional and temporary. Our current answers are themselves open to new questions.

2   Our pictures of the world are always interpretations, based on theories and values. We therefore need to be aware of the need to think reflexively, i.e. to think about the processes of our own thinking. We need to notice how our thinking is derived from our bodies of knowledge and values, and from the personal and cultural experiences which underlie them.

3   It is important to recognise the importance for our thinking of narrative processes. In other words, we order, interpret and make sense of experiences and ideas by embodying them in a selection of characters involved in a sequence of events with a defined beginning and an end (in other words we store experience in the form of stories). Hence the value of undertaking a journey of reflective exploration by starting out from a narrative. Narratives aim at vividness, by including details (so that the reader can better imagine what it was like). These concrete details enable our thinking to start from personal insight and observation, rather than from abstract generalities which easily lapse into the clichés of conventional wisdom.

4   Recounting narratives from our experience can be risky. If they concern areas we really need to think about, they can (for this very reason) be too uncomfortably revealing. There is therefore much to be said for the fictional form, which enables us to present complex and difficult areas of experience in an imaginary context. Discussion of the meaning of a fictional story we have written can thus be separated from discussion of our own particular experiences, which can, if we wish, be kept private. This is one of the reasons why writing fiction plays an important part in the activities of the course.

5   Reflective writing does not need difficult academic skills of a technical nature. It involves drawing on an ability to express ourselves which we all possess, or rather which we used to possess when we were younger, before a constraining educational process gradually squeezed out of us our confi-

dence in our ability as thinkers. The main aim of the course is to restore a sense of expressive confidence that many of us feel that we have lost.

2. First activity: uninterrupted writing

This course is about writing. And many of us feel a certain lack of confidence about our ability to write. Everyone who has undertaken this course in the past, over several years, has ended up being surprised – surprised that they can write much better than they thought they could. So the first thing to do is to get down and write.

- Write for five minutes on anything you like *without stopping*. If you can't think of the next word, then repeat the one you are writing until the one you need occurs to you. Don't spend time wondering what to write about. Just start. No-one will see this piece of writing. It is entirely private. One of the group (or the tutor) needs to act as time-keeper.
- Start writing NOW.
- Read over to yourself what you have written.
- Discuss with one another what sort of thing you found yourself writing about, what you think about what you have written, how you felt as you started to write, and how you feel now.

3. Second writing activity:

'A time when I learned something important'

- Write on this topic for fifteen minutes. Again, you will not be sharing this piece of writing. This time, however, you *can* stop to think of a word! Arrange for someone to act as time-keeper.
- Start writing NOW.
- After you have finished writing, share with one another the ideas you have written about. Did you find that you learned more about the experience through the activity of writing about it? Or was the whole experience and your understanding of it there, complete in your head before you started to write?

4. Ground rules for the sharing process

There will be two main sorts of activity in the course: writing, and sharing your writing with the others in your small group – between three and five is the best number if you are meeting face to face, seven or eight if you are using e-mail or a website. For next week's meeting and for all of the subsequent meetings you will each write something to be shared in the group.

The process of sharing your written work in your small working groups is going to need a sense of trust. An obvious first step towards this is to agree a set of ground rules which will guide (and even to some extent, determine) the process of your working groups. Sometimes it is hard to imagine in advance the sorts of issues that might arise, so here is a set of such ground rules which were agreed by a group undertaking the course. Obviously, you will want to make your own version – adapting the wording of some of them and adding others.

An example of a set of ground rules for the reflective writing course

- Information derived from members' writing should not be discussed outside the reflective writing group.
- Written copies of writing should be returned to writers.
- Discussion should not focus on whether or not readers think the writing is 'good' but on what they think it means, what issues it raises, how the writer might expand or continue it.
- Any disagreement with opinions expressed in the writing should be presented positively and not dogmatically.
- Discussion should be guided by a principle of mutual support.
- Where discussions of writing are conducted face to face:

  - Time should be allowed for thinking; i.e. periods of silence are OK;
  - Time for discussion should be divided up equally, and all members have the right to intervene as time-keepers;
  - It is important to arrive punctually;
  - All members must bring along some writing to share.

5. Some further notes on sharing your writing

- The writing is not to be 'assessed' (positively or negatively): the purpose of the sharing of writing is to help writers take their work forward, through probing and exploring aspects of the writing.
- Good questions for readers to ask and answer (in making their responses) are:

  - Why do you think this piece started where it did?
  - Why do you think this piece ended where it did?
  - What overall impression do you get from this?
  - What point do you think the writer seems to be making by writing this?
  - Which phrase(s) or passage(s) in the piece stand(s) out as being particularly interesting or unexpected?

- Do NOT try to focus directly on the writer behind the writing – that is for writers to do on their own. So don't discuss what the writer thinks but what this piece of writing is expressing. In particular, where the piece is presented as an imagined situation, remember that in principle we don't know where the writer stands in relation to it. Indeed, writers may change their view on where they stand in relation to their writing after receiving readers' feedback.
- Where the group is meeting face to face, don't make the writer feel they are being interrogated. In fact it is a good idea if at first the writer listens to the discussion between the various readers ('eavesdropping' you might call it). During this time the writer should make notes on what they hear, especially anything which surprises them. Because the writer's task is to learn as much as possible from what they hear the readers say.

6. Some suggestions for your first piece of writing

Although the final theme of your writing will be relevant to your professional work, this first piece need not have a professional focus. Write about anything that seems of interest. It can be a description, a poem, a story, an incident, an account of a person, etc. The following titles are merely presented as a set of possible triggers. If they trigger off another title for you, write on that.

- A learning experience
- Two journeys
- A misunderstanding
- Home
- 'Suddenly I understood what it was all about. It all began when ... '
- Anger
- 'Why have I remembered this incident all these years?'
- Compassion
- Coping
- An odious person
- One event, different points of view
- Evocative details: the contents of a room; the contents of a person's pockets/handbag

Acknowledgements: this list of titles is adapted from the work of Gillie Bolton, University of Sheffield, and Natalie Goldberg's book Wild Mind *(Rider, 1991).*

Before you start, read the following passage by Valerie Hannagan.

'Starting where we are: one way of warming up'
by Valerie Hannagan[*]

Like me, you may occasionally find yourself wrestling with the notion that you have nothing to write. At least, nothing 'important'. As you know, there is no greater turn-off than that. It's awful … a horrid little voice inside us says, 'Why don't you give up the whole idea?' … Not surprisingly, we freeze.

I would like to suggest one of the many ways in which we can make friends with that voice and gently ease ourselves into writing.

Start where you are. Do not seek out special places, special times. Just get out your writing materials, whatever they may be, and keep them close to you. It may help if you can have silence; but if noise is where you are, do not attempt to shut it out. A dog barks in a neighbour's garden. Without thinking too much, try to get hold of that sound. Perhaps it embodies your frustration, your despair – you think of the cooped-up animal trying to get out; or else you are afraid of it – the dog wants to attack you. Maybe the barking is pleasurable, reminding you of a beloved childhood pet. Whatever it is, write it down, and if words refuse to come, then draw, doodle or scribble. Find a simple title: 'This is the dog barking; this is where I am'. Write the date, the time, the place. Perhaps your starting point will be visual: you may find yourself drawing the outline of your hand, or copying in words and pictures the grain of a wooden object. Or you will close your eyes, recapturing a fragment of conversation. The important thing is not to expect artistic miracles, but to meet yourself as you are now. If the horrid voice is uppermost, write out what it says, then draw a wavy line around your words and decorate them in any way you choose. Play with them, mix them up, cut them out if it helps, or contain them within other words. Once, when very depressed, all I could produce was a vertical line. But that was already something; the terrifying blankness of the page was split, I had created two spaces out of one – an early life form.

---

[*] From S. Sellers (ed.) (1991) *Taking Reality by Surprise*, p. 7.

SESSION 2

- Begin by sharing your writing with each other. Remind yourself before you start of the ground rules you agreed in session 1 and remember to make notes on the comments made by the other members of your group on your piece of writing. Remember also to share out the time equally. Discuss each piece after your have read it. Don't try to read them all and then discuss them together, otherwise you will find it difficult to spend an equal amount of time on each piece.
- After you have shared all the pieces of writing, take fifteen minutes to sum up, in turn, what you think you have learned and any general thoughts on the process.
- Then leave yourselves an hour or so for the further work described below.

1. Getting started

If you found difficulty in getting started you might find the following passage from Natalie Goldberg helpful.

> Drink a full glass of water continuously and slowly without taking the glass away from your lips. Watch your breath as you drink. Watch how your mouth fills with water before it swallows. Feel your swallow. Look down through the glass. Keep drinking. Finish the whole glass. Now put down the glass, take your pen and list five to ten clear subjects to write about. Number one can be 'how I swallow'. Number two can be 'plastic glasses'. Then 'my hand', 'my arm', 'rivers', 'where I love water', 'summer and ice cubes', 'feeling cold on my lips'. Get it? Go.
>
> (Goldberg 1991: p. 50)

The general point is that one way of starting to write is to focus one's mind on the details of an experience, and then allow associated ideas, images and thoughts to spring up in response to the details. In this way we can draw on the richness of all that we have stored away, 'somewhere'.

After you have read Goldberg's piece, discuss other possible examples.

2. Beginnings

What makes a good opening sentence? Let us begin by answering: 'something that draws the reader in'. (Think of the famous opening of George Orwell's *Nineteen Eighty-four*: 'It was a bright cold day in April, and the clocks were striking thirteen'.) We all do beginnings quite naturally: think of how you get the attention of a group of friends when you want to tell an anecdote: how do you start?

- Read the beginning of Marion Bromfield's piece in Chapter 3 (example 5) and notice how it is both dramatic and also slightly puzzling: it is some time before we realise that it is a horse that has died.
- Look back at the beginnings of the pieces you have just read. How does the first sentence get your attention? Do some do it better than others? How? Do you have any other answers to the question, what makes a good opening?

3. Endings

What makes a good ending? What rounds off a piece of writing? Is it something that sums it all up? Is it a sort of generalisation? Or is that too crude and obvious? Is it more like a point at which a 'new beginning' comes into view? Or the point at which the key ambiguity in the piece becomes apparent – a final question?

- How did you know when you had come to the end of your piece of writing?
- Look at the endings of the pieces you have just read. In what way are they endings? Discuss this: there may an interesting variety of opinions.
- Finally, have a look at the stories in Chapter 2, and notice how the beginnings and endings work – the opening sentence announcing the theme (although when we first read it we don't know that, of course) and the ending often coming as a sudden surprise which reveals what the story has been about (e.g. story 3) or echoing the beginning in a new way (e.g. stories 1 and 6).

4. Continuations (suggestions for your next piece of writing)

Your next piece of writing could be something quite separate, if you wish, especially if you feel you already know what it is going to be and feel enthusiastic about it. But, equally, your next writing might attempt to build on what you did last time, to explore aspects of the theme or the situation that your first piece of writing has brought into view. The various pieces of writing included in Chapter 3 illustrate a number of different ways of doing this, but here are some suggestions which you might find useful.

- Describe the incident from the point of view of one of the other characters in the situation (or from the point of view of the cat, which everyone has ignored, or the old armchair in which someone is sitting, etc.).
- Imagine a different ending.
- Write a diary entry for one of the characters.

- Write what one (or several) of the characters is thinking and feeling at a particular moment, bringing out the contrasts.
- Rewrite the incident with the centre of power altered.
- Write a dialogue in which two characters in this situation argue strongly their different points of view – and write it so that readers cannot easily tell which point of view you personally sympathise with!
- Expain what it is that puzzles you about the incident.

Acknowledgements to Gillie Bolton, University of Sheffield, for some of the above ideas.

Before you write your next piece, look at the following work by Richard Ball as a further example of how one can write a continuation which explores the different perspectives on a situation. (Richard Ball is a forensic psychiatric nurse, working in a special hospital for patients whose mental disturbance renders them dangerous. Before taking part in the reflective writing course he had no prior experience of writing in this way.) After you have read it, ask yourself:

- Why does Richard begin each piece in the way he does?
- Why does he use the same word to end both pieces? (What effect does that have?)
- How does Richard bring out professional issues by writing this continuation?
- If you were the author of these pieces, what would be your next piece of writing?

'FINALLY ... ' by Richard Ball

1. Jessica

Victory. Fear. Sadness. Anger.

The gentle, subtle creaking of Barney's lead failed to indicate the enormity of the situation.

Jessica was hanging herself.

For a while she felt pain. A dreadful squeezing pressure, her head seemingly pumped up like a balloon. Her eyes threatening to burst from her face.

Her face. How often had she sat staring into her mirror, exploring every crease, blemish and scar? How many razors had she sliced into her fresh teenage skin whilst whispering curses upon her mother for not understanding? The pain of the lead cutting into her throat had gradually subsided and now a pleasant numbness began to wash over her.

Now she could think, how dreamy it was.

This will show them. Bastards. Nobody at the hospital cares, they're too concerned with saving their jobs to worry about the patients. Well, a patient dying will screw their jobs. They always run around when someone cuts up or puts a bra around their neck, and always that same look is in the nurses' eyes. The expression that shouts out their real thoughts – patients are problems. Cutting up makes staff angry. But they don't care, do they? They don't actually care, these so called carers.

How long has it been? How long had she been up here? She had caught them out this time. Mum will cry, but then she's good at that. It's what she does best, crying. She cried when Jessica had first gone into hospital and then she cried when she came out. Mum cried after the rape, but she didn't tell anyone. Jessica had only been nine when the bastard had defiled her. Mum's bastard boyfriend. Mum kept it quiet. It's all her fault.

Everything is going dark. Good.

Who would find her – Richard, perhaps? That would be a shame, he's alright. At least he would listen, usually. But he had been strange when she took the overdose, the paracetamol one. He looked like the rest then, that same expression. That had annoyed Jessica. She thought he was her friend. She couldn't trust any of them.

Barney's lead creaked.

Barney! She wouldn't see him again. Panic! A struggle to get down, a sudden fear. But her arms weren't listening.

She couldn't see. Bitterness. A wracking sob. But was it a sob?

More of a gargle.

This will teach them.

So sad.

It doesn't hurt.

I have done it.

I've really done it.

Finally …

2. Richard

Anger. Fear. Sadness.

Jessica is dead.

She has been my problem for a year. Now she is dead. Questions and mixed emotions are tumbling through me, never resolved, never stable but ever present.

Was there something I could have done? She was always telling me that she was going to kill herself. Of course she was – they all are. Never a week passes without an overdose here, a self-inflicted injury there. It is their nature, it is why they are in hospital. But it is so easy to forget that. Them and Us. Always Them and Us. But Jessica was different.

Oh, she cut herself and munched on tablets like smarties. She wanted the attention, but she would never actually risk herself.

I really, really thought that I had got through to her. She had been institutionalised for ten years, how on earth did I think that I would make a difference? I am a professional who cared for her, but there must have been so many before me. What made me think I could change her?

Selfish bitch! Did she know the heartache and trouble she was going to cause? Typical of her scheming manipulative character. Typical. And the poor bloke that found her, I doubt he will sleep well tonight.

But she can't be blamed, can she?

What is the point of a care plan if it's not utilised? I wrote that staff should always know her whereabouts, particularly when her mood was low. Her mood was always low after seeing her mother and going out with the dog. Yet she was hanging for twenty minutes! From the dog's lead! How the hell did she get that back on the ward?

Heads are going to roll for this one.

Thank God I wasn't on duty. I was her primary nurse though. They are going to tear her care plan apart. Was it overdue an evaluation? Was it thorough enough? Was it workable, realistic? There will be an inquest.

Why did she do it? I did my best for her and this is how she repays me. What was the point of all that work – all that effort?

All those times I counselled her, challenged her, sometimes physically restraining her to stop her hurting herself.

Perhaps I should have let her bang her head. She may have released her tension then instead of bottling it up and hanging herself.

This could jeopardise my job. They will tear me apart. God, I knew something like this would happen. I was doing so well. I always feared something like this would happen. And now it has.

Finally.

SESSION 3

- Begin by sharing the work you have written this week.
- Remind yourselves of the ground rules from the first session.
- Remember to make notes on the comments made by different readers, especially any comments which you had not anticipated.
- Then leave yourselves about an hour and a half for the further work described below.

Writing a (fictional) story

One way of learning more about a professional situation or theme is to write a fictional story about it and notice the different interpretations that different readers make. When we write a story we usually have an idea of what it is about, but stories are always ambiguous – they can always be seen from different points of view, because the author's intention is always implicit rather than explicit. So readers can draw conclusions from it that the author had not intended. That doesn't mean that someone is right and someone is wrong. The point of the exercise (within the reflective writing course) is not for readers to discover what the author actually intended, but for writers to discover what other aspects there are to the situation about which they have written, which they may not have been fully aware of until they heard how readers interpreted their story.

Another advantage of writing a fiction is that it places a clear distance between the writer and the situation written about, unlike more factual writing. Since it is a fiction, the writer is not 'admitting' that any of this actually happened. So one can write about more risky matters and still feel relatively safe. (Remember that the discussion will be about the story as a story, what it means, how it might be continued – not about the writer and their own practice. A story thus provides a safe haven in which to do your thinking about the experiences you have written about.

Many of you will not have written a story for many years, but don't worry: students on this course *always* surprise themselves by discovering that they *can* write interesting and powerful stories, even though they may have had no prior experience (at least since they were at primary school). The stories included in Chapter 2 were all written by people who initially doubted their ability to write fiction.

- First of all, read the first part of the introduction to Chapter 2. As you read, sideline any passages which seem helpful or which you disagree with or don't fully understand. Discuss these with one another.
- Then read the first story in Chapter 2 – 'Brave' by Brenda Landgrebe – and before you read the commentary discuss what you think was the purpose of the writer; what is the point she is making? Then compare

your thoughts with the ideas in the commentary, which include Brenda's own explanation.

- Next, read the following story by Ann Leontovitsch. After you have read the story answer the questions listed at the end, first for yourself and then comparing your answers with the other members of the group. (Ann Leontovitsch was acting head of a school for children with severe learning difficulties when she wrote her story. Again, it was the first story she had written, and she had previously found writing generally 'difficult'. The title of her story – 'The Magi' – refers to the 'Three Wise Men' who came to give gifts at the birth of Jesus. The title indicates that the events refer to taking part in the school nativity play as the writer imagines it experienced by one of her pupils.)

'The Magi' by Ann Leontovitsch

Peter looked at the blur of colours on the table. He picked up the wooden peg board and threw it onto the floor. It made a clunk and clatter as all the pegs flew under the desks and chairs. Peter smiled. He waited for the teacher to come to him. He liked it when she held his hands and made loud noises with her face close to his. But today she looked round and sighed and continued to rustle something shiny. Why didn't she come? Jane didn't come either. Peter liked her too. She was busy wrapping another child in a piece of striped material. A girl started to pick up the pegs and put them on the table in front of Peter. He threw them on the floor again. Miss Smith made some sharp noises and the pegs were taken away and a jigsaw puzzle put on the table. Peter threw it on the floor but it didn't make a nice noise only a dull sound and no-one came to him. He sat there watching the patterns of shadows on the window.

Someone was pulling at his jumper. He lifted his arms. He saw dark and smelt warmth, then it was light again and Jane was talking quietly to him. Peter smiled. Jane pushed his arms into some stiff material which scratched him and smelt strange. Peter tried to move away but she held his arms firmly and pulled the material around him. She took his hands and pulled him to his feet then pushed something onto his head. It hurt his ears. He shook his head but it wouldn't come off. Jane held his hands tightly. Peter was afraid. His arms hurt, his ears hurt and there was a strange smell. He started to cry. Jane heard the thin distressed wail and spoke softly to him. She wiped his face. Peter liked Jane, he didn't feel so frightened now. She pushed his tongue back into his mouth and pushed his chin to close his mouth. Peter tried to swallow but couldn't, he opened his mouth and allowed his tongue to feel free again. Jane put a shiny box into his hand. Peter liked the pattern on the box and held it up in front of his face.

Someone was pushing him in his back. He put his foot down carefully on the floor and moved forward to avoid the push but it happened again and again. At each step another push. Peter looked at the shiny patterns of his box. Someone snatched the box from him. Peter stood there. He had nothing to watch now. Jane pulled his arm and he walked with her. The piano started to play. Peter smiled. He liked the feelings the music made through his feet but Jane led him out of the door. He stopped. He wanted to stay with the music but Jane gripped firmly on his arm and pulled him back into the classroom.

Questions

- What, briefly, is the sequence of events as Peter experienced them in the story?
- What is the difference between how he experiences the events and how the teachers experience them?
- What is the significance of the title?
- What point is the writer making about her professional work with chilrden with learning difficulties?
- How does the writer make this point? Are there any key words or phrases which bring it out?
- How does the way the story is written contribute to our understanding of Peter's experience?

Finally, read the following story 'Moments of truth' and discuss what point you think the story is making before going on to read the various readers' interpretations of it on the following pages.

'Moments of truth' (a story about interviewers and interviewees) by Richard Winter

I looked down at the official application form for the course.

There I was:

My name: the social definition I was born with, overlaid by the accidents of my parents' choice of mythological tradition, and my own choice of husband.

My education: a chapter of agonies and disasters, but ultimately of trials overcome.

My career: the schools whose culture I had fought my way into, the colleagues whose trust I had won, the psychic bruises I had suffered and inflicted, the children with whose survival I had briefly been entrusted, and in whose own careers I had been an early influence, for better or for worse.

Inservice courses attended: a combination of my own shifting hopes and politically inspired prescriptions from on high.

My current area of interest: an arbitrary pinpoint within an infinite yet incomplete and uncompletable mystery.

MY LIFE …

Well, here goes.

I sealed the envelope and placed it carefully in the school secretary's mail tray.

'Right, this is the next one: "Helen Freya Watkins, *née* Blumberg. Head of Infants. Interested in parental involvement in reading schemes". Any thoughts?'

'Well we are a bit low on the infants side, although there are three other people from infants schools who have applied for the course. She looked rather bitty to me. I don't see what it all adds up to. Sort of vague, but she seems to have done quite a lot. Not strong, but in with a chance, I think. What did her referee say?'

'Didn't reply.'

'Oh dear. Well, let's have her in, then.'

O, God, this is awful. I don't understand their questions. One of them is half asleep, and the other keeps interrupting to say, 'Yes, absolutely' every half sentence. Does he think I'm talking too much? I'll try and keep my answers short. This chair is so low – I'm sure that smarmy looking one is trying to look up my skirt. Who do they think they are, these people? Do I really want to do a higher degree anyway? What's it all for?

She seems nervous. Bad sign. Doesn't respond well to pressure. Also, she doesn't seem to be following the drift of Arthur's questioning; so will she be able to cope with the intellectual demands of the course (make a note of that)? Nice legs though. She's obviously sincere and committed, but so what – aren't we all? The question is: can she *articulate* it? I know what I'll ask her, after Arthur's finished …

'Right, now, Mrs Watkins: can I slightly change tack here? You've said you're interested in the role of parents. How does this relate to your general *philosophy* of education?'

(Neat question, that: puts a bit more pressure on her than Arthur's waffly stuff; no wonder she ended up just describing her job to us.)

(My 'philosophy of education'! What on earth am I supposed to say? Keep it brief this time, though.) 'I suppose I would say that my philosophy of education is child-centred, and so I see the parents working alongside us, for the children's benefit.'

(Pause)

(Well, that is pretty weak, I must say. She ducked my challenge there, I'm afraid. Oh God, now she's clammed up completely. What do I say now, for goodness sake?) 'Do you mean, then, that unless you had a child-centred philosophy of education, you wouldn't be concerned with the parents' role?'

'No. I don't mean that. It's a mixture, really, isn't it?'

(A 'mixture'! Like a bag of sweets? What in hell does she mean?)

(I shouldn't have said 'mixture', sounds a bit silly. But: children, parents, teachers, they're all mixed up together in the educational process; it's unreal to try to separate them. So what on earth does he mean? Surely, all teachers are 'concerned' about the children's parents. What's he on about?)

'Mrs Watkins, perhaps I can help out here: tell me a bit about some of the parents of the children at your school.'

(Thank God, Arthur's got her going again. I can't see her standing the pace, though. Can't put her thoughts into words.)

'Thank you, Mrs Watkins. We'll be in touch in a day or two … So, Arthur, what did you think?'

'Basically I thought you gave her a hard time.'

'Really? Surely not. But the course is going to give them all a hard time. I thought she just couldn't articulate, except at a fairly naive level.'

'Well, I'm not so sure. She panicked, but she seemed to be thinking very carefully about everything. She didn't have any pat answers. That made it difficult for her, but in the long run, you know, that's perhaps not such a bad thing.'

'Well, maybe. I see what you mean. OK; good: we'll give her a provisional tick then. Certainly, she seemed willing enough. How many more have we got to get through before lunch?'

At that moment our proceedings were interrupted by the ringing of the telephone. I lifted the receiver.

'Hello.'

'Hello. Dr Jones?'

'Yes.'

'This is the University of Dorset here. About your application for the Senior Lectureship in Primary Education … '

'Yes.'

'Could you attend for interview at 11 o'clock this coming Monday? I'm sorry to spring it on you at such short notice, but the Head of Department has been at a conference in Oslo, so our procedures got rather behind-hand. That's why I'm phoning – to make sure. The details are in the post.'

* * *

The following Monday I'm sitting in a tatty armchair outside a hideous yellow door marked 'Professor D. Miller, Head of Education'. The University is only 20 miles from the College, so it would be a great job to get: a lot more status without all the hassle of moving house.

Ten minutes to go. Just time to skim over my application form once more; remind myself what I wrote. Quite an interesting-looking career, on paper, I think. Plenty of variety, plenty of publications, plus that spell of research with the Commission for Racial Equality. They're bound to ask about that. What are they likely to ask? Where are my notes? ... Oh God, the door's opening. Fingers crossed. Here we go.

'Ah, good morning, Dr Jones. Glad you could make it. I'm Derek Miller, Head of Department. May I introduce my colleagues Dr Linda Small, from Psychology and Child Development, Dr Ray Heathcote, from Curriculum Studies, and also Mrs Helen Watkins. She's a local infant head teacher. We always include people from the chalk-face when we're appointing education staff. Important principle, as I'm sure you'd agree. Mrs Watkins, would you like to lead off the questioning?'

Responses to 'Moments of truth': themes identified in the story by different readers (either in written notes or in discussion with the writer)

Reader no. 1

The application form is a means whereby one delivers oneself over to the power of another. There is a contrast between the emotional levels and concerns of the interviewer and of the interviewee. The relationship between the cognitive and the affective criteria for judgement are not articulated. The power relationship between the two interviewers affects the judgements made. The decision-making process seems to be superficial and arbitrary. Vulnerability is socially constructed (the roles of Dr Jones and Mrs Watkins are about to be reversed). In general: underlying the story is a sense of guilt about exercising power, linked to a theme that power undermines effective communication. This guilt has a sexual dimension, leading to a fear of 'The revenge of the woman'.

Reader no. 2

The story is very pessimistic: misunderstanding is taken to be inevitable; hence the theme of sadistic power. This is *not* inevitable: interviews don't have to be arranged in such a way that some *must* be rejected. Dr Jones is not really objectionable; his weaknesses are commonplace, except for the sexual theme, which is implausible: if the story was really about gender relationships then Professor Miller should have been a woman.

Reader no. 3

The people in the story are constructing roles for one another. The characters are in separate bubbles, and cannot communicate. The interviewer sets himself up on a 'high horse'. The question is: how is true communication possible? (In this sense the interview process is like a teaching–learning relationship.)

Reader no. 4

The interview here seems like a competitive game (of tennis, perhaps) in which opponents try to out-fox each other, and score points by correctly anticipating cunning moves. But it is an unfair game, in which the interviewer always serves *and* does the scoring! The interviewers patronise the interviewee because she is an infant teacher, and seem on that basis to have decided in advance that she is intellectually weak. The interview creates a dependency which makes it difficult for the interviewee to be critical of the process. Dr Jones' complacency on reviewing his application contrasts with Helen Watkins' tentativeness: will the reversal of the hierarchical relationship really take place? The theme is that of power leading to injustice, and thus to the distortion of communication.

Reader no. 5

The overall theme seems to me to be the potential for revenge. It reminds me of the theme of much of Alice Miller's writing, particularly in *For Your Own Good*. This title seems to express for me very well the justification for most interview procedures. Her theme is that adults as parents are engaged in a cycle in which the abuse they suffered as children is unconsciously visited upon their own children. Perhaps interviews, of which many people have painful memories, are another vehicle for unconsciously passing on abuses suffered in the past. I am particularly struck by the way in which the story reproduces the parental couple (the interviewers) and the child (the interviewee). I also find it interesting that the theme of parents and children is an overt aspect of the interview presented, which, to me, strengthens the metaphor I am suggesting …

The writer's ambivalence is suggested through the use of a switching first person. It starts with an identification with the female victim and then becomes an identification with the male aggressor (the interviewer), with some switches back, and this then becomes the potential male victim by the end. This is almost a developmental sequence.

Final note

As the writer of the story I am in a position to say quite definitely that I found some of the readers' comments quite surprising. In particular, the comments by readers nos 1 and 5 about the theme of 'revenge' started a new train of thought: perhaps, indeed, one theme in the story is that we take pleasure in exercising power in adult life as a way of 'getting our own back' after all our childhood experience of being on the receiving end of other people's power. That link between power and 'revenge' was certainly not in my mind as I wrote it, but it seems quite plausible, because the structure of the story itelf is one of 'revenge' – Mrs Watkins gets her revenge on Dr Jones. That makes an interesting link between what I had thought of as a professional/organisational theme (power) and the personal, emotional level.

For next week, try to write a fictional story which brings out a theme related to your own professional experience. Keep it short. One or (at most) two sides of A4 is usually enough space to develop a thought, and if it is too long the process of reading and sharing can get rather cumbersome. Type out your story, since reading handwriting often slows down the reading process, and bring along enough copies for the other members of your working group.

SESSION 4

- Begin by sharing your stories.
- Remind yourselves of the ground rules, and remember that the point is not to judge the writing or to interrogate the writer as to what they 'meant' but to provide the writer with interpretations and thoughts that they can learn from (privately). So writers should make sure that they take careful notes on what readers say about their work.
- Then allow about an hour to read and discuss the following material.

1. Writing as an exploration

By now, you should have some experience of how writing itself can be a sort of journey of self discovery, even without the added resource of other people's interpretations. The following piece by V. S. Naipaul brings out this aspect quite clearly.

Notice how the piece works – how the writer begins with concrete memories and how these memories stimulate a range of general themes. This is a description of the process of finding what it is one wishes (or needs) to write about. Naipaul's two titles seem in themselves to say something quite useful: writing a 'prologue' to an autobiography is necessary, because one needs to 'find the centre' (the centre of what?).

'Prologue to an autobiography' by V. S. Naipaul[*]

It is now nearly thirty years since, in a BBC room in London, on an old BBC typewriter, and on smooth, 'non-rustle' BBC script paper, I wrote the first sentence of my first publishable book. I was some three months short of my twenty-third birthday. I had left Oxford ten months before, and was living in London, trying to keep afloat and, in between, hoping to alleviate my anxiety but always only adding to it, trying to get started as a writer.

At Oxford I had been supported by a Trinidad government scholarship. In London I was on my own. The only money I got – eight guineas a week, less 'deductions' – came from the BBC Caribbean Service. My only piece of luck in the past year, and even in the past two years, had been to get a part-time job editing and presenting a weekly literary programme for the Caribbean.

The Caribbean Service was on the second floor of what had been the Langham Hotel, opposite Broadcasting House. On this floor the BBC had set aside a room for people like me, 'freelances' – to me then not a word suggesting freedom and valour, but suggesting only people on the fringe of a mighty enterprise, a depressed and suppliant class: I would have given a lot to be 'staff'.

The freelances' room didn't encourage thoughts of radio glory; it was strictly for the production of little scripts. Something of the hotel atmosphere remained: in the great Victorian-Edwardian days of the Langham Hotel (it was mentioned in at least one Sherlock Holmes story), the freelances' room might have been a pantry. It was at the back of the heavy brick building, and gloomy when the ceiling lights were turned off. It wasn't cheerful when the lights were on: ochre walls with a pea-green dado, the gloss paint tarnished; a radiator below the window, with grit on the sill; two or three chairs, a telephone, two tables and two old standard typewriters.

[*] From V. S. Naipaul (1985) *Finding the Centre*, pp. 15–16, 27–8.

It was in that Victorian-Edwardian gloom, and at one of those type-writers, that late one afternoon, without having any idea where I was going, and not perhaps intending to type to the end of the page, I wrote:

Every morning when he got up Hat would sit on the banister of his back veranda and shout across, 'What happening there, Bogart?'

That was a Port of Spain memory.

* * *

There was much in that call of 'Bogart!' that had to be examined. It was spoken by a Port of Spain Indian, a descendant of nineteenth-century indentured immigrants from South India: and Bogart was linked in a special Hindu way with my mother's family. So there was a migration from India to be considered, a migration within the British Empire. There was my Hindu family, with its fading memories of India; there was India itself. And there was Trinidad, with its past of slavery, its mixed population, its racial antagonisms and its changing political life; once part of Venezuela and the Spanish Empire, now English-speaking, with the American base and an open-air cinema at the end of Bogart's street. And just across the Gulf of Paria was Venezuela, the sixteenth-century land of El Dorado, now a country of dictators, but drawing Bogart out of his servant room with its promise of Spanish sexual adventure and the promise of a job in its oilfields.

And there was my own presence in England, writing: the career wasn't possible in Trinidad, a small, mainly agricultural colony: my vision of the world couldn't exclude that important fact.

So step by step, book by book, though seeking each time only to write another book, I eased myself into knowledge. To write was to learn. Beginning a book, I always felt I was in possession of all the facts about myself; at the end I was always surprised. The book before always turned out to have been written by a man with incomplete knowledge. And the very first, the one begun in the freelances' room, seemed to have been written by an innocent, a man at the beginning of knowledge.

2. Moving from detail to generalisation and 'theory'

Natalie Goldberg makes the interesting statement, 'You have to earn the right to make an abstract statement' (Goldberg 1991: p. 208). Put another way: generalisations can easily seem superficial, glib, unless they emerge from a specific experience, which gives the generalisation your own personal angle, and meaning. Much writing takes this form, of moving from particular experiences to general insights. Indeed, one way in which a piece of writing can be interesting is when it takes us (both the writer and the reader) on that journey outwards, from a particular experience to its possible general implications. Often we can do this by seeing a link between an experience and a piece of theory from our stock of professional knowledge. This link then both illuminates the experience (by indicating its general significance) and also illuminates the theory, because the specific experience can enable us to see a new significance in the theory. The following piece by Brenda Landgrebe, written during the reflective writing course, is a good example of this process at work.

'Kyoko: learning from a patient' by Brenda Landgrebe

Kyoko was beautiful. She stood quite still by the window of the bedroom as I entered.

She was wearing a simple shift dress that fell to her knees. Her arms were bare, slightly bronzed and very slim. Her wrists and hands were tiny; her fingers laced together at waist height.

Her legs were slim but shapely and her feet, like her hands, were very small and were clad in thonged sandals anchored at a point between each first and second toe.

I looked at her face. Slightly arched, narrow black eyebrows accentuated deep, black-lashed, almond shaped eyes. High, rounded cheekbones supported faint shadows which further enhanced their prominence. A small flat nose, testifying to her antecedents, sat above full pale lips.

Her hair was blue/black and glossy, parted at the centre of her head and tucked behind her ears to fall straight down her back. When she stepped towards me I could see that it reached almost to the hem of her dress.

She smiled; a small, hesitant, gentle smile which hardly disturbed her serene countenance but which signalled nevertheless untold emotions – timidity, warmth, fear and confusion.

Kyoko was beautiful and she was dying.

I had been asked to visit Kyoko in my capacity of Continuing Care Nurse. As is customary, the referring General Practitioner had given me the information I needed to make a first visit.

Kyoko was thirty-six years old and had had a recurrence of breast cancer which had been treated initially in the Philippines. She had had a mastectomy and chemotherapy. Eighteen months later cancer was diagnosed in the remaining breast and it was decided that she would come to England for further treatment and to be with her husband who was studying here. Although from the Philippines, Kyoko was of Japanese origin. Her husband was also Japanese. Kyoko was going to live in the house of her husband's brother and his French wife, whilst receiving treatment.

During our first conversation I discovered that Kyoko had been to the local General Hospital and, following tests, had been told that the cancer was well advanced and that further curative treatment was not feasible although she would remain under the supervision of the doctors at the hospital.

She spoke excellent English and there was no doubt that she had understood the significance of the doctor's remarks. Kyoko did not cry, did not express any anger but merely told me the facts.

We discussed her present physical condition, spending a short time on those symptoms which appeared minor (in Kyoko's perception), such as nausea, and a longer time on those that she considered important, such as pain.

After ensuring that Kyoko understood how and when to take her drugs and leaving her a contact number, we came to a joint decision that I would visit once a week for the time being but that Kyoko would telephone if she needed to see me sooner. I told Kyoko that I would speak to her sister-in-law before I left the house.

Nicole met me at the foot of the stairs and asked when Kyoko was going to be taken into hospital. We went into the sitting room and I explained that Kyoko did not need to be in hospital right then but that she could go into hospital when this was needed.

Nicole felt that she had been misled by her Japanese in-laws concerning the seriousness of Kyoko's condition. She felt, she said, angry that she was expected to accept the responsibility. While she had been prepared for differences to emerge between her husband's culture and her own, when they married, she could not and would not accept that she should not be consulted about such a major event as a stranger dying in her home.

I let her talk. It transpired that she had had some problems in her marriage first with the in-laws advising their son – 'telling him what we should do' was how she put it – but since the birth of their daughter things had not been so bad. She thought the family had accepted that she had a mind of her own. 'But now this,' she sighed. Leaving a contact number and promising that I would do all I could to help I left the house, feeling sorry for both of the women in it.

Throughout the couple of months that I knew Kyoko she did not complain of anything. If her pain worsened she waited until I made a regular visit to her to tell me, or Nicole asked me to visit.

At one point the hospital consultant decided that another course of chemotherapy might delay the progress of the disease so this was tried. Kyoko reacted violently to the treatment, vomiting almost continuously and unable to eat or drink. She was already losing weight with terrifying speed, was very tired and had gross muscle weakness and, despite changes in her drug regime, when her anti-emetic drugs were either increased or alternatives tried, the vomiting continued. The chemotherapy was discontinued.

During this time Nicole telephoned frequently and I visited often, sometimes alone, at other times with the General Practitioner. At each visit Nicole became more voluble, demanding that we 'do something'. Usually she calmed down enough to agree to Kyoko staying at the house for the time being but it was obvious to the doctor and myself that if the situation became any worse Kyoko would have to be admitted to hospital or a hospice unit.

She, however, despite the vomiting and the weakness, remained calm. She continued to care for herself, never wanting to give Nicole any trouble, and she did not stay in bed for any length of time. In fact I never saw her in bed but always sitting in a chair and always dressed. Only once did she express her dismay at what was happening to her. I arrived to find her sitting in front of the mirror brushing her beautiful hair. Her expression was very sad and when I asked her what was wrong she held up the brush for me to see. Long black strands were matted in the bristles.

'My hair is coming out,' she said. 'My husband does not want to see me like this.'

Eventually Kyoko's condition dictated that she should be admitted to hospital. I went to see her, just once as it turned out, before she died. Ever respectful, she apologised for not being able to get out of bed and admitted that she was 'very weary'.

She talked then of her husband and their families, of Nicole, of the doctors who had tried to help her and of me. She had not been able to be a 'good' wife for her husband she said and she had disappointed both sets of parents because she had not given them a grandchild. Nicole had given her a home and she had made a lot of extra work for her. She was sorry for the trouble she had given the doctors and myself. Everyone had been so kind, given so much, but her body had not been strong enough to get better.

Before I left her she held my hand briefly and thanked me again. She had never voluntarily touched me during our short time of knowing each other and this simple gesture was her gift to me. I never saw her again. Kyoko died less than two days later.

* * *

No amount of theoretical knowledge can prepare any practitioner to cope with the variety of situations and events with which he/she will be presented.

Every effort is made to ensure that adequate preparation is given to the practitioner before he/she practises in specific areas. Nurses involved with the care of dying individuals may choose from several courses validated by professional or academic bodies, or experimental workshops: where they can learn about the physical, psychological, social and spiritual problems which may be experienced by the dying person, and also examine their own feelings and reactions to death. Such courses are also designed to assist practitioners to improve their knowledge and skills in order to help those individuals in a constructive manner.

Not only had I attended a course aptly named 'Care of the Dying Patient and the Family' in which these issues were addressed but I had also been to a series of study days arranged by an organisation founded by Margaret Torrie (herself a doctor's widow) where issues surrounding all aspects of loss were examined.

Armed then with knowledge and skills which I deemed more than adequate to cope with any situation concerning dying people I was confident that I could help Kyoko during her last few weeks of life.

However, to have knowledge in theory only is not only limiting to both practitioners and patient but can be damaging to both.

Most nurses can quote the 'psychological stages' that a dying patient goes through as described by Elizabeth Kubler-Ross (1970) – Denial, Anger, Depression, Acceptance – but the pitfall here might be that the nurse remembers the book and forgets to study the individual. In an attempt to 'stage' the patient, the individual needs of the dying person may well be overlooked.

My own initial reactions to Kyoko's situation reflected more accurately Kubler-Ross stages than did Kyoko's. I could not believe (Denial) that so many bad things could happen to one person. An apparently loveless marriage, a strange country, an irate kinswoman, a recurrence of cancer, sterility following chemotherapy, and the prospect of death. My own inner feelings (Anger) made me want to stop some, if not all, of these things from happening to her. I perceived her to be vulnerable and this made me feel extremely sad (Depression).

All of these feelings, however, were fleeting. Kyoko's calm acceptance of her situation was infectious. From our first meeting to the last her serenity influenced not only my relationship with her but ultimately relationships with patients and others to this day. I learned from Kyoko what theorists, writers and lecturers could never teach me. That each individual with whom we have contact as practitioners can add a new dimension to our lives, even while we believe that we are teaching them.

Kyoko, whilst making use of my knowledge and experience, especially concerning the use of drugs to control her distressing symptoms, taught me that no matter what my feelings were about a situation I should in no way impose those feelings on another and indeed in Kyoko's case, her own attitude towards her circumstances could not be influenced!

In the *Meno*, Socrates is quoted as saying 'we shall be better, braver and more active men if we believe it right to look for what we don't know than if we believe there is no point in looking because what we don't know we can never discover'.

After Kyoko's death I made a promise to myself that I would in future not only resist pre-judging any situation but that I would endeavour to learn something new from each patient I met.

---

3. Further possible titles

You may well have plenty of ideas by now about what you are going to write about next. But just in case they are helpful, here are some more titles which might stimulate ideas for your next piece:

A new beginning
Conflict
Pain
Integrity
Keeping things going
Forgiveness

The following suggestions need not initially be explicitly focused on your professional work, but could provoke interesting discussion, about the implications of your choices; and the discussion may well bring out themes which do have a professional relevance:

Write on 'Things I remember' and then on 'Things I don't remember'.
Write on 'Things I know' and then on 'Things I don't know'.

Write on 'Things I want' and then on 'Things I don't want'.

Write on 'Things that make me angry' and then on 'Things that make some people angry but not me'.

This list of titles is adapted from the work of Gillie Bolton, University of Sheffield, and from Natalie Goldberg's book Wild Mind *(Rider, 1991).*

SESSION 5

- Begin by sharing your writing, having reminded yourself again of the ground rules. (It is too easy to start talking about whether or not you think the writing is 'good' or swapping anecdotes about your own experiences in relation to those described by the writer.)
- Remember to keep focusing on helping writers to find ways of amending, revising or extending their writing.
- Also do remember to allocate the time fairly. (It is very easy to spend too long on the first piece and not have enough time to really discuss in detail the one who goes last.) Sometimes it is useful to establish a rota, so that someone who goes first one week goes last the next week, etc.
- Then allow about an hour for discussion of the following material.

1. Ways of structuring a text

Links

We tend to think of a text as being either an argument or a narrative. In both cases it is important to make clear the links. We make our writing clear by making sure we have used the right link. Thus we use linking words to indicate:

- *Sequence* (then, next, beforehand, first, finally, meanwhile)
- *Cause* (so, therefore, because, hence, thus, consequently)
- *Contrast* (however, but, nevertheless, on the one hand/on the other hand)
- *Similarity* (and, also, in addition, moreover, as well)

Different voices

Another aspect of a text is that it often contains different voices. There is 'my' voice – the writer's – and there are the contrasting voices of those we bring into the text – quotations from books or the words and thoughts of characters we are writing about. In a slightly different way we can differentiate between the voice in which we recount an experience (personal, involved, perhaps emotional) from the contrasting voice in which we analyse the experience (cool, abstract, speculative).

So another way of structuring a text is to make clear where one voice ends and another begins. We can do this by using different typefaces or italics (see the story 'Moments of truth', in the material for session 3) and we can also do this by simply using a heading, which is how Richard Ball differentiates between the two voices in his piece (see the material for session 2).

Re-read the piece that you brought along to this session, and examine whether you could have made the links clearer by using linking words more carefully, and/or whether you could have made the different voices clearer by using a heading or a change of typeface.

2. Irony

Having noted that we can choose different voices for different sections of the text, it follows that the writer is not always speaking in their 'own' voice. Indeed one of the basic skills of writing is to impersonate different voices, in order to make our narrative more dramatic, and thus more interesting. We do this quite naturally when we tell an anecdote: 'So he said ... ', 'so I said straight back to him ... ', 'so then he said ... ', and so on.' In another sense we are doing something quite similar when we present an argument and then include possible objections to it.

By a careful control of the voice in the text we can construct a voice so that the reader reads between the lines and receives a message that the text does not actually declare but only suggests. This is one way in which a text can create the effect known as irony. The most obvious example of this aspect of irony is what we usually call sarcasm. Someone makes a mistake, and instead of saying, directly, 'Clumsy fool!' or 'Hard luck!' we say, 'Oh, brilliant!'

Such sarcasm is the crudest form of irony. In contrast, consider the following extracts from Penelope Lively's ironic short story 'A Christmas card to one and all' (from her collection *Beyond the Blue Mountains*, 1997). What is the difference between what the voice of the text appears to be saying and the message that the writer intends the reader to receive? What effect is achieved by the irony?

Happy Christmas!

Well, here I am again, your faithful friend (sister, cousin, aunt, etc.). I can hear you thinking – My Goodness! Here's Lizzie's round robin, it must be December already. Too right, doesn't time fly and here we are at number twenty-seven with another year gone by and lots to tell as usual …

It's lovely having Kate and her Sam and the children just a few streets away. Thank heaven they *are* because I can be in and out to lend Kate a hand whenever I've got a moment. And, frankly, to keep an eye on things. I mean, if there's one thing I do know about it's bringing up children. I didn't have four of my own for nothing. Not to speak of running a house – I mean that's what I'm all about and I think I've made a pretty good job of it. I know it's unfashionable these days but I've always believed in putting family first and I'm proud of it! So there! Good for Lizzie! I can hear you saying. Anyway … obviously I'm only too happy to show Kate what's what and take some of the load off her when I can. Of course, her ways aren't my ways entirely – in fact if you ask me that house is a bit of a mess (ssh!), but at least I've been able to make an impact here and there. They were away for the weekend last month so I slipped round while they were gone and gave the whole place a good scrub and clear out. I really went to town, I can tell you – I was ever so pleased with myself. I switched the sitting room furniture round while I was about it, for a surprise – I've always thought they had that sofa in the wrong place. And I went through the wardrobe and sorted out all the things that were fit only for Oxfam (Kate and I never have seen eye to eye about clothes) and I had a good go at the garden. Of course, I hadn't realised Sam wanted all those old computer magazines or I wouldn't have thrown them out, and frankly to my mind all that stuff I pulled up was weed, but gardening's never been my strong point, that I will admit. But as I say, it's wonderful having them near enough to be able to pop in and out and help. Actually Kate says they're thinking of moving, which seems barmy to me. People don't know when they're well off …

Ron joins me in saying Hello! God bless! to all of you. He's gone out fishing for the day. Fishing's something he's taken up lately, funny old thing – I wouldn't have thought it was his cup of tea, really, sitting on the edge of a reservoir in the rain. I mean, he likes his creature comforts, does our Ron. Anyone would think he wanted to get out of the house!

So – here's Lizzie signing off at the end of another year of happy family life here at number twenty-seven, and wishing all of you the same for the year ahead.

The gap between what the text says directly and what the writer is intending to convey is used very effectively in J. Bernlef's novel *Out of Mind* (1988). Here Bernlef portrays the stages through which a sufferer from Alzheimer's Disease gradually loses contact with his immediate reality. But he does this by writing throughout in the first person, 'from the inside'. Thus Bernlef gradually creates an ironic gap between the narrator's words and the reader's response, and the reader slowly finds that they are no longer taking what the text says at face value but as a symptom of what is going wrong with the narrator's view of his reality.

In the following extract (pp. 27–8) notice how Bernlef enables the readers to see how Maarten (the central character) is experiencing his reality in a way which creates a sense of fear and tension both for himself and for others (Vera is his wife).

I look at my face in the mirror over the washstand. No one can tell from it what I used to look like. Not even I myself. Be that as it may … I wet my face, squirt a blob of shaving cream on my fingertips and with the fingers of my left hand rub the slithery foam over my cheeks and chin.

'There, now you look smart again, Maarten.'

Don't talk to yourself. At least not when other people can hear you. When you talk you should be addressing another person, not yourself.

It is as if I can hear two voices, women's voices. Surely we don't have company? Maybe the radio.

Cautiously I open the door and go into the hall. Vera's voice. I try not to listen to what the voice in the living room says, and press my nails into the palms of my hands I stand very still.

'I'm really worried. You can't see there's anything wrong with him. But that makes it all the more alarming. Sometimes he tells me things about us that I was never part of. As if I were a different person in his eyes. And then suddenly he can't remember a whole chunk of his own past. I feel so helpless because I don't know how to help him. And it has happened so suddenly. Practically overnight he has become like this.'

Vera shouldn't worry herself so. I quickly enter the room and then stop in my tracks, stiff with fright.

A big robust woman is sitting in my place at the table. A stern female in a mouse-grey suit and black hair in a bun with a wooden pin stuck through it on the back of her head. She says my name and then I recognise her. Of course …

'Hello Ellen … How is Jack?' I ask.

Their faces stiffen ... 'I always recognise people best by their voices,' I say. 'I have a bad memory for faces, but voices I recognise at once.'

The conversation must proceed. Their faces, on either side of the round patch of light from the lamp, still wear that rigid, plaster-cast expression.

'And when someone is dead,' says Ellen ... Her voice trembles and Vera puts her hand on Ellen's arm in a protective gesture.

- How does Bernlef make us realise the fragility of Maarten's grasp of reality?
- How does Bernlef enable us to understand things that Maarten doesn't?
- What are your feelings about Maarten at this point?
- For your next piece of writing try to manage the voice in your text so that the reader is made to see through the actual words to what they imply but do not explicitly say.

SESSION 6

Check the ground rules and begin by sharing your work as usual. Then allow about an hour for discussion of the following material.

1. Metaphor

Metaphors make comparisons and links. This is a natural thing to do with words, because words always have many different meanings at the same time. And it's a natural thing for the human mind to do, because we often use a comparison as a way of explaining or describing things.

For example, read the following extract from Jonathan Raban's book *Old Glory* (Raban 1986: 46) about his boat trip down the Mississippi, and consider the effect of the two contrasting sets of comparisons he makes.

> On Tuesday I drove out to see my boat. I had firm ideas about what a boat should be. One of the river-books over which I'd pored during the summer had been Henry Thoreau's *A Week on the Concord and Merrimack Rivers*. Thoreau had made his inland voyage in a green and blue dory, 'a creature of two elements, related by one half of its structure to some swift and shapely fish, and by the other to some strong and graceful bird'. I had been tempted to send this lovely specification on an airmail postcard to Crystal Marine.
>
> The boatyard lay far out of town, away from the river, at the end of a dismal suburban boulevard. In the lot at the back, a hundred boats

were tipped up on trailers, identifiable only by their numbers. Mine was WS 1368 DD. It was just a mustard-coloured shell of aluminium. Blunt backed, broad in the beam, this bare piece of riveted alloy did not look like a craft in which one might float at all easily into an idyll. It was related to neither fish nor bird, but to some new, efficient brand of non-stick saucepan.

Try to explain the point Raban is making without using any sort of comparison: what is the difference now that the comparisons have gone?

2. The variety of writing formats

By now you will have become aware of the many different ways of writing you can use to convey a point. Let us call them formats, but 'method' or 'genre' would do equally well.

To remind yourself of the variety of possibilities, begin by reading the following pieces in the earlier chapters:

'The contents of a bedside locker', by Bernadette Saharoy (Chapter 3: p. 77) (beginning from a description)

'Through the eyes of a child', by Bernadette Saharoy (Chapter 3: p. 78) (an incident as described by someone who does not understand what is happening)

'Moments of truth', by Richard Winter (material for session 3 above, p. 122) (contrasting what people are saying in a situation with what they are thinking)

'Every number is a student', by Jayne Crow (Chapter 3: p. 104) (a poem)

' "And the word was made flesh and dwelt amongst us" ', by Tricia Hill (Chapter 2: p. 60) (a kaleidoscope of contrasting fragments of quotations)

'Mary', by Jeannette Yems (Chapter 2: p. 34) (an incident described in such a way that the reader only realises what the situation is right at the end)

'The Sainsbury's Guide to Good Management: a recipe for success?', by Liz Morris (Chapter 1: p. 12) (a parody; one could also write a parody of, for example:

- an advertisement
- a mission statement
- a job advertisement
- a set of case notes
- a course syllabus
- an annual appraisal, etc.)

Discuss in your group what possible format you might experiment with in your next piece – perhaps one of the methods used in the examples you have just read or another quite different format that now springs to mind.

For your next piece of writing, try to use a format which you haven't yet used.

SESSION 7

Check the ground rules and share your writing, as usual, remembering to make notes on the comments made in response to it.

Then allow about an hour for discussion of the following material.

Constructing a patchwork text

The time has come to start to consider how the various pieces of writing you have done can be linked together to form a single text, rather as different pieces of textile fabric are sewn together to form the unified pattern of a patchwork quilt.

The technique of building a text out of the contrast between different voices can also be thought of as resembling the film technique of cutting from one scene to another – a process of assembling and editing together different types of material. One of the ways in which modern films (both fictional stories and documentaries) draw us in and get us interested is by presenting us with several different scenes, so that we are posed the question: what is the link going to be between all these? The same method can be adapted in putting together a series of short pieces of writing to form a longer text, consisting of different sections, using a variety of styles, adopting different voices, and even focusing on what appear at first to be different topics.

You may already be aware of obvious links between some of the different pieces of writing that you have done so far, and can therefore see how your final assignment for the course can be assembled from the pieces of writing you have done, including extracts from your notes from the discussion sessions and using analytical commentaries to explore the linking theme. This is the format which many participants in the reflective writing course have used, and various different ways of doing so are presented and discussed in Chapter 3.

Sometimes the link between your various pieces may not seem immediately obvious. But don't conclude too rapidly that there is no link at all, that you have no theme. For example, consider the following piece of writing by Paul Chidgey. When he wrote it, he was not aware of its having any specifically professional relevance, but then in his commentary at the end, he notes how in discussion with the other members of his group he did become aware of a professional angle which was linked to the general theme of the rest of his writing.

'Sunday dinner' by Paul Chidgey

There is something curiously contradictory about a late Sunday afternoon. After the best part of a gentle and uncluttered day, I have a sense of relaxed calmness. And yet I can feel rising within me a tension which is in anticipation of all the demands that will inevitably be upon me when the new week, now uncomfortably close, arrives. Perhaps that's why preparing our Sunday dinner has become an important part of my weekend; it's about creating a climax to our special time together as a family over the last two days, while at the same time distracting me from the pressures I envisage over the next five days.

The others are out, so the house is quiet as the oven gives a muffled thud as the gas is ignited. A meal seems a long way away as I carry over the leg of lamb on the roasting rack. The uncooked flesh, to be absolutely honest, looks very unappetising and it's only the sanitised plastic carton in which it was bought that allows me to distance myself from the origin of the meat that I am about to cook.

The early stages of cooking a roast dinner seem quite slow, pleasantly though. This period calls for a glass of cool beer, which enhances a kind of reflective mood and is an easy companion as I approach the task of preparing the vegetables.

There's a sack of spuds in the pantry. I choose a number of assorted sizes, all of which are caked in dry mud. I have always found peeling potatoes a largely satisfying job. As I peel the trails away I like to see if I can manage an unbroken skin for the whole potato. This modest vegetable will eventually be a golden bedrock to our meal. The pan spits hot fat slightly as I add the potatoes, carefully salted.

I have cut the carrots, green beans and broccoli just as the others get home. One daughter is imbued with the smell of woodsmoke, having spent the day with the Brownies. The other, looking crestfallen, is in her Judo suit having been unsuccessful in her grading. We hug and I offer some words of consolation, but anyway we're going to have a scrumptious dinner.

By now there are some delicious aromas flowing from the kitchen around the house. The others show interest in what we're going to be eating and I find this to be infectious. Although I had not noticed until this moment, I am now beginning to feel hungry. The girls are off to have a bath and my momentum in the kitchen increases. The vegetables are cooking and I am whisking the batter mix for the Yorkshire pudding. I am feeling well on top of things when the telephone rings. It's my brother wanting a chat. Ordinarily, this is not a big deal. However at this stage in the proceedings I experience his call as an intrusion as I eye the clock and check the timings of the beans and the carrots, and the Yorkshire pudding, and the gravy which I haven't made yet ... !

I like to lay the table as near to the arrival of the meal as possible. There is a coolness and tidiness about the dining room which is quite soothing compared to the steamy clutter of the kitchen at this stage. I am looking forward to opening Granny's mint jelly.

I think we're finally there, the sizzling and succulent joint that I retrieve from the oven is scarcely the same object I dealt with some considerable time ago. I call for help with the carving. Even though I've roasted this and other meats on Sundays for weeks and weeks, I still find myself seeking reassurance with, 'Is it cooked okay?'

As our family assembles at the table, I have a sense of pleasure and satisfaction that all the component parts of this meal have come together. I receive comments of appreciation which I enjoy. And yet, it's strange that in the eating of my meal, enjoyable though it is, it never quite tastes as perfect as I planned it to be.

I wonder what the perfect Sunday meal does taste like?

Commentary

The first piece, entitled 'Sunday dinner' was written without any deliberate intention (i.e. awareness of professional relevance) shortly after just such an event as described. However it immediately draws the reader's attention to the contrast of a 'relaxed calmness' of Sunday afternoon and the 'demands' and 'pressures' of the remainder of the week. In this context the preparation of a particular meal takes on a special significance involving a high level of control, order and precision. My peer group (i.e. those with whom I shared my writing) observed that although this activity seeks a high level of skill, it could be seen as the pursuit of a state of perfection that can never be achieved.

So how does one deal with the pace and change of a world where it is not possible to have such precise control over events?

- Now read the first five sections of example six in Chapter 3, by Jayne Crow, but *don't* read her Epilogue. Discuss in your group what link you can see between Jayne Crow's first piece (her Preface) and the rest of her work.

- After you have discussed it, read her Epilogue, in which she gives her own interpretation.
- Finally, have a preliminary discussion, as a group, about the possible themes underlying the various pieces of writing you have each done. You may find that hearing how other people see the unifying themes underlying their writing is quite helpful in starting off your own train of thought.
- For next week, re-read the whole of Chapter 3 carefully, and then re-read all the pieces of writing you have done so far, making notes on possible unifying themes which could be used to provide a structure for your own patchwork text.
- In particular, consider what your title might be – one which both arouses the reader's interest and also indicates the essential point behind your writing as a whole.
- For the next session bring along copies of everything you have written and also your notes on the links and themes.

SESSION 8

This is the final session of the course (unless you intend to combine the fictional approach outlined here with other forms of writing – see next section of this chapter, 'Two notes for course tutors').

Begin by discussing with your group the notes you have made on how you see your various pieces of writing fitting together. Members of the group will remember the pieces you refer to since they will have discussed them in previous sessions. Perhaps you can suggest unifying angles which the writer has not mentioned, but remember also that you will probably be partly projecting your own themes into other people's writing and that in the end everyone has to make their own decision on what emphasis is important to them.

The remaining task is to put together a draft of your final patchwork text.

To begin with, consider the objectives of this piece of writing, i.e. your patchwork text. If you are undertaking it as part of a formal course there will be published criteria, which may be similar to those presented at the beginning of this chapter. So make sure that your writing fulfils the various criteria. If you are doing the work as an informal staff development exercise, then consider who is going to read your work. Do you intend to distribute a collection of the group's work to colleagues in the organisation or more widely? Both of these considerations should usually be borne in mind. The advantage of the patchwork text is that it usually fulfils professional course criteria quite naturally while at the same time being of interest to professional colleagues.

In putting together your final text the key decisions are:

1   Are you going to include all of your pieces of writing, or are there one or two which you are going to leave out? (On what basis would you do so? Perhaps one or two pieces really do not fit into your theme; perhaps two pieces are working over exactly the same ground in a similar way and you only want to include one of them, to avoid repetition; perhaps by including all of the pieces the balance and emphasis of your text would not be right.)

2   What is the best sequence for your pieces? (This might not necessarily be the same as the order in which you wrote them.)

3   What is your title going to be? (It must somehow arouse the reader's interest and also give the reader some guidance when they start to read as to the overall topic.)

4   Do you need to write an introduction, or can one of the pieces themselves serve as an introduction?

5   Do you need to write linking commentaries (see Chapter 3: example 1) or do the pieces fit together in such a way (once the theme is clear, e. g. through the title) that no linking explanation is needed (see Chapter 3: example 2)?

6   Does your text need a 'conclusion' to round it off? (Or does one of the pieces you have already written seem to do this quite well?) There are different approaches to conclusions. Funghai Nhiwtiwa's conclusion (Chapter 3: example 3) is very practice-oriented and thus works perfectly well as a way of rounding off his text, but it does not try to sum up the whole of the writing he has done. In contrast, Jayne Crow's 'Epilogue' (Chapter 3: example 6) revisits each of the earlier pieces and draws out an interpretation of its significance in the form of a little reflexive essay. This also is highly effective as a concluding section.

When you have done a first draft of your text, try to show it to someone else – a colleague perhaps, or a tutor, if you are working through the material as a course. Writing is always a combination of exploring one's own mind and presenting the outcomes of this exploration in such a way that other people can follow you even though they inevitably have their own themes in mind as they read what you have written. So you will need to check the clarity of your final text with a reader (or two) just as you did earlier with your individual pieces of writing.

TWO NOTES FOR COURSE TUTORS

Incorporating other forms of reflective writing into a patchwork text

The work suggested in the eight sessions above is intended to be complete in itself, leading to the sort of work presented in Chapter 3. However, it is quite possible to combine the fictional emphasis presented here with more conventional approaches to reflective writing, like those discussed at the end of Chapter 1. There may even be advantages in doing so, especially if the work is to be assessed as part of a university course, where analytical and academic dimensions to reflection are stressed (see below). Some suggestions on how to manage this combination are given as follows, based on our experience with a reflective writing course at master's degree level.

- Participants could keep a 'reflective diary' during the course and include extracts from, and comments upon, the diary as part of their patchwork text.
- Participants could use the work described in session 7 (identifying linking themes) as a way of clarifying the focus for a 'critical incident analysis'. In this way the critical incident work becomes an opportunity to draw together, in an experience-based analytical summary, the various lines of reflection stimulated by the earlier fictional work.
- Having explored and clarified their professional themes, participants could do a piece of writing in which they engage critically with some of the published literature on this theme, using their own previous writing as a resource. This might help them move beyond using published work merely as confirmation or support. In other words, it might help them approach others' writing with a sense that they also are writers on these matters and are thus in a position to take issue with what others have written, on the basis of understandings which they know they have thoroughly explored.

A text which incorporates such approaches will still be a patchwork text in the sense outlined in Chapter 3, but its later sections will have more in common with the concluding sections of a conventional essay or 'reflective practice report'.

Assessment

The question of how a fiction-based patchwork text can be assessed as an assignment for an academic course is an interesting one, and one which brings up some of the problems of academic assessment in general.

To begin with, it is important to note that the objectives and assessment criteria for the work are professional (to do with observation, empathy, understanding complexities, making links, etc. – see the list at the beginning of this chapter). They were originally framed so that they could be demonstrated by a file of work-based evidence which would include material in many forms – notes, reports, audio recordings of discussions, analytical commentaries, etc. There is thus no suggestion that the patchwork text needs special criteria; rather, the implication intended is that the patchwork text is an alternative format in which professional understanding can be realised and presented. Thus the key question is: are patchwork texts so varied and so personal that examiners find it particularly difficult to agree how far those (or similar) criteria have been met?

The first step in answering this question is to accept that it is always difficult to assess work presented in a new format: examiners will, by definition, have seen relatively few examples of the new format and until experience begins to accumulate, judgements will lack confidence, relative to assessments of work in familiar formats. For example, tutors involved in the development of work-based curricula initially found it extremely worrying when they were confronted with the task of assessing 'portfolios' of practice evidence (see Winter and Maisch 1996: pp. 87, 91). The issue of familiarity is thus just as significant as that of objectivity: in only very few contexts can academic judgements appropriately be made in the wholly objective form of ticks on a multiple-choice answer sheet, and issues of subjectivity and reliability arise regularly in the marking of essays and reflective reports.

Second, the objectivity of academic judgements is based in a community which shares understandings. There is no substitute for this; lists of detailed requirements can never be wholly exhaustive: in the end examiners have to make interpretations, and with a new format they will need to check their interpretations with each other in meetings where texts are compared and discussed (see Winter and Maisch 1996: ch. 6, 'Assessment: the development of an expert community').

Third, in responding to a piece of work, examiners are guided not only by explicit criteria but also by a general impression – what Alison Wolf (1998) calls 'tacit knowledge'. One aspect of this tacit knowledge consists of underlying general criteria which apply to imaginative work just as clearly as to conventional essays: whether it is well written, clear, balanced, coherent, whether it has shape, whether it flows, whether it successfully handles complexity. These can be seen as issues of presentation, but they can also be seen as aesthetic qualities (see Chapter 7) – to do with elegance as much as logic – and their presence or absence is just as important in an essay or a description of a scientific experiment as in a story or a patchwork text.

Finally, given our general argument that most participants on professional courses are capable of producing imaginative, artistic work, it should follow that most examiners are capable of appreciating and evaluating it. After all, we all live in a culture where novels are awarded prizes, where films are given between one and five stars in weekly TV guides, and ice dancers are awarded 5.7, 5.8 or 5.9. Human beings are always happy to make discriminative judgements, and there is no reason why this should be more difficult with a patchwork text than with an essay on Wordsworth's poetry, a report on a work-based project, or a bottle of wine. Except that we are not (yet) used to doing so.

In the light of these general considerations, it is not surprising that the three of us initially involved in assessing the portfolio texts from the reflective writing course found it quite worrying to begin with. We felt that the work was so personal and varied that we doubted whether we would be able to reach agreement. But the same arguments also explain why, when we actually compared our responses to a set of texts, we found that we could indeed agree, even to the extent of grading the work on an A–E scale – as the University, regrettably in many ways, required. And only relatively little further discussion was needed to establish agreement with external examiners from other universities. Indeed, one examiner recently appointed to the reflective writing course wrote that reading the patchwork texts had been his 'most pleasurable experience' in eight years of external examining.

To sum up: academic assessment of fiction-based patchwork texts is not without its difficulties, but in the end these difficulties can be resolved, and they are essentially not very different from the problems of academic assessment in general (see Atkins *et al.* 1993: p. 26). As with any assessment decisions other than those involving multiple choice tests, there is an inevitable component of subjectivity. But if assessment is explicitly based on the professional criteria presented at the beginning of this chapter (or an equivalent specification), and if examiners devote time initially to sharing and discussing their responses to groups of texts, judgements *can* be agreed as to whether the work fulfils the given criteria and with what varying degrees of success.

5

PARTICIPANTS' VIEWS
'What was it like and what effect did it have?'

The general approach to 'reflection' presented in this book is the outcome of what may be thought of as a long-term research study, and this chapter is intended as an evaluation of its effectiveness, addressed particularly to readers seeking a full and systematic appraisal of the work. To begin with, a summary of participants' experience is presented, illustrated by their own accounts of the work and their observations on what they felt to be its impact on their professional practice. Most of the material in the first two sections is derived from a series of interviews carried out by Paula Sobiechowska with a mixed group of social workers, nurses and professional tutors after one of the reflective writing courses (based on Sobiechowska 1998). The first section of the chapter focuses on participants' experience of producing and sharing 'imaginative' written work in the context of the reflective writing course, and the second section concentrates on participants' accounts of the impact of the course on their practice. The third and final section contains an analysis of responses to the rather different experience of the story-writing workshops, by two different groups of participants.

Participants' experience of the reflective writing course

The main investigation into participants' experience was conducted through a series of individual personal interviews undertaken with a particular cohort. The interviews were semi-structured, partially informed by a 'prompt' list of questions, which interviewees had requested. On the whole this seemed to work well; individuals took the opportunity to 'roam' in their responses and noted the things most significant to themselves. The development of ideas and themes followed on either from what interviewees were already suggesting, or through attempts to check and clarify their opinions on specific matters. Nine out of the eleven participants in the group were interviewed, the other two being unavailable. All of the interviews were tape-recorded and transcribed.

The course overall

Eight of the nine respondents commented favourably and enthusiastically on their overall experience of the course. For seven of the participants the course was a particularly positive experience; 'enjoyment' was the word most often used to describe it. Two interviewees described it as the best and most valuable professional development course they had undertaken. It appears to have offered the participants a number of opportunities, the most significant among these being a sense of 'permission':

> ND: It [the course] is quite a freeing experience because, especially at the beginning, you're able to write about whatever you want. Just to get into the habit of writing, I suppose, and away from report writing and bureaucratic-type writing that you have to do in a set way. I'm used to writing reports for court, so it is very factual and laid out specifically for court. ... Now reflective writing, unless you had been on it, it would be difficult to know how beneficial it can be.... The way social work seems to be going a lot of the time is ... they are not interested in ... only want factual, brief reports; and probably don't want you to think too much!

Another participant (RS) notes:

> I've always tried to hold on to different life experiences but over time it becomes quite difficult to do that because of the bureaucratic framework in which we work and the lack of encouragement to do it. Now, I think, I write much more using the whole of me rather than the parts that are trained and schooled in bureaucratic writing. ... It was the kind of way teaching should be, showing the person what things might be like, not what they should be like. ... Opening up possibilities, creating a sense of freedom and liberation.

In reading through the interviews it is also apparent that the course offered participants some structured space to think about aspects of themselves and their work that they might not otherwise have considered. For example, ND wrote about an exchange visit she undertook to Romania, an experience she had not previously shared or explored in any great depth. She describes her surprise in finding her attention so absorbed by Romania and welcomed the opportunity the writing gave her to revisit the experience. Equally LN discusses how she wrote about things she thought well buried and found that the writing gave her permission to explore some apparently unresolved personal issues in the guise of professional inquiry. KH too found herself exploring professional issues she had not previously appreciated to be of any account.

Small group learning

All nine interviewees commented on the small group experience and eight of them found the learning in the small group an especially positive and enabling experience. Each respondent reflected the initial anxieties of exposure in the small group but commented as well on how quickly the anxiety was broken down in the group. As a consequence most participants felt they experienced almost unconditional support and trust in the groups. Although the success of the small groups should not be dismissed or minimised it does raise some critical issues about small group work. Facilitators certainly want to encourage support and trust in the groups, which would not work without such an ambience, but too much support can undermine the group's ability to explore critically ideas and material with each other. The effects of this were commented upon by the interviewees, who acknowledged a degree of over-politeness in the groups, and difficulties inherent in offering constructive criticism or any critique at all.

However, despite reservations, all of the participants gained positively from the small group experience, valuing the close, cooperative working with peers. The small groups seem to have worked well, in the opinion of the respondents, because of commitment and consistency in the group and the associated high degree of personal investment. 'Intimacy' is the word used to describe the small group experience, an intimacy which seems to have been generated by the sharing itself and the nature of the material shared.

The initial exercise

The first activity of the very first session on the course requires participants to write for five minutes on an unspecified subject, from 'off the top of the head'. This is immediately followed by a second exercise during which they are asked to write for ten minutes about a time they learnt something. The primary aim of this exercise is to break the icy barrier between the writer and the page.

In the interviews five of the respondents commented directly on this initial five-minute writing exercise. Each noted the immediate anxiety generated by the exercise but also commented on the unexpected and favourable outcomes of the exercise. Four of the respondents averred that it was the first time they had approached writing in such a way. It seems the exercise proved two things to people: that they could actually write and that there were things going on in their heads that they had not been consciously aware of:

> CF: One of the things that impressed me right on the very first day was getting everybody to write for five minutes, and saying we could write anything at all. … And I was amazed there were things in your brain you could actually write. And that you could fill five minutes completely and needed a bit more. … And it made me think 'Well, there is life in the old dog yet! Maybe there is something I can write'. So that was

quite confidence-inspiring in its way. ... I think it made us all feel 'Yes, probably we could write if we put our minds to it.'

Such sentiments are echoed by other participants, RS and AC. Both CF and RS describe the exercise as 'freeing' by virtue of the fact they were given permission to write about anything; this was a feeling shared by most participants. It was CF's opinion that this exercise set the tone for the course; ironically, CF had started off hoping that she would be given a theme to write on; had she known she was to be thrown on her own resources she would have been even more anxious. There is a strong sense that the exercise opened up possibilities for participants primarily by demonstrating to them that they could write something. The freedom of the writing in the first session unsuspectingly generated themes that many followed through to the final piece of work.

Personal learning

It appears that learning for all of the participants generated personal insight. LN particularly felt that she had gained a much deeper understanding of herself, and was especially impressed by the validating nature of the whole process. For LN the fictionalised accounts of her experience apparently made them more real: through discussions with the peer group she was able to confirm and appropriate her experience.

Another participant (MG) also believed she had undergone some kind of personal development, but found it difficult to articulate and did not think it could be measured because there was not an obvious, immediately applicable product and this caused her some unease and discomfort. MG thought that she would experience concern if she were asked to account for and justify the time she spent on the course, which she herself regarded as a luxury. RS expressed a similar opinion: he was not able to 'audit' what had been learnt but offered the following point of view:

> I really enjoyed the adventure, going into a different way of thinking, way of being, in a sense, which was uncharted for me, which hadn't got a direct and obvious, quantifiable relevance to my everyday work. I could see that it could grow and help and develop me in a way which education should ... I was really thrilled to get that spark back, which I haven't had for some time. ... There was an almost soul-expanding feeling, going into territory that was unknown, and it being really both at once exciting and a little bit nerve-wracking. It needed a bit of confidence to do it, but while doing it finding one was being exhilarated and challenged. Good from that point of view.

Personal learning among the interviewees is most often expressed in terms of further developments in self-awareness and self-confidence, as well as a renewal of the battle for professional integrity.

On being 'a writer'

The participants did not consider themselves to be 'writers', but they did recognise that they spend a lot of time writing. However, they described the writing they do as more often a functional, rather than expressive, activity:

> CF: I was sitting there thinking 'I am not a writer. I wonder if these people are writers?' I am not a writer, I write reports, I write letters but I am not a writer.

> MG: It is entirely different from how I write reports and how we have to write about our clients, which makes it a relaxing and creative exercise to do.

ND expressed the rigidity of the writing she had to do at work most forcibly, and more than once:

> We do so much writing at work you get bogged down in it.

On the other hand, most of us are story-tellers, full of gossip, anecdotes and incidents, and the task of the course is to encourage individuals to commit their stories to paper in order to examine them to see what can be learnt. Reflective writing might be seen as a method of mining and capturing a vast wealth of experience that is often unrecognised and rarely given any value. However, many participants not only do not regard themselves as writers but also feel themselves to be disinherited learners with a lack of confidence in their own ability to write and (at first) with little faith in the inherent worth and value of their 'stories'.

Through the interviews participants reflected on the lack of confidence they had in their writing ability. In describing her experience CF did not overtly acknowledge a lack of confidence but recognised the impact of the initial exercises in uncovering her ability to write *something*, which apparently came as a relief and was confidence-inspiring, enabling her to see that she 'could probably write if [she] put [her] mind to it'. In the concluding comments of the interview CF notes:

> I suppose that it felt quite powerful that you could do it [write]. I write personal letters and I write reports, but it was quite a feeling of power that maybe I could write something other than that. And write differently. … It was valuable, it made me feel if I wanted to write an article or something I could do it.

HT was quite open in expressing her lack of confidence in her writing ability; she notes:

> I am quite conscious about my own writing, I don't feel I am particu-
> larly good at it. Even with assignments or reports, I will often do them
> two or three times. Because I am quite conscious that I do not think my
> English is that good.

Such negative feelings were allayed for HT through the group sharing process which both valued her experience and made her feel that her writing was:

> Not that bad and, also, that everybody writes differently; so there is no
> right or wrong. We all have a different way of putting things. So that
> was good for me. Definitely.

HT believed that her experience on the course released her from some of the rigidity and constraint she previously exercised in her writing, released her from the idea that there might be only one proper way to write. It is this sense of a prescribed way to write that also appears to have initially inhibited KH, who struggled with her personal history of academic experience and conventional expectation. Superficially it is similar to MG's struggle, as she continued to think that her writing was too imaginative and lacking in credibility because it did not carry enough authoritative quotations.

BB did not directly discuss any personal anxiety about writing but thought that in the first couple of weeks she and her peers wrote 'to impress'; she consid-ered this to be an expression of people's nervousness in their writing abilities, and naturally the exposure of one's writing to an audience does add another dimension to the whole process. Notwithstanding her apparent confidence, BB did remark that she appreciated feeling that there was not necessarily a right or wrong way of writing something, as long as the reader 'got the message'. Thus the interview with BB suggests that in recognising that writing was neither 'right' nor 'wrong' she also achieved a liberation from previously held notions about writing. In the closing statements of the interview she openly acknowledges that through the course of the programme she gained confidence in her writing ability. She states:

> I feel less stressed out now about what I write. ... I feel more comfort-
> able because I am actually getting better at writing it. ... I've also learnt
> that I am not bad at writing, either. ... I can write something that is
> worthwhile reading. These are two quite important things for me.

In discussing her writing, BB's primary concern was to ensure that 'the message' she wanted to convey was heard and understood by her readers. She comments on this a number of times:

There isn't a wrong or right way of producing a piece of work, as long as the reader actually picks up on what the writer intended to say. It doesn't matter really how you present it, as long as you get your message across.

To write about what you want as you want is a real challenge. Most of those interviewed had not previously engaged with such a challenge; their writing had always been addressed to a specific topic, predetermined by another, or contained by a predefined purpose. Many found that the classroom writing of the first week, or the random topics suggested by the tutorial material, provided a starting point for the work. The undertaking of the task was approached differently by all participants. AC, for example, took a pragmatic approach in deciding to explore a very obviously work-related theme; RS decided to work with the intensity that was exposed in his first piece of 'automatic' writing; LN spent some time consciously searching for suitable material, discarding the same thing two or three times before settling with it in a different manifestation; and by her own admission CF endeavoured at first to 'play safe' with bland contributions.

On the therapeutic effect of writing

For LN, writing validated her experiences and made them real in a way they had not been before:

> I think, for me, seeing it on paper was the impact because then I had to read it and know it really happened to me.

She felt that her writing had uncovered aspects of herself and her experience that she had believed to be 'well buried' and resolved. She felt that she had little control over the writing activity; apparently things 'just came out' and 'flowed', she felt she exercised no censorship over her work. This experience was shared by others on the programme; for example, RS, ND and KH. In contrast, LN believed that when she related the same tales to a *listening* audience she *could* exercise editorial control: under such circumstances she saw herself as being actively selective in the detail and the framing of the story. LN wrote her stories knowing that they would be received by an audience, but she attests that she felt safe in this process because the material was based on a professional theme and ostensibly merely a matter of professional concern. It was only in the re-reading of the work (and admitted only to herself) that she realised she was telling a personal story. It was the professionalisation of the theme which made the sharing safe: she was (perhaps) 'fooling' others, but not herself.

Through the interview discussion it becomes clear that LN experienced her writing and the sharing of it on the course as therapeutic. This process was also at work for other learners: KH directly describes the course as having been 'therapeutic' as well as 'illuminating'; she tells how she uncovered, through the use of particular words and phrases, aspects of her personality, her approach to work and associated thoughts and feelings. She says, for example:

> There were things in the writing that wouldn't have come out, I don't think, unless I'd written them down. Although I have mulled over certain aspects, there were clues in the words and things that I used that came out of nowhere, that must have been in my subconscious some-where, that then perhaps illuminated something that wouldn't have come to the surface if I had just thought about it. ... For instance, about the photocopying card in my briefcase: I was talking about how I love to give photocopies of things to people and being able to give out photocopies in class is a very bountiful, lovely thing to be able to do. ... I hadn't really realised how much I like doing that. And how much it is a part of the way I see myself, see my role, as this sort of giver of knowledge and facilitator. And looking at photocopies in that way hadn't really occurred to me until I wrote it down, and I'm sure it never would have occurred to me, because it was just the way it was written that it made me go back and think about that.
>
> *(These comments refer to example 6 in Chapter 3)*

Similarly, ND, through her writing, found an arena in which to explore her experiences of Romania; an opportunity that had not previously been available to her. She notes that once she started telling her stories she found it hard to stop. Coincidentally, RS believed that the course came at the right time for him, a time when he was already engaged in a personal reflective process encompassing all aspects of his life. He felt that the writing and the sharing of it helped him untangle and reveal his thoughts and feelings. He says that he was:

> Surprised in that analysing, or looking back at what came out of it, was quite instructive and informative in ways which were surprising about what was going on inside of us. ... I think it gives, if you do it atten-tively, it gives an insight into what is going on deep down, maybe even at a subconscious level, or it can do.

RS describes the opportunity to write from the heart as both extraordinary and freeing, allowing a subsequent recognition of the personal processes that were going on. He felt the opportunity allowed him to 'by-pass' the usual 'custodians' of his mind.

In a similar vein HT notes the effect of her own writing on herself:

> There were times when I found it quite ... quite upsetting really. To reflect on what I'd written and what other people saw in that. ... I wrote a piece, I think it was about when I was a child, and it just sort of

came out quite naturally. And then, when somebody else read it, it was quite emotional really.

HT's appreciation of her work illustrates how the subconscious and well defended in us can be brought to the surface really quite easily, despite perhaps our desire to control it. This reveals the risk factor in creative/reflective writing – in the process of creation and intuition and in the subsequent reflective process.

As is suggested by the interviewees themselves, the initial intuitive writing seems to have been subject to little conscious constraint. Interestingly, they were happy enough to share their work with each other, perhaps in part because the revelatory aspects of the writing may only have become apparent when shared. However, it appears that authors on the course gradually began to pay more attention to their potential audience and thus to exert more discretion over their public work. This is suggested by RS:

> The writing itself. The first two or three were lovely. The writing for publication required a much more attentive approach, attentive to what you're writing for and the purpose, and that it was for others' consumption, and you had to make sure certain things were visible in the writing. It had to achieve certain things. That was the academic side, but really it would have been enough to carry on with the other side ... to see where that led.

On revision and reflection

In the interview it seems that RS found the need to amend and edit his work almost irritating, he did not seem to think that any such amendments would naturally improve the quality or intent of his work and was pleased enough with what seemed to 'come off the top of [his] head'. The same was true for other participants, such as KH and ND. In contrast, CF, for example, was surprised at her drive and anxiety to play with and alter the work in progress, on Sunday afternoons, and even at the expense of family visits! And AC explicitly recognises the merit of editing and revision – she says:

> The course tutor said something about repetition, and there was. I've actually re-edited it, taking into account some of the comments made, things about better wording ... I think it is much better to read.

Her work on the course was interrupted by a domestic crisis; she hoped that under different circumstances she would have re-edited the writing as a matter of course. In order to revise, Graves suggests, the writer has to be able to anticipate the direction of the work in hand; that is, the writer has to have a plan, a message to convey, the desire to make a certain statement (Graves 1983). However, as has been suggested, writers may nonetheless surprise themselves, or be surprised by the interpretations of others. Thus, although BB was strongly aware of the need to communicate a 'message' (see pp. 154–5) she was nonetheless of the opinion that were she to write the same piece again it would be different, as though by reflecting on her writing, her ideas had developed and changed: she said, 'I no longer feel quite the same about the piece. I feel now there are bits I would add to it that weren't there three months ago.'

The impact of the course on participants' practice

For obvious reasons this is not an easy question to answer in terms of direct cause-and-effect. But some tentative suggestions may be made. To begin with, it is notable that many participants felt some degree of tension, between the ideals of the reflective writing course and their prior experience of the workplace and of writing. For example, in her interview MG was insistent that her combination of confusion and lack of confidence with regard to the course was a consequence of the nature and demands of previous learning experiences. Although she wrote well and imaginatively on the programme, she could not be convinced of the legitimacy of her work. This was primarily because it carried no direct quotations from other authorities, nor did it have an overt theoretical perspective. Therefore it seems, for MG, it was not properly academic. MG's most recent educational experiences had been on teacher training and social work training programmes. Such programmes rightly demand rigour, the exercise of intellect and the testing of hypotheses and theories. These requirements of themselves do not preclude the use of imagination and reflection in academic work; in fact both might be considered as essential ingredients. However, as Freire and Schor (1991) suggest, it may be that rigour and validity are sometimes subject to very narrow definitions and this, in conjunction with tight time-frames and outcome-driven assessment schedules, curtails the opportunities for individuals to share their true experience and their learning from it. It has to fit into the boxes.

The work of educationalists such as Dewey, Brookfield and Freire suggests that the constraining process begins at a very early age where the emphasis in schooling is to transmit the dominant cultural truth without any significant critical analysis of that truth. It is a process that Freire has described as the 'banking' of knowledge (1972a). As Jones and Novak (1993) argue, it is possible that a constraining educational process can compound the limiting experiences of daily professional practice and so undermine professional autonomy and the worth of critically reflective practice.

This is a point of view subscribed to by a number of those interviewed, most particularly ND, who, as we have seen already, was not sure that the job actually wanted her to 'think':

> [The course] has helped me to reflect generally upon things to do with work. We *never* have enough time to think, we're always rushing and

doing things. I think I've slowed down in my writing, but I don't know if that is a good thing!! It might not be a good thing as far as managers are concerned. I think I make time (as a consequence of the course) to put more thought into things.

Arguably, it is through the grind of daily professional practice and debilitating educational experiences that potential learners lose confidence in their ability and cannot properly value and learn from their own understanding. It may be that for some the reflective writing course helps to counteract some of the worse excesses, as summed up by RS:

What I've learnt. ... I know about the value of seeing things from different points of view and bringing in different life experiences to the work I do. ... I've always tried to hold on to different life experiences, but over time it becomes quite difficult to do that because of the bureaucratic framework in which we work and the lack of encouragement to do it. Now, I think, I write very much more using the whole of me rather than the parts of me which are trained and schooled in bureaucratic writing. I've always sought to retain integrity in my work but it has been a really difficult struggle and I don't know that I've succeeded in doing that. In fact I'm sure quite a lot of the time I haven't. But I felt I was re-investing in that personal integrity in a way I haven't been able to do for some time. Yes, it was a re-investment, not something completely new.

Thus, as a consequence of having been on the course, four participants specifically noted an improvement in, and even a reclamation of, their practice skills. RS felt he had regained a more 'holistic' approach to his practice, BB and HT had recognised a direct improvement in their writing skills, and AC had benefited from the course on a 'meta' level, in that she used some of its methods in her own training work with practitioners.

More generally, all nine participants commented on the relevance of the course to everyday work. Six of them believed that being on the course had improved the quality of the work they did and the services they delivered as social workers. They seemed to register the effect in three discrete areas: an enhancement of knowledge in their specialist area of practice, directly improved writing skills (and so an improvement in general communication skills), and the immediate transfer of some of the learning exercises to their direct work with clients.

Three participants discussed how they used different 'tools' from the course in direct practice with clients: RS has used the five minute free-writing exercise with clients to help open up areas for discussion and intervention. ND, in her work placing children for adoption, has used activities derived from the course actively to encourage prospective adopters to imagine how adoptees might feel.

And AC has used the idea of a developmental journey in her work with trainees, no longer expecting them to have 'got it all' by the end of a training programme.

Similarly, in an interview with a different group of participants, who had worked through the distance learning materials presented in Chapter 4, one interviewee described how she had applied her learning from the course to her work with a client who found it difficult to express her feelings 'at the time' but who was able to write down her responses for later discussion:

> I told [her] to write down what she feels and maybe reflect on it. I probably would not have been so keen to do that before this [course] and now it is something I can use more with clients, because if it feels good for me it probably feels good for them. It has really opened things up, and made a difference to working with her. It has been tremendously empowering for her. So it is almost like taking the lessons from the [course] and giving that to a client. I feel like she is part of the [reflective writing] group now. It is almost evangelical.

In a separate interview, Brenda Landgrebe, whose work appears in Chapter 2 (story 1) and in Chapter 4 (session 4), was asked whether there were any ways in which she felt she might now act differently as a practitioner after her experience of writing about her practice on the reflective writing course. She replied:

> Yes, I am certainly more aware of cultural differences in attitude to illness and health, definitely, and I'm really intent on studying Buddhism. I'm really going to try to find out why this girl [Kyoko – see Chapter 4: p. 130] was as she was. So I'm going to look at some cultural things and some religious factors, beacuse we have a multicultural and multireligious society, and I know how easily I could have tried to impose my western ideas on Kyoko.

At the time of the interview Brenda was undertaking a course on care for the dying. She commented:

> For this other course, I've had to write a 'care study'. But having written about Kyoko I actually approached this 'care study' with a very sociological outlook, rather than a medical approach. So already it has changed me, because I'm trying to find out why this man (who is dying) is acting in the way he is. I actually went to visit him and his wife at home, to talk to them in a situation where I was not really in a nursing role, to try to find out about his life.
>
> [Interviewer: So if you hadn't written about Kyoko …]
>
> No, I wouldn't have bothered; I would just have looked at the notes. But I actually wanted to know what made him the individual that he is. Because we have to let people find their own way of coping.

Finally, and beyond this development of her awareness of the cultural dimensions of nursing theory and practice, Brenda made a further and yet more general point concerning the effect of her work:

> I want to emphasise the *communication* aspect: I really do feel I have been shown (or have discovered) another way to communicate, and this is of great importance to me.

Responses to the story-writing workshops

The material presented so far relates to participants' experience of a ten-week reflective writing course. This is a sustained experience which allows plenty of time for participants to come to terms with a new method of working. The following material concerns the responses of two separate groups to a rather different and more 'sudden' experience, the story-writing workshop sessions described in the introduction to Chapter 2 – an introductory session, followed by a week or so to write a story, and finally a session in which the stories are shared.

To begin with here is a set of comments, in their own words, made by a group of eight schoolteachers about two story-writing workshops which were included as an introduction to a course on research methods. The comments are not a selection, but a verbatim presentation of the written evaluation comments given by a complete group of participants, excluding comments about the way the sessions themselves were managed. They are not arranged in any order.

> I enjoyed writing the story and found that I got more out of the story than the readers did. They did, however, find one point I had made had an overriding importance. I had not intended it to carry so much weight. I found the exercise quite revealing.

> Although I was doubtful about the point of writing a story I enjoyed the sessions very much and in fact the worry was groundless. The discussion about the stories was informative and has led me into thinking more about my own role as a teacher. I find fiction easier to read than non-fiction, and I feel this was purposeful and worthwhile.

> Very useful sessions. I think the use of fiction to convey idea, fears, perceptions and so on is a very powerful method. Response to fiction also is an important way to elicit people's feelings and thoughts. I shall certainly consider seriously using this technique in my own research.

> I have thoroughly enjoyed both sessions and feel I have gained a lot out of them and out of writing my story, both personally and professionally. The emotions which I felt when writing the story came back just as powerfully today [during the discussion].

Extremely useful, very powerful, very 'freeing', revealing. Is there enough preparation for the emotional content of the story?

I found writing the story very therapeutic. When I finished writing I felt a slight weight had lifted from my shoulders.

In fiction there is often a vivid clarity of reality. What I have gained: a greater depth of understanding of others' ideas and thoughts; a clarification of some of my own thoughts.

I find my story very personal, and I am not yet sure I fully understand the issues raised, although the discussions regarding it I found to be helpful. However, I have been aware for some time that these were the issues which concerned me.

It might be argued that, as evaluative evidence, this is somewhat anecdotal. In contrast, the following evidence is derived from a group which is large enough for some simple quantitative analysis. On this occasion the group consisted of forty-nine participants, mainly nurses and community nurses. This group took part in the two story-writing sessions as part of their preparation for reflective journal work. At the end of the second session, after they had written and shared their stories, they were all asked to write 'five key words' to describe their feelings about the two sessions.

The largeness of this group and the form of their evaluation gives an opportunity to present an analytical evaluation of the participants' experience of the work, even though not all of them followed the instructions very accurately: some wrote only four (or even only three) key words, some included phrases rather than words, and quite a few included words which gave no indication of their feelings, e.g. 'story' or 'writing' or 'sharing ideas'. Moreover, some of the responses probably merely reflected concern and disappointment that the story-writing sessions had not provided the detailed guidance on journal writing that they were hoping for, and in other respects also this was not the most helpful context for the work: the group was really rather too large for this sort of work, and that also led to very cramped conditions for group sharing of the stories. So in many ways, this was an extremely severe test of the robustness of the story-writing method. Nevertheless, the following observations may be made.

Out of a total of 49 responses, 24 (nearly 50 per cent) were entirely positive, like the following examples:

* 'Interesting, beneficial, enlightening, surprising, refreshing'
* 'Surprising, revealing, informative, educational, therapeutic'
* 'Useful, interesting, informative, surprising, cathartic'

A large number of responses were clearly positive but included one word (out of the five) indicating initial anxiety, something like the following examples:

- 'Bewildering (initially), enlightening, inspiring, thought-provoking, challenging'
- 'Surprise, fun, thought-provoking, anxiety, relief'

Out of the 49 responses, only 4 (less than 10 per cent) seemed ambivalent, in that they included negative comments:

- '(At this particular time): irrelevant, superficial, childish *but* thought-provoking'
- 'I felt confused at the beginning and thought that the work was pointless *but* I enjoyed the discussion with my colleagues of my story and some aspects were enlightening'
- 'Too long, not relevant, restricting *but* opened further discussion on feelings and learned a lot about general writing'
- 'Disappointed – can't see the point of sessions on timetable, puzzled *but* enjoyed sessions'

Another way of approaching the data is to consider the overall pattern of the key words used by the forty-nine students. A list was drawn up of all the words participants used to describe their feelings (i.e. omitting purely descriptive terms such as 'story', 'sharing', etc.) – an overall total of 151 'choices'. (The difference between 151 choices and 49 students × 5 key words [= 245] choices is accounted for by the various ways in which students did not follow the instruction, as indicated earlier.)

The following points are derived from this listing:

- The words most frequently used were: 'interesting' (which occurred 15 times), 'enjoyable' (13) and 'thought-provoking' (13).
- Other terms which occurred repeatedly were: 'surprising' (9), 'enlightening' (7), 'stimulating' (6) and 'therapeutic' (6).
- The general tone of the responses is very positive. Of the total of 151 there are only 24 terms which could be thought of as having negative connotations, mostly referring to anxiety and uncertainty, which would not be unexpected since the approach would have been wholly new to every member of the group.
- The number of references to anxiety, uncertainty, stress, etc. (total: 17) is balanced by references which suggest 'relief' that the process turned out to be 'non-critical', 'non-threatening' and therefore, in the end, 'safe', 'positive', 'relaxing', 'confidence-building', 'rewarding' and 'therapeutic' (total: 19).

- A large number of terms seem to refer to a sense of discovery (i.e. 'thought-provoking', 'surprising', 'enlightening', 'stimulating', 'informative', 'challenging', 'revealing', 'curiosity-provoking', 'illuminating', 'searching', 'developmental', 'educational', 'mind-searching', 'refreshing' (total: 57).

In the end, of course, such calculations are very much a matter of interpretation, but the analysis as a whole does offer a broad basis of confirmation for the students' responses quoted in the first part of this section, namely that writing and sharing stories is, first, initially worrying, but second, enjoyable, and third, helpful and revealing – both personally and professionally.

* * *

This chapter has presented evaluative data and discussion, indicating how participants respond to workshops and courses where the emphasis is on writing fiction as a mode of reflective analysis of practice. The next chapter provides a further perspective, in the form of a case study of one participant's experience, first of the course and second of its subsequent effects.

6

'BREAKING THE MOULD': A CASE STUDY

Experiencing the reflective writing course

Introduction

The previous chapter presented an 'outsider' evaluation of the participants' experience of the reflective writing course. In contrast, this chapter presents the view 'from the inside', a personal account, written by Alyson Buck, describing how she became involved in the reflective writing course, first as a 'student' and then as a tutor. It includes the work she wrote during the course, the impact of the course experience on her subsequent work with her own students on other courses, and finally how this experience affected her response to the death of her father.

How it all began

The flyer landed on my desk and immediately roused my curiosity. 'Reflective Writing for Professional Practitioners' it said, but gave little other information on what to expect. My imagination ran wild and I had written an international best-seller before I'd even finished completing the application form. I'd always been interested in writing and, like many others perhaps, spent my childhood years compiling stories and my adolescence writing angst-filled poems. I had even been told I was quite good at it over the years, but never explored the possibilities further. Life gradually took over and I settled down into nursing, where any creativity and individual thought was trained out of me. In the early 1970s nurses were not encouraged to think for themselves ('What!' I can hear colleagues crying, whilst throwing their hands up in horror, but it's true). I completed my Registered General Nurse (RGN) training in Scotland and got an excellent basis for my career: I absorbed what I was told, generally believed it and sought very little else. Of course there were moments of reflection, though it wasn't called that then. The only reflection I saw was my own when I looked in the mirror to see if my cap was on straight and my apron fastened properly (this being of prime concern to the nursing hierarchy). There were moments of wondering what things meant for patients in your care, of course – the woman who had been in a coma for ten years following a routine operation; the young man left permanently disabled following a brain haemorrhage. But perhaps most of all, contemplating the effect of all this on the relatives who sat and waited, with endless patience, for a sign or some small word from you, the nurse, that there had been a minor improvement.

These remain in the memory more for their emotional impact however, not necessarily because they were serious reflection points in terms of performance or practice. No, we did what was expected of us (which was a great deal), rarely questioned (certainly not in a challenging way) and gathered this 'wealth of untapped knowledge' (Benner 1984) which few seemed interested in at that time.

Over the years things changed of course, as did I, and, following several years as a midwife, I moved into a field which had always interested me – mental health. After a spell of clinical practice where I had a chance to see the effects of mental ill-health on individuals and families, I moved into teaching and remain there to this day.

Much of my interest in recent years has been taken up with this question: How do I get students to see the 'other side' of the story and not fall into the 'professional knows best' trap? I have tried to encourage them to be open in discussions and role-play for experiential learning. My overriding interest in the reflective writing course was totally selfish, however. I wanted to write and I hoped this course would tell me how. So with those thoughts in my head and with not a little trepidation in my heart, I joined the group, little knowing the effect it was to have on my educational practice and myself.

Becoming a student

'I want you to write,' said the tutor. 'Write anything at all for five minutes.' I sat for a moment and then started writing my thoughts down as they were coming into my head:

> I don't really know what's expected of me here. Write anything he said, well I am. Writing I mean. Maybe that's it. Maybe that's what's expected – that I write. That I *can* write.

Five minutes flew by and we were then instructed to 'write now about a time you learned something'. Ten minutes was the allotted time, and again I filled it with thoughts written onto a page. There was a difference this time though, as I noticed when we were asked to read again what we'd written and make comments on both our writing and the exercise we had undertaken. The first piece of work was very much in the 'here and now', catching thoughts as they flitted in and out of my mind, following them to a certain extent, but not allowing them to develop at all. Just acknowledging they were there and recording them on paper. The second piece, however, was much more struc-tured. First of all I had to identify a time when I felt I had learned something, I recorded the details of the event, the characters in it, and so on. Then I had started to deconstruct it to try to establish just what it was I *had* learned and put it in some kind of context. All in ten minutes! I hadn't quite finished it when time was called but I know I could have gone on for a lot longer, delving deeper and deeper into the various components of the situation and my own reactions to it. One thing that did surprise me was that I was writing about something which had happened years ago in my Registered Mental Nurse (RMN) training, and I was somewhat intrigued as to why it should have surfaced at that particular moment in time. I did not explore this further, however, as we moved on into outlines of the course, and established a set of ground rules for the sharing of our work with others.

As a mental health nurse I was used to group work, and the establishment of ground rules was a familiar practice to me. I know that one or two other members of the group found the prospect of sharing their work with others a little daunting at this stage, though, and was pleased at the way that their concerns and anxieties were handled. Overall I left the first session with a feeling of excitement and a motivation to find out more. The excitement was generated by the knowledge that there was a way to write for professional practice which was not confined to the rather stifling academic format which I had so far been used to, but which I (and numerous others) was far from happy with. The motivation was to write more and to enjoy the fact that it was OK for me to spend time thinking. This is something which in nursing we have been somewhat reluctant to embrace. 'Reflection' has become a significant concept within nursing, but it seems that diverse understandings of the term exist. Whilst various materials and activities have been introduced into the curricula to foster reflective development, the practice of reflection is carried out and encouraged in many different ways.

There is one thing we cannot deny, however, and that is that reflection needs time, and for me this was one of the vital aspects of the course. I was actively encouraged to spend time reflecting not only on professional issues, but personal issues from which links to professional practice were then made. There was a sense of luxury about it – those Thursday mornings were time spent discussing reflections we had made over the previous week and written down in a variety of formats. Each week we discussed a different aspect of writing and saw examples from published authors of the myriad ways in which to make a point, use language and find a voice. The groups we had formed came to be very important in this sense. Information was shared with them which, in some cases, had not been shared with anyone before; and they were not only commenting on related issues, but, more importantly, were discussing the work itself and the way in which it was written. Did it get the message across? What about style and language used? And so on. In this way group members began to explore personal issues more, and came to see how their own circumstances had a bearing on their professional practice.

It was a process that both liberated and enabled in a number of different ways. Through it I came to realise that reflection was much more involved than I had previously considered, that there were different levels and that there were numerous ways I could demonstrate reflection to students in the hope that they would find one to match their individual needs. I moved from my previous notion of reflection being triggered by a problem or concern, as proposed by writers such as Boyd and Fales (1983), and inclined towards the work of the philosopher Heidegger, who considers reflection to be the prominent component of thought:

> What is thought is the gift given in thinking back, given because we incline toward it. Only when we are so inclined toward what in itself is to be thought about, only then are we capable of thinking.
>
> (Heidegger, cited in Pierson 1998: p. 166)

So Heidegger suggests that reflection is thinking *back*, about something of interest. Through the process of sharing my writing with others and having them discuss it and offer alternative viewpoints and thoughts, I came to see that 'something of interest' to me held links not only for professional practice, but was often of interest to others also. Although situations hold different meanings for individuals, there is invariably a shared component, which can be explored through the emotions engendered by the experience.

Thus the course provided me with the opportunity and time to explore the writing process explicitly and the reflective process implicitly. I was able to explore experiences of the personal and professional and effect new insights. It was at the end of the course that I wrote the following piece entitled 'Role on … role off … ' in which I explored the way in which we constantly move between roles in our interactions with others – a theme which was later to recur in a most significant way whilst caring for my father who developed Alzheimer's disease.

'Role on … role off … '

The situation described in the following pages led me to thinking about the various roles which a person may have in their professional life and how we slip in and out of these roles to suit the various situations we find ourselves in.

Each status in life is accompanied by a set of norms, which dictates how a person in that particular status is expected to act. This group of norms is known as a 'role' and individuals perform these roles in relation to other roles involved in social relationships. Individuals interact in terms of these roles. Haralambos says (1991: p. 7) that 'Social roles regulate and organise behaviour. In particular they provide means for accomplishing certain tasks'. So when individuals adopt their appropriate roles, social life becomes ordered and predictable and the various individuals know what to do and how to do it. 'With knowledge of each other's roles they are able to predict and comprehend the actions of the other' (*ibid*.: p. 7). But what happens when roles become confused or when individuals' notions or role expectations don't quite match? Individuals then have to find alternative ways of dealing with these familiar situations.

* * *

I walked down the long corridor and entered the day room at the end. The three nurses grouped around the open drug trolley looked up somewhat disinterestedly as I approached. No-one spoke. No-one smiled, but I could tell they were staff from the badges they wore that displayed name and rank. 'Hello,' I ventured, 'I'd like to see Sarah Scott please.'

'Over there,' the nurse nearest to me muttered, barely giving me a second glance as she gestured across the room. She never moved away from the radiator she was leaning on and the other two nurses paid me no attention at all.

I looked across the room to where she had pointed and for a moment didn't recognise the girl I'd come to see. Then as she spotted me I realised that this was indeed Sarah, but not the Sarah I had seen just two weeks ago, this was a young woman with a haunted look of hopelessness on her face. I moved towards her and with a smile said 'Hello Sarah.' She was already on her feet and in a tight, tense voice said, 'Thanks for coming. I do appreciate it.' She moved across the room and I noticed the way she avoided eye contact and held her shoulders and arms hunched in close to her body. 'Is there somewhere we can talk?' I asked. 'Yes, out here,' she replied as we went back into the corridor and she moved towards some seats in the corner. 'We'll be alright here, we won't be disturbed.'

We sat down and I noticed the fine tremor of her hands, the anxious way her gaze kept shifting backwards and forwards but always avoiding mine, the small gauze dressing on her right arm, the dark circles under her eyes. I studied her face, devoid of expression yet at the same time screaming out in silent anguish for someone to give her that most basic of human needs – love. I touched her arm gently. 'Do you want to talk about it?'

She paused for a moment as if struggling to find the words to express herself and then, with a deep breath, she started to speak, slowly at first, testing me, judging my reactions and attitudes; but once she found a willing ear she spoke with greater confidence and relaxed a little. The tremor remained though and the tight, tense face and posture was not dropped completely, but for a short while she was able to talk freely with little interruption, giving vent to the pent up emotions, fears and anxieties that festered beneath the surface.

As I watched and listened I was aware that as she was responding to my reactions, so I was responding to hers. I had come as a tutor to visit a student in need of care, to assure her of my help in whatever way I could and to allay any anxieties regarding impending assessments and other pressing academic issues. Now I found myself taking on a former role, but one that is always there within, that of the nurse. I was now making professional assessments of mental state, the ability to make judgements and of assessing risk to herself. Coinciding with these two roles was a third level: that of a fellow human being giving comfort and support to someone in need.

Conversation continued and I found myself listening to things which as a teacher I would not normally be privy to, only in exceptional circumstances. Information about a loveless family life, a failed marriage, several unsuccessful relationships and the loss of the only person who ever really meant anything to her, her father. Add these to the stresses of a student nurse's life and an inability to cope, and the current situation arises – a torment and tension so great that the only way she could see to release it was to cut her arm. As the blood flowed, so too did the anxiety and fears she had been unable to tell anyone about. The nurse within me was now asking about these acts of self-harm, to which the gauze dressing was testimony, and about the feelings of worthlessness and inadequacy. Was she suicidal? 'No, not now. I did think about it at first, but now I don't want to die, I just want to get my life back in order.'

I let her talk. Many times I have spoken to students of the need to often just 'be with' the client. To allow them to talk freely without interruption or judgement and to listen with their whole being, not just their ears. Here I heard a young girl pour out her heart to someone with whom, though not noticeably close in relationship terms, she obviously felt comfortable enough to trust with at least some of her thoughts. A relationship started on one level was now moving into a totally new arena.

Sarah addressed the 'business' issues first. She was concerned with assignment deadlines and an unseen examination to be taken several weeks later. As a tutor that's what I was there for, right? Once she realised I wasn't going to get up and rush off she went on to other issues – some 'safe' things like life on the ward. The mundanity of it all, the boredom, the wanting someone to talk to. During this stage I was to her like one of the other disinterested nurses she and I had encountered with no time to spend listening to some one else's problems – they had their own to deal with and anyway, they 'did their job' so why put any more into it? She talked of the drugs she was on, how they made her mouth dry and this was reinforced by her tongue darting in and out to try and moisten her cracked lips. As I remained steadfast and sat quietly through this, she moved onto the third level. Now she was trusting me not only as a teacher and nurse and by virtue of those positions; but because I had been tested by her and not been found wanting she reached the personal level. For me it has not been easy working through these states either. I came to the ward as a teacher, not a nurse. I had no right to any information regarding her problems or care, only what she wanted to tell me. When I did move into nurse mode I too was hesitant. How would she react to queries about suicidal intent and so on? I had professional boundaries to consider.

In the situation described I had only been known previously to the student as a teacher and lecturer and I only knew her as a student in a classroom situation. Roles and expectations of each other's behaviour were therefore set and previously determined. She therefore approached me initially in this way – discussion of essays, exams and so on. I likewise responded as 'the teacher', reassuring her of my ability to grant extensions, defer examinations and so on. We were on safe and familiar ground (although in an unfamiliar setting) and so conformed to role.

It wasn't until we had exhausted the set of rules for this particular situation that we moved into different roles. With discussion of her illness now in the conversation, we were moving into an area that was both unfamiliar and a little uncomfortable for both of us. It was at this point I became aware of a shift into a former role of mine, the nurse, and Sarah had returned to her familiar (and current) role of the patient. Schön says of this type of situation that 'the familiar situation functions as a precedent, or metaphor, or exemplar, for the unfamiliar one' (Schön 1983: p. 138).

So once Sarah started discussing her illness, fears, anxieties and so on, the only way I could deal with this 'unfamiliar' situation was to return to a situation I felt comfortable with, and that meant the role of the nurse. As Sarah was largely in 'patient' role anyway, we then interacted fairly comfortably for a while in this way.

* * *

Reflecting on my feelings in this matter led me to think about the third aspect of my experience and that is the aspect of caring in terms of being human, as opposed to the 'caring' of being a professional, in something we like to think of as 'the caring profession'. But that implies that there is a role called 'human' which is separate from the other roles which humans adopt. This says to me that we are 'human' first, above all else, and then other roles are developed to predict, challenge or control our behaviour. Do we then 'care' on different levels? As Waterhouse says:

> Without care – nothing matters and something, myself, always matters to me. This 'mattering' structures my world and determines my interest in things and my relations with others; it is the basis of all motivation ... to the truth that my existence is fundamentally my own ... must be added the truth that fundamentally I care.
>
> (Waterhouse 1981, quoted in Griffin 1983: p. 289)

So whilst relating to Sarah in the various roles, underpinning all of this was the fact that I was socialised to being human and I was also caring from this stance. Roach saw caring as 'the human mode of being and ... caring behaviour is manifested through the attributes of compassion, competence, confidence, conscience and commitment' (Roach 1984, quoted in Forrest 1989: p. 815).

I sometimes hear other nurses and teachers say that 'nurses don't care anymore'. If this is true, how might it have arisen? From my brief interaction with the nurses on the ward where Sarah was a patient, I would have agreed – as they all seemed to be singularly uninterested in either Sarah or myself. But how could one not notice the obvious signs of distress that this girl was displaying and how can one not respond – on any level – to another human being in distress? Have we, as professionals, become so bound up with the trappings of our roles and responsibilities of our positions that we have lost touch with the basic instincts and intuitions that make us inherently human, and therefore lost the ability to care? An important aspect of a caring relationship is intuition, and this is so important to develop if we are to respond creatively to the changing needs of human beings. With intuition I was able to move into a different level and discuss aspects of Sarah's life with her that as a teacher, or perhaps even as a nurse, I was not able to do. But intuition cannot be scientifically measured and nursing is losing a grip on these aspects which help to retain nursing as an art and rather than the science we are trying to make it. We need a careful balance of both to ensure that the caring element – which is fundamental to both the process of becoming human and the process of becoming a professional – is developed, maintained and strengthened to ensure that both professional and client have the potential to benefit and grow within the caring process.

From student to facilitator

It was sometime after I had completed this piece of writing that I began to act as co-facilitator for the course. I was interested in doing so for two reasons. First, for my own development, feeling that I wanted to learn more of the nature of reflection and writing in a style which I readily felt an affinity with. The second reason was that I felt the course had a lot to offer mental health nursing and vice-versa. One thing I had found whilst undertaking the course as a student was how little we really understood of each other's disciplines and work. This was brought home to me by reading some of the pieces of the social workers, and being surprised at both the range and diversity of their work. The social workers in the group in which I participated also expressed interest and surprise at the varied and difficult world of the mental health nurse. The different sides of the same story need to be told, including that of the client's, and this is one factor which the course allowed members to explore in safety, often with surprising results.

My experience of tutoring the reflective writing course went well. The students contributed much to the discussion on writing and related professional issues. The small-group work, the cornerstone of the course, was evaluated as a very valuable and effective teaching method, and in terms of my own develop-ment I learnt an enormous amount, not only from the experience of being a facilitator, but perhaps more from the students themselves. Reflective writing yields a wonderfully rich source of material, and I never cease to be amazed at the variety of both experiences and styles of writing which are presented. Students who feel they cannot write before they start the course are, before long, sharing pieces of writing with colleagues and gaining in confidence to explore and experiment with it. Following on from this comes the discussion on professional issues which are related to their particular piece of work, and which again provided an excellent source of information from which to build up my own knowledge base.

Yes, the experience of being involved in the facilitation of the course provided me with an added dimension from which to explore the reflective process, and I was able to observe this in action at close quarters, over a longer period of time. With student evaluations indicating that writing gave them a tool with which to give voice to their experiences and reflection, I began to wonder how I might use this medium with my own pre-registration students to the advantage of all concerned.

Re-writing reflective journals

One of the biggest barriers to effective reflection appears to be that of time. It often feels that 'time is of the essence' in nursing, as clients require immediate attention for urgent or life-threatening situations. The pressure on nurses' time contributes to what Pierson (1998) calls 'calculative thinking'. This form of thinking is an abstract and practical process confined to organising, managing and controlling, and is a form of thinking which does not consider meaning and yet has the 'power to absorb completely our energy and attention' (Hixon 1978: p. 4). This is a superficial level of reflection and is akin to looking in a mirror, which merely deflects back to the observer a physically similar image just as my early experiences in nursing did. Whilst there may be value in starting students off at this level of reflection, simply describing actions executed in practice 'serves to reinforce positivistic and behaviourist educational traditions' (Pierson 1998: p. 166).

In contrast, my intention now, after the reflective writing course, was to encourage the mental health nurses with whom I was working to reflect at a deeper level. They are at the end of the second year in training when they undertake a module that, like many others, contains a clinical practice placement which confronts them with a wide spectrum of intense human emotions and physical conditions. Initial reactions to some of their experiences also encompass a broad range of emotion, many students never previously having worked with such ill or vulnerable clients. Coupled with the vulnerability of the clients, is the sense of vulnerability of many of the students in dealing with and caring for individuals who were often exhibiting extremes of behaviour and ill health. A strategy frequently used to allow students time to consider their experiences is the written journal (Cameron and Mitchell 1993; Paterson 1995). This technique is considered to offer writers the opportunity to become observers of their own learning and then to reflect on that experience to see what they can learn from it. However, written journals can also be used simply to support students' 'calculative thinking', such as documenting the day's activities as a list of accomplishments, or writing about the effect of medication on client's illness and so on. This was the form that most of the journal writing for the student nurses coming into the module were used to. At best this produced superficial reflection and usually related to content or instrumental tasks.

In order to try to break this mould of thinking I tried to move students on a stage further. I encouraged students to think of their journals as personal diaries in which they were able to make any entries they wished, engaging in conversation with themselves on the issues in question. They were encouraged to write as they thought, using their own language and asking questions in any manner they wished; in other words, to explore the situations or experiences which presented themselves in any way they felt was appropriate, so long as they did explore them. In order to sever the links between the 'old' journal and the 'new' journal, we decided to change the name we gave to these writings and decided to adopt the term 'reflective diary writing' to distinguish them. These diary entries were then to be shared with others in the group for comment.

Things didn't immediately go to plan. Some students didn't appreciate the need for commitment to the small groups, feeling they could opt out and either not attend, or not bring any work to share. We discussed this in the large group, though, and were able to make parallels between how they were feeling and the experience of anxious clients in group situations, the need for attendance to demonstrate respect for others, and so on. It slowly worked and attendance improved. Some students were initially reluctant to share more than the superficial experience with others and I wondered why this might be so. I asked them and received a number of replies, amongst which were:

'Well nurses aren't meant to be emotional are they?'

'If I really told you what I wanted to say to her you'd probably throw me out as being an unfit nurse', and

'Well nothing's going to change, so why are we bothering?'

We were able to discuss each of these issues in the larger group, and gradually students came to be more relaxed about the time we spent in reflection and in sharing their work with others. The plenary session after the small group work was spent looking at common issues which had arisen out of seemingly different experiences. By doing this we enabled all students to share in the experiences and discussions of the other groups. Often the theoretical content of the next week's sessions would arise out of discussions from the 'reflective practice' time. Students were thus able to not only deepen their level of reflection through dialogic writing and discussion, but they were able to relate this to practice issues and analyse care given to a particular individual, as was required for the written assignment of the module.

The length of time needed to write the diary entries and to reflect on their content is quite considerable, and it is not always possible to fit it in during periods of heavy scheduled activity. I tried to counteract this by combining it with preparation for the assignment, but there were inevitably some students who preferred to work individually and the combination was not effective for all students. The quality of reflection seemed to improve, however, and students have commented on the usefulness of writing as a valuable aid to reflective practice.

174

A multiplicity of notions regarding the concept of reflection exists, yet conclusive answers to what it is and how it is taught/learnt in relation to nursing practice are not yet apparent. My personal feeling is that reflection can and does give rise to a more intuitive and sensitive practitioner and that reflective writing, whether it be of reflective diaries, fictional accounts, poems or the like, is an appropriate medium for many practitioners to explore their own practice and should be encouraged.

In order to highlight the change in the level of reflection, I have included a few entries from both 'traditional' journal writing and from the new 'reflective' approach I tried with the third-year students. These are obviously selected extracts and not complete entries. The first three are from 'traditional' entries:

(a) Gave an intramuscular injection of Clopixol. Ensured that the correct procedure was followed, checking the drug with the staff nurse on duty. The patient needed to be restrained by two other staff, as he didn't think he needed it. Restraint was carried out using approved Home Office methods and all relevant records were completed. No problems encountered.

(b) Carried out special observation on a suicidal patient. This meant, according to unit policy, I had to be within arm's length of her at all times. She didn't like this much, particularly when she wanted to go to the toilet, but I had explained why we had to do it, several times. She tried to abscond on several occasions, but was prevented from doing so by staff. Observation is one of the most important aspects of suicide prevention and includes observation of mental state and interactions with others, as well as behaviour.

(c) Had to administer first aid to a patient who had injured herself through smashing a universal specimen container and cutting her arm with it. I called for help, applied pressure to the wound (there were no fragments of container left in) and elevated her arm. Doctor was called and patient was transferred to A&E, with an escort, for emergency care.

It is worth noting that these examples contain some highly dramatic situations, yet these are virtually hidden in the routine presentation. These are examples of how 'calculative thinking' generates no more than superficial reflection, as Pierson (1998) observed.

Following the 'reflection sessions' however, some entries changed qualitatively as outlined below. Whilst acknowledging this is a different student group, they had also engaged in the superficial reporting style of entries in their former placements, and I therefore have no reason to doubt that without the sessions they would have continued in the same vein.

(a) I was shocked when I saw Liz [not her real name]. She had blood pouring down her arm and this big gash on her wrist. I'm sure I froze for a minute, not knowing what to do, but hearing this voice (which I know was me) saying, 'My God, Liz! What have you done?' I felt frightened, angry and guilty all at once. I suppose fright because it was a new situation, I didn't know what to do; anger at her for putting me in this situation in the first place and guilt because I was supposed to have been observing her and should have prevented it. Now I'm beginning to see that 'observation' isn't just about having an easy time.

(b)   When I saw Martha lying there, with two male nurses holding her tight in restraint, I felt awful. She was sixty-three years old and here we were having to hold her down to give her an injection. For a moment I saw my grandmother in the same situation and was horrified to think that, in different circumstances, it could be her lying there. Can we really say we're helping her, when we're having to give this drug to her in such a harrowing way, two or three times a day? What does 'care' actually mean?

(c)   I think if I was in Stephen's place [a patient] I'd be angry too. He said to me once, 'Who the hell do you people think you are, running other people's lives like this? Now, I've made a sensible request in a civil manner. What is your problem?' and I had to ask myself the same question. What is the problem? Why are we treating him in such a way? The answer seemed to be, unfortunately, that he wasn't liked. He was young, male, articulate, challenging and had attracted the label of 'psychopath'. With that label, he didn't need a reason, he was on a losing streak right from the word go.

When I read these accounts the complexity of the various situations was immediately apparent, unlike in the first examples where the issues were obscured by the desire to illustrate 'correct procedures'. These second examples do justice to the dramatic reality of the situation and there is greater opportunity to open up the discussion in a variety of ways. Thus the promotion of 'reflective' writing enables personal and professional issues to be explored alongside each other whilst also encouraging other perspectives to be considered.

Caring for my father

All this has been brought home to me recently by becoming carer to my father, who suffered from Alzheimer's disease before his death earlier this year. Mayeroff, in his philosophy of the nature of 'caring', suggests that it involves helping another to grow and actualise, and that whether the caring is that of husband for wife, or daughter for father, it will result in 'a qualitative transformation of the relationship' (Mayeroff 1971: p. 11). By reflecting again and again on an idea, we are 'caring for the idea' (*ibid.*) which will result in qualitative transformation of the idea as it grows. Writing can give us many ways in which to explore the same idea over and over again from differing perspectives. Jottings can help to illustrate points and to highlight what it was like to cross the professional boundaries of caring and take it into the personal domain, and its effect on our other roles and relationships.

The following poem was written when I realised that my father hadn't spoken for a while and yet couldn't remember when it was that this occurred. Often in times of terminal illness all parties are able to prepare for the event, make their arrangements together and say goodbye. Not to do so has been one of the hardest things to come to terms with. He was with us in body (just) but his mind was definitely elsewhere. Dementia has been called the 'Long goodbye'. It's not; there is no goodbye. Just a gradual fading away.

> I can't quite remember when
> I heard your voice for the last time
> Or you spoke my name
> Or smiled
>
> I can't quite remember when
> I saw you walking for the last time
> Upright, proud and alone
> Without help
>
> I can't quite remember when
> I felt you knew for the last time
> Who we were
> And understood
>
> Instead, I remember a slow, yet seemingly sudden
> Decline into confusion, unhappiness and despair
> When your life continued in some strange, vaguely recognisable way
> Yet you were gone
> And you never even said
> Goodbye

One of the essential insights from psychology which most of us learn at some stage is that whatever we would do or be to others, we have to do or be to ourselves first. This would seem particularly true of the professions, and nurses have to learn to nurse themselves before they can truly nurse other people (Tschudin 1997). We must therefore find ways in which to encourage this learning, though it may be many years into nursing before an individual comes to this insight. So I have written down things which occurred to me during the various phases of my father's illness, things which I found difficult to deal with or things he said which made me think in some way and, looking back on them, I find them both sad and enlightening. Like the time early on in his illness before his problems had been given a name, he came into my house and, noticing he had his shoes on the wrong feet, I pointed it out to him. Laughing, he said 'Don't tell your mother, she'll think I'm going mad!' He knew there was something wrong and he knew that I knew, but there was a silent beseeching of me not to delve into things. He was afraid, and I feel I never really found a way to help him express his fears. For a patient I might have been able to, for my father I could not.

But writing is in itself a therapeutic process, and in some way gives vent to the grief that has to be curtailed somewhat at the time. The following piece was written after something my brother had said when he too realised that our father was no longer able to communicate verbally in any meaningful way, apart from asking for physical things, but that too disappeared soon after. By writing from a distance I was able to note the detail and content of the interaction which, without the benefit of knowledge, looked like a cosy encounter between two people.

I turned the corner and the café loomed into view. The lights piercing the increasing gloom and the neon sign offering a somewhat artificial welcome against the chill of the late autumn evening. Condensation covered the windows and lent everything a slightly hazy look – like a photograph with a soft filter used to blur the edges and take on a warm and mellow look. Customers were sheltering from the cold and damp, cupping steaming mugs of coffee in their hands to warm numb fingers and tucking into the 'all day breakfast' or plates piled high with sausages and chips. It looked safe. It looked comfortable.

Two men sat in the corner, to all intents and purposes deep in conversation. Both had drinks in front of them and one, the older of the two, was demolishing an apple turnover with great gusto. He nodded every now and then, seemingly in response to the younger man's conversation, and contributed to it on occasion with words of his own. A father and son, deep in conversation. Talking about what? Life, memories, arrangements to go out together? I reached the door and went in, greeting the staff cheerily as I did so, for I knew them as I did the two men.

Approaching the table I heard the younger man say, 'Dad, what's happened to you? You really don't know what I'm saying to you, do you? I never dreamed it would be like this. I wanted to spend long evenings by the fire debating things with you and now, suddenly, you've gone and I didn't even have a chance to say goodbye. Dad, Dad … are you listening?' He turned to me as I reached the table, smiling sadly. 'He doesn't know me anymore. He's gone.'

'No, not gone, not yet, he's still here, just different now, but I don't think he really understands much anymore. We must all try to help each other through this.'

My father looked up at me and, with an expression that I think was a smile and which nearly broke my heart, held up his mug: 'More.'

The notion of being an informal carer within a professional carer's world is the idea which gave rise to this 'qualitative change in the relationship' that Mayeroff spoke of, and it is this change in relationships which I focus on in my work as a mental health nurse and teacher. To understand the world from the client's perspective you have to be part of that world, to get inside it in whatever way you can so you really feel it.

My mother spoke to me of a time when once, in a particularly black mood, my father said to her, 'There must be more to life than this … if there isn't what's the point of going on? You'd be better off without me.' Mercifully for him and all concerned, his torment did not last too long, but for others it continues, and any way we can find of shedding light on that world to help ease it, must be pursued.

* * *

Compiling this chapter has raised several issues for me, not least of which is the fact that writing about certain events in my life has been somewhat therapeutic. The piece moves back and forth between professional and personal life, with interlinking threads weaving their way throughout. As this is how we generally live our lives, much can be learned from picking up these threads and tracing them back to their origins. To be in one domain and ignore the effects of the other on it is to deny ourselves a rich source of learning. Reflective writing encourages this learning process.

The other observation I made as I re-read the chapter is that the structure and format of the work, with the links between the pieces of writing, unintentionally illustrates one of the very concepts that has been highlighted throughout this book. I have created a patchwork text.

7

ARTISTRY, FICTION AND REFLECTION

The strange absence of the creative imagination in professional education

Introduction

In some respects our argument is straightforward: we emphasise the possibility and the value of exploring the meanings of our experience through writing and sharing fiction; we argue that, as professional workers (and indeed as human beings), we possess a general capacity for effectively representing our experience in artistic form; we suggest that in order to realise our capacity for reflection we can (and should) draw upon our intuitive grasp of aesthetic processes as well as our capacity for conceptual and logical analysis. So far we have presented the argument largely through examples and concrete reports of participants' experience, because unless the argument is convincing at that level, no amount of theoretical rationale is of any avail. But the time has come to present a fuller account of the theoretical considerations underlying the argument.

There are a number of reasons for this. First, this chapter is particularly (though not exclusively) addressed to staff responsible for professional education and training, in universities and elsewhere, who will wish to be reassured, before they decide to spend precious time and resources engaging in the sort of work described in the previous chapters, that there is a soundly based theoretical framework within which they can work. After all, there are reasons why writing fiction is *not* usually included in courses of professional education. Second, our argument concerning the parallel between imaginative creation and reflection on experience also has something important to say to staff engaged in teaching 'literature' in higher and adult education, concerning the sorts of activities they might include in their courses. For both of these groups of readers this chapter tries to present a novel yet coherent synthesis of key arguments in education and aesthetic theory, to show how each can support and illuminate each other in ways which have not so far been recognised. Third, practitioners about to engage in writing fiction as a method of exploring their practice may wish to appreciate fully the theoretical reasoning underlying the approach. Finally, the argument challenges a number of basic assumptions: about what we mean by 'reflection' and literary 'art', about the relationship between artistic expression and the general processes of understanding, about the various ways in which our understanding of experience can be represented, and (even more generally) about the role of imagination and artistic creativity in the learning process – in professional work and in a democratic society. And to re-think assumptions involves revisiting the theoretical traditions and the historical contexts where those assumptions were created.

For these reasons, then, this final chapter attempts to trace the arguments presented so far back to their philosophical starting points and to make sure that each stage of the argument is grounded both in its historical context and in an analysis of its key concepts. The first section is a brief reminder of the ideas conventionally associated with the notion of the reflective practitioner, and the second section goes on to examine the historical, philosophical and political context of those ideas, with particular reference to the themes of individual creativity, 'artistry' and participatory democracy. This is followed by an examination of the parallels between the processes of professional reflection and artistic (specifically literary) creation, taking 'imagination' as the key linking concept. This is conducted in two stages, first focusing on the writing of 'stories' and second on the conception of the patchwork text. Finally, it is suggested that writing fiction is a way of ordering experience which we can all engage in, and that sharing fictions involves writers and readers in a collaborative relationship, embodying key educational and democratic values of crucial relevance in a society where 'work' is increasingly concerned with the development of innovatory understanding.

The reflective paradigm (I): a summary

When a phrase catches on in the way that 'The Reflective Practitioner' has done, in the years since Donald Schön first published his book with that title in 1983, we can be sure that it has connected with something historically significant. For example, just yesterday (as I write this) at the end of a day conference with the title 'Developing and evaluating practice through inquiry' when we were considering how to develop the work further, one participant said, 'Maybe the title of the conference isn't very clear; maybe a lot of staff don't know what it means; why don't we call i, "Reflective practice", then *everyone* would understand.' It felt, at that moment, as though 'reflective practice' had become the one indispensable phrase with which to define and sum up all the positive meanings that we attach to the experience of professional work.

So, what is reflection, and why has it become such an attractive term that nothing else, it seems, will really do? To say that it has become 'a cliché' explains nothing and has itself become a cliché. To say that it has come to identify a 'paradigm' (Kuhn 1962) may also be a cliché, but it does begin to point towards an explanation. It suggests that we are concerned with a set of methods which imply not only a conception of technique but also an overarching 'philosophy' and a set of social and political values (see Kuhn 1962: ch. 10; Shapin 1994). The concept of 'paradigm' also opens up the argument that the 'reflective practitioner' paradigm (of the relationship between experience and understanding) ignores the central role of imaginative writing as a method because imaginative writing is supposed to belong to a different paradigm, a different way of conceiving of the relationship between experience and understanding, namely 'art', or, more precisely, 'literature'. So the argument will be in part about paradigms as expressing political and cultural 'movements', but also about paradigms as expressing cultural barriers between traditions and roles. The 'reflective writing' course and the story-writing workshops described in earlier chapters are, precisely, attempts to remove the traditional cultural barrier between the activity of writing fiction and the activity of professional reflection.

As a starting point, then, let us review the general ideas embodied in the paradigm of the reflective practitioner (which from now on will be abbreviated to 'the reflective paradigm'). Schön begins his book with an account of what he calls a 'crisis of confidence in professional knowledge' (Schön 1983: ch. 1), a loss of faith in the conventional model of knowledge as 'technical rationality' (p. 29), where professional practice was conceived as posing technical problems that could be 'solved' by the 'application' of 'scientific knowledge' (p. 22). What had caused this loss of faith was a realisation that professional events are characterised by 'complexity, uncertainty, instability, uniqueness and value conflict' (p. 18). The model of technical rationality, therefore, does not account for the actual experience of effective professional work, which typically includes making sense of uncertainty, setting problems (as well as solving them), and – generally – performing in a way which is not so much scientific as 'artistic' (p. 20). Thus, instead of simply applying predefined theories, professionals must 'reflect in action' (p. 69): 'the unique and uncertain situation comes to be understood through the attempt to change it, and changed through the attempt to understand it' (p. 132). But if the situation is unique, how does the practitioner make use of previous experience? And if understanding a situation involves changing it, how is 'understanding' to be evaluated? The scientific logic of controlled experiment clearly will not fit (p. 132); instead Schön refers, repeatedly, to reflection-in-action as embodying 'the artistry' of practice (p. 162, and a further eleven lines of references in the index under 'Artistry') and presents what he later calls a 'constructionist' model of the relationship between knowledge and experience:

> In the constructionist view, our preceptions, appreciations and beliefs
> are rooted in worlds of our own making that we come to *accept* as reality.
> (Schön 1987: p. 36)

The 'epistemological' crisis of confidence in professional knowledge thus arises because we no longer have a simple belief in an 'objective' world of facts which could resolve disagreements of opinion and interpretation: as professional workers we have to recognise our fundamental underlying subjectivity. Our expertise is not directly guaranteed by our mastery of a body of scientific knowledge, and we do not make decisions on the basis of simply following rules; instead we have to rely on 'appreciating and reframing' the details of experience in order to invoke the relevance of previous 'cases' (Schön 1987: pp. 132, 138).

In arguing against the scientific model of rationality, Schön emphasises the tacit, intuitive basis to expert knowledge. The general argument is quite familiar: in order to follow any given rule or instruction we always need further understandings which the rule itself doesn't give (Wittgenstein 1967: pp. 39–42). We are reminded of this, often with some annoyance, every time we try to assemble a piece of furniture from a kit, using the manufacturer's instruction sheet: it always seems as though some crucial piece of information has been omitted – until we 'suddenly see how to do it', at which point, in retrospect, the meaning of the instruction becomes clear! As Polanyi says:

> The practical interpretation of a definition must rely *all the time* on its *undefined* understanding by the person relying on it.
>
> (Polanyi 1962: p. 250)

Applying knowledge in a particular case, therefore, is always an act of interpretation.

However, the reflective paradigm not only emphasises that understanding relies on personal, intuitive awareness, but that this awareness needs to be made explicit in order that we may go beyond it, following Vygotsky's familiar contention that verbalisation is part of the creative development of understanding (Vygotsky 1962). This aspect is announced at the beginning of the other seminal text of the reflective paradigm, conceived at the same time as, but independently of Schön's work: *Reflection: Turning Experience into Learning* (Boud *et al.* 1985):

> Reflection in the context of learning is a generic term for those intellectual and affective activities in which individuals engage to explore their experiences in order to lead to new understandings and appreciations.
>
> (p. 19)

'Experience' here refers to 'the total response of a person to a situation', and 'reflection' includes 'affective' activity in attempting to recapture that experience and thus to evaluate and learn from it (pp. 18–19). In other words, the conception of reflection in Boud's work includes an important emphasis on the whole person, including the affective domain.

The reflective paradigm of adult learning, then, announces a renewed emphasis on the individual as a *maker* of meanings, on the individual's capacity to construct new patterns of significance in response to the complexities of experience. In thus evoking the creative and critical autonomy of the individual, it clearly carries political implications as well as a set of suggestions for effective learning. This political dimension is explicit from the outset in Schön's account of how the reflective paradigm transforms the client/professional relationship (and the relationship between colleagues in work organisations) from one in which expertise is projected and accepted (a model of authority and compliance) to a negotiated relationship, in which trust is earned through public discussion of available choices and responsibility is accepted on both sides of the transaction. More generally, the demystification of technical rationality and the recognition of reflection as the basis for understanding are necessary for the secure establishment of the democratic process (Schön 1983: pp. 226–31; ch. 10, esp. p. 342).

It is this aspect of the reflective paradigm which receives particular emphasis in the influential work of Jack Mezirow and his colleagues, whose book *Fostering Critical Reflection in Adulthood* is subtitled 'A guide to transformative and emancipatory learning' (1990). In his introductory chapter, Mezirow distinguishes between 'instrumental learning' (characteristic of the natural sciences) where the purpose is to 'control and manipulate the environment or other people' (p. 8), and 'communicative learning' – i.e. 'understanding the meaning of what other people communicate concerning values, ideas, moral decisions and such concepts as freedom, justice, love, labour, autonomy, commitment and democracy' (p. 8). Thus, whereas in instrumental learning we attempt to encompass the object of our learning within our own categories and experimental procedures, communicative learning entails the *exchange* of ideas and reasons between autonomous beings, each with a different scheme of meanings:

> In communicative learning … the learner attempts to understand what is meant by another person, through speech, writing, drama, art or dance.
>
> (p. 9)

And if we succeed in communicating effectively, we can learn from each other's different, unfamiliar interpretations of reality (p. 9), allowing our perspectives to be transformed by discussion, so that we become more 'inclusive' and more 'integrative' with respect to others' ideas (p. 14). '*Nonreflective* learning', Mezirow suggests, involves accepting or rejecting claims that something or other is valid, 'without discursive consideration' (p. 10). 'Critical reflection', in contrast, is an 'emancipatory', 'transformative' process whereby we overcome the limitations of our thoughts and attitudes by subjecting our underlying presuppositions to challenge and reassessment in the light of alternatives derived from critical dialogue with others (p. 18). In this way we can correct the 'distortions' in our meaning schemes derived from social ideologies (e.g. prejudice, rigid categorisations) and from unconscious psychic processes (pp. 15–17).

To sum up: this brief review of the key texts suggests that the reflective paradigm can be understood in terms of the following themes:

1   The reflective paradigm asserts the origins of understanding in the totality of personal experience rather than in the specialised bodies of knowledge institutionalised as 'disciplines'.

2   It emphasises that the development of understanding involves emotional and unconscious psychic processes – not merely the cognitive and logical processing of factual information.

3   It emphasises that theoretical understanding is derived from a response to the complexities of experience – rather than prescribing in advance the interpretation we are to place upon experience.

4   It emphasises that understanding is never final, but always in process of development, through introspection and through interaction with others.

5   It emphasises that the proper exercise of authority based on professional expertise involves recognising the contribution to one's professional understanding made by clients (students, patients, service users, organisational subordinates, etc.). The necessary partner of the reflective practitioner is the reflective client; both are to be conceived as reflective citizens in a participatory democracy.

The next section will elaborate the origins of these themes, partly by considering some of the theoretical writings frequently cited in the reflective paradigm texts, and partly by considering the social and political context in which these themes have recently and currently achieved a coherent historical relevance. Meanwhile, we have also noted a number of fleeting references and suggestions which imply that developmental reflection on experience not only requires the objective, cognitive and analytical procedures of 'science', but also the subjective, creative and appreciative processes characteristic of 'art'.

The reflective paradigm (II): theoretical and political context

Reflection and the construction of meaning

In order to get the concept of a 'paradigm' into perspective, and also for other reasons which should become clear shortly, it is important to remember that for Kuhn, the Mother and Father Of All Paradigm Shifts was Copernicus' proposal that the earth revolves round the sun, and not vice-versa. The critical response of the church to his work showed that radically new ideas in astronomy, like radically new ideas concerning anything else, can turn out to be full of political implications, because any existing definition of 'how things are', once it comes to be taken for granted as a background assumption, also comes to embody part of the overall structure of power relations in society. To question definitions and assumptions may thus be interpreted as a questioning of general aspects of cultural authority. Hence, there are political implications both in the reflective paradigm (as we have seen) and also (as we shall see) in the argument that the artistic paradigm of knowledge and understanding should play a part in professional reflection.

Copernicus' paradigm shift involved rejecting the basis for what had previously been accepted as an external religious authority regulating human affairs, and substituting instead the anxieties and the opportunities of individual human responsibility. (If the earth goes round the sun, rather than vice-versa, then God may not, after all, be watching closely over us with any clearly prescribed purpose, and humanity must accept the painful responsibilities of freedom.) All this has a direct link with the themes of the reflective paradigm in general (e.g. the creativity and autonomy of learning) and, in particular, with the rise of the concept of the artistic imagination, to be considered later. At the end of the eighteenth century Kant drew a specific analogy between his own philosophical proposals and the implications of Copernican astronomy. Kant's claim was that our ideas cannot be directly derived from objective facts of nature (because we can never have any evidence which is independent of those very same ideas) and so our ideas about the world can never have the direct authority of claiming to mirror the structure of Nature itself (Kant 1966 [1781–7]: p. xxxiii). Like Copernicus' revolution in astronomy, Kant's argument frees our thinking from being directly determined by an objective world, at the cost of undermining the authority of our concepts and interpretations. Hence Mary Warnock refers to:

> The Kantian Copernican revolution, according to which we must regulate the world by our own concepts before we can learn the regularities of the world, and according to which we could not even perceive the world of objects unless we constituted it first by our own schematism of the imagination.
>
> (Warnock 1976: p. 126)

This Kantian/Copernican revolution is an important element in the reflective paradigm, as we have already seen: the individual as a creative 'meaning maker' is asserted against a model of learning which suggests that the structures of thought are already 'there' – to be acquired and used. To begin with, therefore, the reflective paradigm rejects behaviourist psychology, with its implicit suggestion that human beings can in principle be understood as predictable objects, using similar methods to those of natural science. Instead, the reflective paradigm emphasises the creativity of human subjectivity: experience is not simply a succession of 'actions' or 'behaviours' which can be directly 'observed', but a complex process including unconscious residues from long-forgotten events. 'Understanding' therefore requires more than observation; it requires us to engage in a process of introspection leading to self-clarification. Hence the frequent references, in the reflective paradigm texts, to Kelly's 'personal construct' psychology (Kelly 1955) focusing on 'the whole person' as a source of categories for interpreting individual experience. Hence, also, the influence within the reflective paradigm of the ideas of Carl Rogers, who suggests that, in order to be 'effective', education needs to be redefined in terms of 'becoming an authentic autonomous person' and overcoming one's defensive fears in order to engage in exploring the meanings of one's experience (Rogers 1983: pp. 279–88).

In some respects, these ideas go back a long way, at least as far as the work of John Dewey, one of the most widely acknowledged precursors of the reflective paradigm. Dewey is generally associated with the movement for 'progressive' school education in the United States in the 1920s and 1930s, which opposed a traditional pedagogy in which 'what is taught is thought of as essentially static ... a finished product ... [as] imposed from above and from outside' (Dewey 1963 [1938]: pp. 18–19). Instead, Dewey proposes an educational process in which the individual's experience undergoes 'progressive' enrichment and developmental organisation (1963: ch. 3, ch. 7). The reflective paradigm is, of course, a model for *adult* education, and its emphasis on the role of experience in learning specifically invokes not only Dewey but Kolb's universally quoted 'experiential learning cycle', shown in Figure 7.1.

Kolb also emphasises that learning is a 'holistic' process (p. 31) involving 'transformation of experience' (p. 38) and 'creation of knowledge' (p. 36). However, there is an ambiguity here which has an important bearing on the overall argument, and thus needs clarification. In spite of the emphasis on an 'open', creative, developmental dialectic involving the whole of personal experience, including unconscious affective dimensions, there remains an apparent emphasis on a 'rationalistic', cognitive model of reflection based on the experimental testing of concepts (see the wording in the Kolb model in Figure 7.1). This ambiguity is there in Schön's original book. Schön makes frequent references to the 'artistry' of practice, and most of his references to 'science' are made in order to stress that scientific method does not provide an adequate

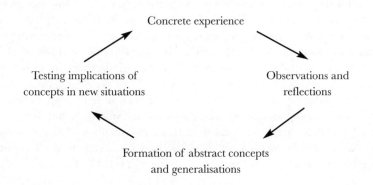

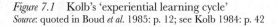

Figure 7.1   Kolb's 'experiential learning cycle'
Source: quoted in Boud *et al.* 1985: p. 12; see Kolb 1984: p. 42

understanding of professional reflection; but when he describes in detail the reflective process he uses terms derived precisely from the vocabulary of scientific inquiry: 'experimentation', 'exploratory experiment', 'hypothesis testing', and the testing of 'moves' (as in 'game theory'), to see whether the move is 'affirmed or 'negated' by the 'outcome' (Schön 1983: pp. 140–56). In this sense, Schön's argument does not seem to move much beyond a purely cognitive, analytical conception of 'reflection'. It is therefore much narrower in its scope than the work of Boud *et al.*, whose collection includes several chapters emphasising that reflection may also involve an interactive process, and is thus dependent on factors such as trust and freedom in dialogue (see for example Knights 1985). (In Schön's own later collection of examples (Schön 1991) he includes chapters on 'organising feelings' (Hirschhorn 1991) and on the use of stories (Mattingly 1991).

Let us, then, examine the place of 'experimental' thinking in the reflective paradigm. Like so much else in the reflective paradigm it has its roots in the work of John Dewey; but Dewey's basic argument is not so much about an opposition between, on the one hand 'science' (as a purely cognitive mode of knowing) and 'art' (as including 'the whole person'), but about elitism and empowerment, i.e. about the *politics* of knowledge. Dewey's thinking about educational processes and about the methods of science was always inseparable from his thinking about democracy. On the one hand he saw the free interchange of ideas characteristic of the experimental method in the natural sciences as inherently 'democratic' (Dewey 1966 [1916]: p. v) because it means that beliefs are not accepted as 'fixed by authority' (p. 339) but as always open to revision (p. 219). On the other hand he emphasised that 'scientific method' (i.e. hypothesis testing and experiment) is embodied in the problem-solving and interpretation of experience carried out by ordinary citizens in the course of their everyday lives (Dewey 1960 [1933]: pp. 166–8). In other words, he presents 'experience *as* experimentation' (1966: p. 271). 'Thinking' is precipitated by an experience which makes us aware of a 'problem' – of ambiguities, dilemmas and alternatives – and thereby forces us through 'perplexity' into 'reflection' (1960: p. 14). So Dewey anticipates the 'empowerment' theme in the reflective paradigm by attempting to 'demystify' the potentially exclusive notion of 'scientific method': he treats it not as the rare prerogative and mysterious expertise of an elite ('scientists') but as describing a mental activity in which we all, simply as human beings, already participate, especially if we are given the right support, stimulation and encouragement. This is a particularly important argument, since, as we shall see later, it is equally relevant to another potentially exclusive and elitist notion – 'art' – and Dewey himself proposes the same argument in that context also (see 'From "literature" to "storying experience" ', p. 206).

The politics of reflection

This brings us to the specifically 'political' dimension of the reflective paradigm, namely its concern for what Mezirow *et al.* (1990) calls 'emancipatory' learning. The two writers most frequently cited in support of this theme are Habermas and Freire. Habermas stresses the importance of the distinction between the different 'cognitive interests' served by the pursuit of different forms of knowledge. Thus he distinguishes between the 'practical' interest of simply 'understanding' the variety of our fellow human beings' interpretations of experience and the 'emancipatory ... interest which aims at the pursuit of reflection' in the search for 'autonomy and responsibility' (1978: pp. 176, 198). For this we need to engage 'critically' with those aspects of our understanding which preserve our dependency on power relations, ideologies and neuroses (1974: p. 9). 'Reflection' thus requires forms of communication which embody the democratic ideals shared by philosophy, politics and education, namely that they must be freed from the distorting effects of power relations:

> Only in an emancipated society, which had realised the autonomy of its members, would communication have developed into that free dialogue of all with all which we always hold up as the very paradigm of a mutually formed self-identity as well as the ideal conditions of true consensus. To this extent the truth of statements is based on the anticipation of a life without repression.
>
> (Habermas 1970: p. 50)

In the absence of this ideal, we live within various forms of power relationship which are oppressive precisely because they limit the freedom of dialogue and thereby distort and undermine 'the truth of statements'.

The attraction of Freire's work is that he claims to provide a practical realisation of Habermas' ideal. He describes in detail how an adult literacy programme for Brazilian peasants was effective as a broadly conceived educational process even under conditions of severe political oppression; and the enduring and widespread appeal of his work for writers within the reflective paradigm suggests that, in an important sense, the educational and political plight of Freire's peasants touches a chord in all of us. For Freire, a passive model of learning is one of the key aspects of an oppressive social order which prevents the development of the 'creative powers' and 'critical awareness' needed to transform a world which deeply requires transformation (Freire 1972a: pp. 46–7). What is needed, says Freire, is a model of learning which is 'problem-posing' (p. 57), and 'authentic' (p. 66) precisely because it is 'dialogical' (p. 59) and involves non-hierarchical 'cooperation' (p. 135ff.). Thus teaching adults to read and write is not merely a matter of transmitting technical skills but a process of working with them to 'reflect critically' on their experience (1972b:

p. 33), through the negotiation of its key 'contradictions' and 'generative themes' (1972a: pp. 68, 69):

> The important thing, from the point of view of libertarian education is for men [*sic*] to come to feel like masters of their thinking by discussing the thinking and views of the world explicitly or implicitly manifest in their own suggestions and those of their comrades.
>
> (Freire: 1972a: p. 95)

The current historical relevance of the reflective paradigm

This brief review of the theoretical origins of the reflective paradigm shows that its underlying themes were already quite familiar by the early 1980s. Indeed, Schön himself had already published his ideas in 1971. So we need to ask, what it is about the recent political and historical context of adult and professional education which has fostered so readily and so intensely a sense of the renewed relevance of these themes – the assertion of creativity and autonomy against compliance, the assertion of experiential holism (including the emotions) against purely conceptual analysis, and the assertion of empowerment and dialogue against the hierarchical exercise of cultural power. A tentative answer may be given which, although certainly incomplete and highly simplified, at least brings into view the beginnings of an important parallel between the historical position of the professional worker in the 1980s and the position of the artist in modern society, namely a stance of defensiveness (of what are felt to be crucial values) in response to a sense that in society at large those values have been rejected or lost.

In general terms, then, the reflective paradigm represents the response of certain key professions to finding themselves, quite suddenly, in the 1980s, in an embattled position. For Talcott Parsons, in the 1950s, professional work embodied the general application to social affairs both of scientific rationality and of altruism, giving professional work a substantial sense of cognitive and moral authority (Parsons 1954). There were, of course, critical voices questioning this authority, and this is indeed the starting point for Schön's work (see Schön 1983: ch. 1). But, overall, the rise of a 'welfare state' (in Europe) and the adoption of various social policies which combined to form what has been called a 'semi-welfare state' in the USA (see Roche 1992: p. 82) institutionalised a number of professions in a position which provided for its members a very clear sense of cultural authority. As teachers, nurses, doctors, social workers, local government officials, etc., our social role was expressed in terms of general values (concerning care and the promotion of welfare) and individual responsibility for interpreting how these values were to be realised (justly and equitably) in particular cases. But the 1980s saw a powerful political attack upon the welfare state as the key to social justice. Instead of a welfare state staffed by 'caring' professionals representing 'values', there was to be a 'market in the provision of services', where the key task was the efficient management of resources. And if professional work was to be 'managed', the lessons of Frederick Taylor's advice to industrial managers seventy years earlier (see Braverman 1974: ch. 4) needed to be applied: professional knowledge needed to be 'codified' (in terms of 'competences' and official 'codes of practice') so that individual workers could be held accountable to corporately defined goals and procedures. Thus the late 1980s saw professional staff beginning to experience a sense of having their autonomy reduced, their decision-making mechanised, their expertise fragmented and their 'artistry' abolished (see Field 1991; Norris 1991; Avis *et al.* 1996).

Behind this experience of devaluation, deskilling and alienation lay a massive economic shift. Whereas previously Keynesian welfare economics had emphasised the positive economic benefits of public expenditure, 'monetarist' economic policies defined public expenditure as never anything but a regrettable distortion of idealised market forces. At the same time, advances in information technology and the removal of national restraints on the movement of capital led to a global 'vicious circle of competitive austerity' (Albo 1994: p. 147) as all economies were forced to try to match the lowest cost levels achieved anywhere in the world, even where profitability was being achieved at the expense of workers' health and human rights. For professional workers, this meant (and means) that professional artistry and value commitments are further threatened by the simple fact that staffing levels and all other resources for meeting the needs of clients are continually being reduced, creating an ever widening gap between what budgets make available and what professional judgement would propose as desirable. Thus Palmer, introducing his collection *Reflective Practice in Nursing*, writes:

'Reflective practice' [is] a means for addressing the alienation [brought about by] the high speed manner in which nurses are expected to care for their patients. ... Today's nurses, more than at any other time, are faced with an increasing obligation to evaluate and improve their practice [and yet] nursing in our present climate often does not appear to foster professional self-evaluation. ... The drive for efficiency and cost effectiveness ... often leaves little time for an individual nurse or group of nurses to reflect on their clinical practice.

(Palmer 1994: p. 1)

The reflective paradigm, then, is not merely about methods for effective professional education, but also about re-claiming and rescuing the professional values which are implicit in the structure of professional knowledge and in the methods of professional thinking. The reflective paradigm assembles its theoretical resources in order to defend professional values, creativity and autonomy in a context where they are generally felt to be under attack from political and economic forces which threaten to transform the professional from an artist into an operative. The notion of the reflective practitioner thus contains aspects of a heroic stance for the professional worker: the professional as an embattled fighter for the values of practice and for the rights of vulnerable clients (students, patients, etc.) against 'un-caring' bureaucracy and discriminatory cultural attitudes, and thus, implicitly, against the distorted values and priorities of an unjust society. Such themes, of course, fit perfectly into the structures of fictional narrative, and indeed we see myths of the professional-as-hero enacted every evening on our TV screens – countless episodes in which compassion is rescued from red-tape and truth from corruption and concealment, by doctors, nurses, journalists, pathologists, lawyers, vets, even ambassadors, and – above all, of course – by police officers.

Reflection, postmodernism and the crisis of 'truth'

But all this, although appealing and entertaining, is of course very one-sided and somewhat suspicious. 'Pity the land where heroes are needed', says Brecht's Galileo (*The Life of Galileo*, scene 13), and myths are the expression of a cultural problem – the fantasy resolution of some sort of contradiction (Lévi-Strauss 1981: p. 603). So what is the contradiction inherent in this profoundly appealing image of the reflective practitioner as mythic cultural hero, struggling against external circumstances and social authority for authenticity, rationality, artistry, autonomy and truth? Basically the contradiction is that, as professional workers we are ourselves authority figures. There is thus an irony in celebrating our struggle against external authority (bureaucratic procedures, managerial imposition, routinised theoretical curricula, 'science', 'technical rationality') in order to assert our own individualised, personal authority for making decisions affecting others' lives. Because the same arguments which undermine the basis for external prescriptive authority also question the conceptions of 'authentic' personhood, 'free' experimentation and 'undistorted' modes of communication which the reflective paradigm proposes: for example, where shall we seek the criteria for judging that this communication here, now, *is* 'free', 'undistorted', 'authentic'? For our clients and our students, and even for ourselves, we as practitioners also represent a cultural authority whose basis has become unclear. The crisis of legitimate authority thus runs deeper than we have so far admitted, involving a lack of certainty concerning the basis of 'valid' knowledge in general and thus the basis for professional work itself.

The term which has been used over the last few years to refer to this very general level of philosophical and cultural uncertainty is 'postmodernism', and its particular relevance for our argument is that it emphasises, among other things, the limitations of purely rational, analytical knowledge and focuses instead on the significance of aesthetic, artistic modes of understanding. The postmodernist thesis explicitly denies that we can, any longer, have faith in the 'grand historical narratives' of modernism, i.e. those which proclaim progress, through history, towards the realisation of emancipation, truth, justice or reason (Lyotard 1984). Postmodernists argue that meaning is determined within the overall terms of a 'discourse' or a 'language game' (*ibid.*: p. 15) and, consequently, that all these key ideas (truth, justice, freedom, etc.) merely have different meanings within different cultural contexts. There can be no simple 'progress towards' truth, justice etc, because there can be no universal discourse which can prescribe a general consensus about their meaning. Instead, any agreements (about the meaning of truth, justice, etc.) must be negotiated pragmatically and for the time being, on the basis of perceived interests and localised norms (pp. 60–1, p. 66). Conceptions of justice are thus limited both in time and space (p. 66), what is acceptable as truth depends on the distribution of wealth and power (p. 45), and we cannot even have confidence that we can 'represent' reality but must be content with what we know to be mere tentative 'allusions' (p. 81).

Although such arguments are currently influential (see Jameson 1998), many would argue that they go too far, pushing legitimate doubt over the edge into incoherence and self-contradiction (see Eagleton 1996). But for professional workers wishing to assert the values inherent in their role, the postmodernist argument certainly raises a crucial question: how can we seriously exercise our responsibilities if we cannot even be sure how to frame our questions, our goals or our interpretive categories? Indeed, it is exactly this form of radical self-questioning which is at the centre of several of the papers in two recent volumes on reflective practice and reflective learning in the social work profession (Yelloly and Henkel 1995; Gould and Taylor 1996), and the concluding chapter of the latter uses postmodernism as its organising theme:

> Reflective learning may be conceptualised as a response to postmodernism, as a positive and creative approach to the prospect of living with contingency … variety, relativism and ambivalence.
>
> (Taylor 1996: pp. 159, 156)

As Taylor suggests, arguments which question the universal basis of rationality should not lead us to mere scepticism, but they do return us to what we have already seen as one of the central ambiguities in the reflective paradigm: on the one hand reflection has been presented as a process of emancipatory reason – liberating the intellects of learners to reconstruct for themselves the meaning of experience through hypothesis-testing, mental experimentation and conceptualisation; on the other hand, reflection is seen as involving the whole person, including emotional awareness, unconscious dynamics, the narrative of experiential growth, and the search for 'artistry'. The postmodernist rejection of a universal rationality brings these two aspects of the reflective paradigm together, suggesting that artistic and pragmatic criteria are not simply the 'enemy' of reason, but helpful collaborators in the processes of reason itself: reason is only undone if it places all its faith in the authority of facts and concepts, attempting to exclude emotion, context and motive, and ignoring artistic modes of understanding. Hence Lyotard conducts much of his argument against Habermas' proposal that democratic emancipation can have the form of a consensus guided only by 'the force of the better argument' (Habermas 1976: p. 108). And in his 'Postscript' he presents the 'concept' of postmodernism largely in terms of the work of painters and novelists (pp. 79–81). In other words, Lyotard concludes his 'Report on knowledge' in terms of a theory of art.

Exactly how theories of art can contribute to our understanding of 'reflection' is the theme of the remainder of this chapter, but by way of preparation it is interesting to see just how clearly and directly the basis of our argument is expressed by one of the most generally influential of contemporary philosophers, Richard Rorty. In *Contingency, Irony, Solidarity* he argues that the social 'solidarity' of democratic values is encapsulated in one key principle: avoiding cruelty to others (Rorty 1989). But this commitment cannot be justified through a purely philosophical analysis, since all analysis is 'contingent', i.e. dependent on the norms and values of particular cultures and the languages which embody them. One can (and should) make moral and political commitments, but this must be combined with an 'ironic' sense that our commitments are always 'contingent', and are thus always open to question from within other systems of meaning. Hence, the suggestion that one should avoid cruelty to others can only be represented in a persuasive form – e.g. through evocative descriptions which promote empathy with others' suffering. Any attempt to present it in a form which claimed absolute validity (based on 'philosophical' analysis or 'scientific' evidence) would be prescriptive, and would thus carry, in itself, the risk of political oppression and consequently a further round of 'cruelty' (Rorty 1989: pp. xv, 46, 61, 196). And the form of representation which combines commitment, irony and empathy is 'poetry' (p. 61) and fiction:

> Human solidarity ... is to be achieved not by inquiry but by imagination, the imaginative ability to see strange people as fellow suffers. This process of coming to see other human beings as 'one of us' rather than as 'them' is a matter of detailed description of what unfamiliar people are like and of redescription of what we ourselves are like. This is a task not for theory but for genres such as ethnography, the journalist's report ... and especially the novel. ... The novel, the movie and the TV program have, gradually but steadily, replaced the sermon and the treatise as the principal vehicles of moral change and progress. In my liberal utopia this replacement ... would be part of a general turn against theory and toward narrative.
>
> (Rorty 1989: p. xvi)

Rorty thus makes explicit and central a theme which is exemplified in the work presented in the earlier chapters of this book but which is, as we have seen, only implicit and peripheral in most writings of the reflective paradigm. And this is the theme to which we now turn directly: the development of understanding by means of an analytical process grounded in an 'aesthetic' shaping of experience; empathy, sensitivity and ironic self-awareness achieved through the imagination and embodied in fictions.

Reflection and the 'shaping spirit of imagination'

The general significance of the artistic imagination and of 'aesthetic' judgements

It takes no great effort of mental agility to see the links between the key elements of the reflective paradigm, as described so far, and what we know as 'imagination'. Imagination is a pivotal term here, because it has both a very general meaning (which can easily be located in the process of reflecting on experience) and a much more specific one (which takes us straight to the heart of artistic creativity).

In its general meaning it refers to the ability – characteristic of all human minds, and probably the minds of other mammals too – to go beyond, in some sense, what is directly present to our senses. What we experience in our minds is always an interpretation of what we see and hear, which thus creates a space of freedom: our thoughts are not mechanically determined by the immediate inputs of our senses. Neither are we determined by past experiences. The term 'imagination' is linked with the idea that our memories are stocked with images of remembered events, but we can manipulate these images almost at will: we can conjure them up in sequences and combinations quite different from how they originally occurred, and we can create images of events that never happened. It is the imagination which enables us to generalise from immediate fragments of experience by reviewing the relationship between this, here and now, and other experiences with which it might in some way be linked. It is thus the imagination which allows us to classify experiences in the first place as well as to explore alternative ways of classifying them (Warnock 1976: p. 28). Hence Gareth Morgan, writing about 'creative organisational management', uses the term 'imaginization' to describe the process of improving 'our ability to see and understand situations in new ways' and of 'finding new images' with which to interpret events and situations (Morgan 1993: pp. 2–10).

But the imagination is more than an ability to make links and associations; it refers to a creative capacity (Coleridge 1960 [1817]: p. 167). There are two typical activities of the imagination which provide its creative power. First, 'it reconciles opposites or discordant qualities', i.e. it plays with the question of what is 'the same' and what is 'different' (*ibid.*: p. 174). Hence the imagination creates 'metaphorical' links between things and situations (Morgan 1993: p. 1). For example, a school or a hospital or a social services agency can be seen as, in interesting ways, 'the same as' a culture, or an organism, or a mechanism, or a political system or even a hologram, in which each component part embodies the structure of the whole (Morgan 1993: pp. 5, 9). Koestler (1964) uses the term 'bisociation' (bringing disparate frames of reference to bear on a single phenomenon) to describe the acts of creative imagination involved not only in scientific discovery and artistic production but in the everyday activity of telling and understanding jokes (pp. 35ff.). Second, the imagination finds general significance in particular concrete experiences (Coleridge 1960: p. 174). The imagination is 'something working actively from within, to enable us to perceive the general in the particular, to make us treat the particular ... as symbolic, as meaning something beyond itself' (Warnock 1976: pp. 53–4). In these various ways, the imagination can be thought of as lying at the root of human beings' existential freedom. We are always free, ultimately, in the sense that every act of perception involves the capacity to imagine the world as possibly different (Sartre 1972 [1940]: pp. 213–15). Alan White puts it the other way round: 'To imagine something is to think of it as possibly being so' (White 1990: p. 184). But for both writers the imagination, so to speak, intervenes between the inputs of our experience and our mental processes, ensuring that our thoughts are not simply determined and predictable, and giving us the capacity for autonomous judgement.

But when Coleridge laments that he is losing his 'shaping spirit of imagination' (Coleridge, *Dejection: An Ode*, line 86) he is not, of course, complaining that he is losing his autonomy as a human being but that he is losing his ability to write poetry. This brings us back to the second, more restricted meaning of 'imagination', namely the creative capacity of the artist. This in turn introduces our main argument: that artistic creativity and aesthetic modes of judgement are not the preserve of a rare and special type of person ('artists') but a universal capacity, and that they need to be included as a central component of reflection on experience.

In order to begin this argument we need, first of all, to pause on the term 'aesthetic'. According to the dictionary, 'aesthetic' has two quite different meanings, which offer a significant parallel to the two meanings of 'imagination'. The word 'aesthetic' is derived from the Greek word for 'things perceptible to the senses', and so it originally referred to 'the whole region of human perception and sensation, in contrast to the more rarified domain of conceptual thought' (Eagleton 1990: p. 13). To focus on 'the realm of the aesthetic' is thus to focus on lived experience (feelings, desires, aversions, etc.) a rejection of 'the tyranny of the theoretical' (*ibid.*). However, in the currently more familiar sense of the term, 'the aesthetic' means 'pertaining to the appreciation or criticism of the beautiful; having or showing ... good taste' (*Shorter Oxford English Dictionary*). Why on earth, one feels like exclaiming, should one word refer both to the whole of our sensuous experience in such an apparently general and inclusive way and yet also to the making of certain types of rather specialised discriminatory judgements ('beautiful', 'tasteful')?

To answer this question we will need to consider in detail the link between 'experience', 'judgement', 'taste' and 'the beautiful', and we will discover that it is not such a strange assortment of terms as one might initially presume. The link between them is precisely the general issue addressed by Kant in his *Critique of Judgement* (1987 [1790]). Kant's fundamental concern in the *Critique of Judgement* is what we have already seen to be one of the central themes of the reflective paradigm: how do we make and explain our decisions when the one thing we know is that our knowledge has no guarantee of certainty? 'Judgement', says Kant, 'is the ability to think the particular under the universal' (p. 18). If our judgements start from universals in order to deduce particulars (as in solving a mathematical problem for example) then our judgements are 'determinative', i.e. determined, prescribed in advance by a system of axioms and logical operations. 'But if only the particular is given and judgement has to find the universal for it, then [judgement] is merely reflective ['reflektierend']' (pp. 18–19). (He says 'merely' because reflective judgements lack the absolute certainty of judgements deduced from universal rules.) 'Reflective judgement', then, is the process of finding general reasons/explanations/interpretations for the particularities of human experience in those situations for which there are no pre-given universal rules. Such situations, clearly, include most of those we meet in our everyday and professional lives (the general argument anticipates Schön's distinction between 'technical rationality' and 'reflection').

This basic human activity of reflective judgment has close parallels with the general cognitive role of the imagination (Kant 1987: p. 182): it represents our ability to find an objective orderliness in our experience by projecting onto the natural world the cognitive structure of our own minds (p. 19). And since this orderliness is indeed a projection of our own minds *onto* the world (rather than a set of objective facts about the world) we experience a specific sense of satisfaction and pleasure when we find apparent empirical confirmation for our thinking, i.e. when an experience or a group of experiences suddenly falls into place as forming an ordered unity (pp. 23–7). Mary Warnock ends her analysis of imagination by echoing Kant in celebrating the importance of such moments of insight: it is at such moments, she says, that we feel, intensely, the value of our experience through our power to understand it in ways which go beyond our merely subjective impressions (Warnock 1976: pp. 206–7). Our sense of elation at such moments, one might suggest, also following Kant, comes from a sudden, creative sense of being 'at one with' the universe. At such moments, says James Joyce, an experience takes on a sort of radiant clarity, as we grasp a sense of its underlying structure and integrity (Joyce 1956 [1916]: pp. 216–17).

But back to Kant. Having asserted, at the outset, this general argument about the nature of reflective judgement, Kant then devotes nearly three-quarters of his main text to considering the nature of 'taste' and 'the beautiful'. So why does Kant (whose concern, as a philosopher, is the conceptual structure of human knowledge) see questions of taste and beauty as playing such a key role in the operation of reflective judgement in general? But, again, it is not so surprising after all. Checking once more with the dictionary, 'beautiful' simply means 'giving pleasure to the senses or the intellect'. So one could quite properly describe those pleasurable moments of reflective insight just described as moments when we appreciate something (any object or experience) as 'beautiful'.

And this does indeed correspond with our usage. There can be beautiful sounds, beautiful aromas, beautiful views; beautiful faces, beautiful arguments in philosophy and beautiful proofs in mathematics, beautiful passes and goals in football and beautiful phrases spoken at moments of interpersonal tension by lovers or by nurses, teachers and social workers; beautiful prayers, poems, stories, paintings, churches, songs and string quartets; beautiful pebbles, beautiful wallpaper and beautiful spots for a picnic. Beauty, then, is a general mode of judgement in which we can (potentially) appreciate the quality of almost any experience.

But what, specifically, does the judgement of beauty mean? First, it is important to note that to say something is beautiful is more than saying 'I like it'. To say that something is beautiful is to make a claim for it which I could try to justify. It is a judgement to which I make a commitment and would try to elaborate in order to convince others if they disagreed (Kant 1987: p. 54). There can be an interesting discussion about whether something is or is not beautiful, albeit probably an inconclusive one. In contrast, I happen to like peanut butter sandwiches and corduroy jackets but I wouldn't wish to claim that they are 'beautiful', since I recognise that they are purely a personal preference and I therefore have not the slightest reason for engaging in a discussion to try to persuade anyone to agree with me. Second, to say that something is beautiful is not to make a practical judgement or one based on our own personal interests or desires. It would seem like a total misuse of words or a misunderstanding if I were to expain why I think a particular house is beautiful by saying that it looks as though it would be nice and warm in winter and well ventilated in the summer, or that it is very conveniently situated for where I work. Judgements of beauty transcend the merely practical and the merely personal (*ibid.*: pp. 53, 58) and for that reason they are judgements which could be agreed by anyone (p. 54), i.e. even if they were interested in different practical issues and had different personal motives.

Similarly with questions of 'taste', Kant's other main focus. Because, again, matters of taste are more than merely personal inclinations but, rather, judgements with which we hope others will agree. And, moreover, they are social judgements, invoking cultural norms which claim general support for individual decisions. To say that something is 'in poor taste' is to say more than 'I don't like it'; it is to make a judgement that we think others ought to agree with. Indeed it even feels quite close to a moral judgement.

The terms 'beautiful' and 'tasteful', then, are a way of referring to a fundamentally significant feature of reflective judgements – their indeterminate quality. The reflective paradigm, as we have seen, specifically rejects the idea that professional judgement is the direct application of given rules. On the contrary, 'reflection' is open-ended, explorative, seeking possible and tentative generalities rather than prescriptions; it is responsive to the unpredictability of individual experience, seeking some sort of justifiable grounds while recognising that no final proofs are possible; it seeks objective reference points and principles while accepting that these are ultimately subjective and relative to a particular culture;

it recognises that no judgement is ever purely technical or conceptual, but always involves a combination of intellect, emotion, value commitment and politics. And it is precisely this vague but powerful combination of factors which is evoked when we engage in what Kant calls 'aesthetic' judgement. 'The aesthetic' is thus symptomatic of reflective judgement in general.

In some respects there is nothing new about the link between the realm of the aesthetic and the realm of professional reflection. We have already seen how Schön frequently argues against the technical model of professional thinking by evoking its 'artistry', and he quotes Coleridge's description of the act of reading a poem ('the willing suspension of disbelief') to evoke his conception of the professional/client relationship (Schön 1983: pp. 296, 363). Elliot Eisner argues that the work of schoolteachers needs to be understood in the same way as one appreciates paintings, through a form of 'connoisseurship' or 'art criticism' (Eisner 1985), and Hugh England responds to the recognition that social work practice cannot be grasped through the methods of social science by describing how the criteria for the evaluation of works of literature can be applied to the evaluation of social work (England 1986: pp. 119–23). However, the emphasis here is on artistic and literary *criticism*: instead of the authoritative institutions and disciplines of 'science', Eisner and England substitute the equally authoritative institutions of art and literature, from which criteria for the evaluation of professional experience are to be derived. Their arguments therefore miss the emphasis – so crucial within the reflective paradigm – that the basis for reflection is in the experience of the individual rather than in authoritative criteria provided by institutionalised knowledge. And although Maxine Greene's article 'Realising literature's emancipatory potential' (included as one of the 'key approaches' to critical reflection in the volume by Mezirow *et al.*, *1990*) emphasises the *creative* aspect of reading, she does not propose to involve practitioners in writing and sharing their own fictions, but merely to encourage the careful and committed reading of 'Great Literature' (Greene 1990).

We have to return, then, to our earlier problem. One of the key meanings of 'imagination' conventionally focuses on the typical activities of 'the poet' (Coleridge 1960: p. 173) or even 'the genius' (Schopenhauer 1995 [1819]: p. 110), and one of the meanings of 'the aesthetic' ('pertaining to the beautiful, to the criticism of taste') conventionally has distinct overtones of cultural elitism; and both of these run counter to the basic argument of this book, which seeks to define the imagination and the aesthetic in terms of a universal capacity for the creative interpretation and representation of human experience.

So far, in tracing this argument, we have largely followed Kant, but at this point it is important to distance ourselves from one aspect of his thinking. Kant's overall project (two hundred years ago) was to elucidate the structure of reason and of ethics in terms of universal and finally established concepts. But this is precisely what many recent philosophers have abandoned as in theory unsustainable (see references to postmodernism above). Thus, where Kant attempted to provide universal grounds for judgements of taste (e.g. 1987: pp. 89–90, p. 188), we would want to emphasise, now, that there are different 'sub-cultures', each of which would have different notions of what was 'tasteful' and what was 'over the top'. So, even though we still follow Kant in thinking that our judgements of taste and beauty are more than merely personal opinions, we now make them, as Rorty says, 'ironically', i.e. in full recognition that other social groups have different norms, concerns, and reasons. Our century has experienced (and continues to demonstrate) all too painfully the political dangers associated with attempts to enforce a total and unified conception of truth and justice, and we therefore emphasise a conception of moral and political order based on negotiated strategies for accepting and valuing cultural and political plurality (Mouffe 1993: p. 40).

Hence we tend to use the term 'style' alongside 'taste', as part of a recognition of differing 'lifestyles' within which a given choice may or may not be seen as 'tasteful' (i.e. 'stylish') or, alternatively, as 'naff'. Hence also the rapidly changing terms in which everyday judgements of beauty are made. Yes, there are beautiful spots for a picnic, beautiful jumpers and beautiful stories, but although we may perhaps hear the term 'beautiful' used in such contexts, we are equally (or more) likely to hear (at different times and in different places) 'super', 'brilliant', 'neat', 'absolutely fabulous', 'cool' or 'wicked'. The reason for such a plethora of terms and the speed with which they slip in and out of fashion may be not only a simple matter of cultural diversity but also linked with Kant's point that such judgements are, at the same time, highly significant, very indeterminate (i.e. vague), and extremely common. Words lose their precision with frequent usage, which is why language is constantly changing. Thus the rapid turnover in our vocabularies of aesthetic appreciation is in itself a testimony to their importance and their widespread use.

Literary creation as a process of reflection

So far, I have tried to establish a non-elitist conception of the function of aesthetic judgements. Let us now take the argument a stage further, and consider specifically the activity of artistic creation and see how some of the characteristic processes of the literary imagination can be understood in relation to professional reflection.

One important set of ideas has already been mentioned: the literary artist (like the reflective practitioner) brings together apparently disparate ideas, images and events, so as to create a generally significant structure of order from the flux and fragmentation of personal experience. This basic starting point – the artist as a constructor of individualised-but-generalisable meaning – is derived, as we have seen, from Kant and Coleridge, and it is historically specific in the sense that it expresses ideas characteristic of the European Romantic movement. But these ideas also continue to set the terms for contemporary understandings of the role and significance of art, since it was at that time, the beginning of the nineteenth century, that notions of 'art' and 'the artist' first achieved a degree of self-consciousness and popular currency. 'The aesthetic', says Eagleton, was 'the secret prototype of human subjectivity in early capitalist society' (Eagleton 1990: p. 9) and we continue to live in a society structured by capitalism, with its overwhelming emphasis on subjective experience, individuality and individual choice. This is expressed at one level in the general principle of competition, but, more importantly for our argument, by the sense that only individual experience can directly express ethical and spiritual values, since the broader social and politcial pattern of events is essentially driven by financial forces and principles from which values are excluded. This contrasts (in both respects) with 'traditional' society, where, first, the social order as a whole was divinely ordained and thus in itself was supposed to express spiritual and moral values; and second, individual identities were relatively non-problematic, being also divinely ordained and fixed at birth. Hence Giddens refers to 'the reflexive project of the self, which consists in the sustaining of coherent yet continuously revised biographical narratives' as the key characteristic of life in 'the post-traditional order of modernity' (Giddens 1991: p. 5). So, the combined implication of these two quotations (from Eagleton and Giddens) is as follows: the creative subjectivity of the artist, as formulated at the turn of the nineteenth century (often quite explicitly from Kantian theories of knowledge and reflection), continues to represent the nature of modern subjectivity in general: the individual as a creator – constructing meaning from the raw material of experience.

What was relatively new in the early nineteenth century conception of the artist may be summed up in two contrasting metaphors. On the one hand, the work of art as a mirror – on which light impinges to produce a reflection of nature – i.e. as an imitation of reality (the traditional model, ultimately derived from Aristotle's *Poetics*); on the other hand, the work of art as a lamp – an internal source of light, which by shining out upon the world produces a new image of reality which otherwise would not exist (Abrams 1953; Kearney 1988: p. 17). Clearly, the two images are not entirely incompatible, but at the end of the eighteenth century there was an important shift of emphasis: the artist no longer simply represents or imitates reality, but produces an original and personal interpretation. Here is an entry from Coleridge's notebooks:

> In looking at the objects of nature while I am thinking ... I seem to be seeking ... a symbolic language for something within me that already and forever exists ... as if that new phenomenon were the dim Awakening of a forgotten or hidden Truth of my inner Nature.
>
> (quoted in Warnock 1976: p. 83)

The creative process, then, is in part an act of self-exploration. As an example, we might think of Tolstoy's *Anna Karenina* as an apology or an atonement for the 'sins' of his own earlier life, where Vronsky (the seducer) is the self he now wishes to banish and Levin (contented husband, father, farmer) is the self he wishes to be, as Tolstoy makes explicit in his *Confession*, published two years later. Similarly, Jeannette Yems' commentary on her story 'Mary' in Chapter 2 makes it clear that in writing about her fictionalised client she is also writing about herself. There is thus a sense in which creating an artistic structure for experience can be 'therapeutic' – which is indeed, as we have seen, how many of the participants in our reflective writing courses refer to their writing (see Chapter 5: p. 155).

The idea that artistic production is a process of personal creation and exploration also follows closely from the idea that what is satisfying in a work of art is that it 'produces a balance or reconciliation of opposite or discordant qualities' (Coleridge 1960 [1817]: p. 174). This is partly a matter of seeing links between apparently unconnected matters or weaving varied events into an integrated pattern so that individual elements are illuminated from different points of view. As examples of this, see the summary of Naomi Ball's story 'Ignorance' in Chapter 1 and Julia Plunkett's story 'If only she knew' in Chapter 2. On a grander scale the point is illustrated by George Eliot's *Middlemarch*, which combines two main stories originally conceived quite separately (Ashton 1996: pp. 301–12).

This leads on to another important point. When a number of different situations are juxtaposed and set into a closely worked relationship within the unifying artistic structure, then the unity which emerges has a sort of generality, which is partly what the disparate elements share and partly the 'train of thought' started by the relationship between them. There are two sources for this sense that the product of artistic imagination has a general significance beyond the context it immediately refers to (unlike, say, a 'report' or a 'description'). First, it taps into a background mythology of universal themes: patterns of comedy or tragedy; heroes, villains, journeys of discovery, growing up, finding the right partner to fall in love with, solving a mystery, seeking justice, the relationship between dream and reality, sudden catastrophe, reversals of fate, the significance of death, and so on (Frye 1957; Propp 1968). Second, by embedding a concrete experience in an artistic structure, the imagination, as it were, converts it into a pattern of general significance, by revealing it as 'symbolic', making it seem representative of a whole category of experiences (Warnock 1976: pp. 68–9). The operation of this symbolic or mythological process is clearly illustrated by Jane Arnett's ghost story in Chapter 2, and even more clearly by the discussion of Muriel Lace's 'The journey' by her colleagues (also in Chapter 2).

In this way, the 'shaping spirit' of artistic imagination re-creates the individual experience as a potentially general experience, even though its 'meaning' can never be finally or completely formulated (Eagleton 1990: p. 94). The work of literature is at the same time theoretical (in the generality of its meaning) and ambiguous (inviting a variety of interpretations). Thus there is no doubt that Shakespeare's portrayal of the sequence of events leading up to the death of a medieval Danish prince, Hamlet, creates a sense of their general significance; otherwise it would be difficult to understand its continuing appeal to people quite remote in culture and experience from both the author and the events described. But is it a story of youthful idealistic rebellion against a corrupt social order? Or an example of the Oedipus complex in action (Freud's interpretation)? Or about the paralysis of effective action when it is preceded by too much speculation about possibilities? (And if it is about the latter, is the play sympathetic towards the hero, or critical?) Is it about sex, or about politics, or about knowledge? Its artistic structure enables it to be about all of these at once, as well as about the relationship between them. Returning to fictions with no pretension to being great literature, is Pamela Henderson's story 'Cakes and ale' (Chapter 2) optimistic or pessimistic about the social role of community theatre? And is it, indeed, about the social role of theatre or about gender roles?

This 'symbolic' quality which the artistic structure gives to particular events is both a sort of general truth and at the same time a sort of openness and undecidability. It gives a sense that these events have indeed been understood (by being placed within a generalisable pattern of meanings) and at the same time it gives a sense that any attempt at a final and complete interpretation of them is bound to be inadequate, because, in the end, actual events, people and situations are too complex, too multifaceted to be wholly contained within any formula. All of which, of course, echoes many of the key themes of the reflective paradigm for understanding the events of professional practice.

But all this is very intellectual. It misses out the emotional dimension of creating and appreciating artistic structures of meaning. In Coleridge's poem 'Dejection: An Ode', written in 1802, about his sense that he has lost his 'shaping spirit of imagination' he laments that he can see the beauties of nature, but he cannot feel them. The artistic imagination links the operation of the intellect with the operation of powerful feelings; indeed it is the powerful feelings which provide the force which enables us to perceive the symbolic significance of the particular (Warnock 1976: p. 81). By the same token, it is because a work of art creates a sense of general significance that we can identify emotionally with the characters and situations portrayed in films, novels and stories, and frequently do so, responding with tears, horror or jubilation (various readers have reported being moved to tears by some of the stories in Chapter 2). And Coleridge suggests that for the original creator it is the same: the power of the imagination comes from our ability to *feel* the symbolic significance of an experience.

On the other hand, the work of art does not simply *express* powerful emotions. It requires them to be present, but it goes beyond them. It transforms expressions of feeling into art. This transformative effect is particularly noticeable when the emotions are 'negative' – pain, fear, anger, horror. How can such feelings be incorporated into a work which aspires, insofar as it is art, to be beautiful? (we are especially familiar with this question as it applies to 'violent' films). Schopenhauer approaches the issue by asking how it is that we can find beauty in a wild and threatening landscape (Schopenhauer 1995 [1819]: pp. 124–9), and his answer is illuminating: a sense of 'exaltation' is experienced when we manage to triumph over immediate feelings of fear or horror aroused by specific objects and appreciate the 'ideas' which underly them (p. 125). This argument of Schopenhauer's allows us us to see more clearly the significance of the notion (mentioned earlier) that the aesthetic response is disinterested: in responding aesthetically to a phenomenon we find a pattern of meaning which transcends crude feelings of desire or hostility and crude practical motives, and attains a mode of 'contemplation', which is thus a sort of objectivity, a sort of 'truth' (pp. 131–2). And nearly 200 years later, Adorno, concerned with 'modern' rather than 'Romantic' art, specifically accepts Schopenhauer's view: 'Aesthetic experience – and this thought was already familiar to Schopenhauer – transcends the spell of mindless self-preservation, becoming the paradigm for a new stage of consciousness' (Adorno 1984: p. 475).

The 'detachment' of a work of art, then, is not just a process of intellectual abstraction but a form of emotional discipline. Schopenhauer calls it 'exaltation', Coleridge calls it 'joy' ('Dejection: An Ode', lines 64–75), and J. S. Mill calls it 'the imaginative emotion' which arises when we suddenly feel the 'intrinsic value' of our capacity to create meaning from our experience (Warnock 1976: pp. 206–7). One of the sources of this joy in the imaginative creation of meaning lies in the sense that it is an achievement, because it is the outcome of a struggle – a struggle to extend our sympathies and our understanding to experiences from which we may initially feel inclined to recoil. For example, the playwright Bertolt Brecht emphasises that his aim is to prevent the audience feeling an easy empathy with his characters; he wants to force the audience to weep at what appears at first to be comic and to laugh at what seems at first to be tragic (Brecht 1974: p. 71). From this point of view, the artistic success of Irvine Welsh's *Trainspotting* (1993) is that he enables us to appreciate the humour, insight and residual human dignity of the drug addicts whose lives seem at first merely repellent. Similarly, Gary Oldman's film *Nil By Mouth* is carefully structured so that, reluctantly, we find ourselves feeling sympathy with the suffering which lies behind the horrendously destructive violence of the central character. The imaginative shaping of experience, then, is not only an intellectual structuring but a response to an emotional challenge – a sort of emotional discipline.

The relevance of this process of consciously extending our sympathies, for a model of professional reflection, hardly needs spelling out. It corresponds exactly to the argument put forward by Rorty (see above, p. 194) and is perfectly illustrated by Matt Capener's portrayal of 'Frank' in Chapter 3. It also leads directly to the general point that the imaginative structuring of experience constitutes a critique of experience, i.e. a 'critical reflection upon' experience, an examination of experience. It brings together disparate feelings, disparate ideas, disparate situations and events, and constructs for them a tentative, ambiguous unity which escapes any simple summary because its fundamental implications have the form of a question, rather than a statement. Consider, for example, Steven Childs' story 'The judgement' in Chapter 2: does it simply portray the pathos of a failure to understand or the enactment of a real injustice? Works of art leave us with a sense of something understood but never fully or finally. They always leave us with further questions and often with confused emotions. The artistic structuring of experience brings us up against the realisation that we cannot construct the final or total significance of our experience. Hence Brecht explicitly presents the basic process of artistic representation as making familar experiences seem strange or 'alien' (Brecht 1974: p. 71). And in the ancient Tibetan portrayal of the wheel of life, the Buddha is depicted as using the power of art (in this case music) to arouse humankind from complacency (Sangharakshita 1993: p. 77).

But art is 'critique' in a more direct sense as well. Kearney argues that the artistic imagination does (and must) have a specifically ethical dimension. The 'ethical imagination', he says, is the essential response of moral and political commitment, of humanitarian empathy, required by contemporary history (Kearney 1988: pp. 362–6). And Kearney is doing no more than echo Shelley's assertion nearly 200 years earlier: 'Poetry acts to produce the moral improvement of man' by enabling him to 'put himself in the place of another and of many others'. In this way 'the great instrument of moral good is the imagination.' (Shelley 1988 [1821]: pp. 483–4). However, a work of art does not critique experience from an external standpoint or in terms of established moral or cognitive rules. Artistic judgements are more open, more ambiguous than moral judgements (Kant 1987 [1790]: p. 56; Goldman 1995: p. 146). Insofar as the structure of a work of art coincides point-for-point with a specifiable set of moral or political concepts it is propaganda rather than art, and propaganda becomes more artistic insofar as it creates ambiguities which transcend its moral or political programme. For example, one of the ways in which TV series about the police and detectives retain their appeal is that they avoid being simple law-and-order propaganda by often encouraging us to sympathise to some extent with the villains, so that at one level we may even want them to get away with it – another example of the challenge posed by the artwork's ambiguity.

Thus the artist's critique is conducted not as an outside observer but as a fellow sufferer. An artistic structuring of experience is an attempt by an individual to create meaning by picking a way through the various ideological structures which always threaten to predetermine the meanings of our lives. It expresses, at the same time, commitment and detachment, freedom and constraint. Art, says Eagleton, is 'a critique of alienation', offering a 'glimpse' of our freedom to offer resistance to the rationality of markets, commodities and bureaucratic administration (Eagleton 1990: p. 369). It expresses this all the more plausibly because it presents it as a possibility rather than as a fact or a programme. The work of art is 'enigmatic', says Adorno (1984: p. 186). On the one hand, it is fundamentally concerned with 'political authenticity' (p. 351), with 'truth' (p. 186) and indeed with 'truth of the kind also associated … with philosophy and social theory' (Bowie 1997: p. 117). Yet, on the other hand, the work of art cannot escape 'complicity with untruth – the untruth of the world outside' (Adorno 1984: p. 475). And, we might add, complicity with the world inside our heads: the culturally formed limitations of our concepts and desires.

Much the same might be said for the reflective practitioner, enmeshed in the struggle to preserve the ethical values embodied in their professional responsibilities, within an always-ambiguous organisational and cultural context.

To sum up: in this section I have tried to establish that the realm of the aesthetic is not merely a narrow specialist concern, but is closely linked with the structure of reflective judgements in general. I have also tried to indicate how the basic processes of creative fiction correspond to many of the themes of the reflective paradigm: the subjective construction of meaning from experience, self-exploration, playing with new possibilities, reconciling contradictions, generalising from the particular, coming to terms with complex and difficult emotions, extending one's sympathies into the lives of others in order to 'understand'. And in tracing the link between professional reflection and the imaginative process of writing fiction I have referred frequently to examples from the work of practitioners exploring their professional practice, in order to challenge the assumption that writing effective and interesting fiction is necessarily the exclusive prerogative of those who define themselves as artists or authors. However, this assumption, which limits the cultural role of imaginative fiction to the institutions of 'literature', is so deeply embedded in contemporary culture that a systematic theoretical dismantling of it seems important, and this is the task of the next section of the argument.

From 'literature' to 'storying experience'

At the beginning of the last section I argued that one of the meanings of 'imagination' refers to a universal mental process, and that one meaning of 'aesthetic' refers to the totality of our sense experience. So how did the realm of artistic creation get so separated off as the prerogative of a tiny minority? The basic assumption dates back to the Romantics, who thought that the artist, by creating another world from the resources of their imagination, re-enacted the original act of creation on the part of a deity (Coleridge 1960: p. 167). And it was Kant's 'Copernican revolution' which precipitated this conception, by making human beings the creators of the world we perceive: suddenly there was an absence, a void, where previously we could intuit the presence of 'God' by observing directly 'His' works in nature. In this way, therefore, the conception of the artistic genius was invented to fill a newly created philosophical and religious vacuum, by affirming the richness of the human spirit. But this was an aesthetic *ideology*, which combined an acceptance of social hierarchy with the assertion of individualism, an individualism for the few in an age when opportunities for education were limited and when capitalism was beginning to construct a mass workforce destined for obedient drudgery (Eagleton 1990: p. 28). Now, we might be tempted to say that not much has changed. But this would be too simple. We have had nearly a century of universal suffrage, and we currently think of society as poised to enter an age of mass higher education, of 'lifelong learning'. The reflective paradigm is above all about the extension of the individual capacity for creative selfhood – it evokes a world in which work is not mere obedience to rules, but an opportunity for exercising precisely those reflective judgements which Kant himself sees as exemplified typically in art. We are entitled to ask, therefore, why our conception of 'the artist' still seems to lag behind (in its implicit elitism) the broad advances in our thinking about democracy, education and self-fulfilment.

Part of an explanation may be that our conception of 'the artist' is a phenomenon of an increasingly specialised society: the artist has a sort of profession or craft, and is thus 'special' in the same way as the doctor, the lawyer, the nurse, the teacher or the carpenter. But although professional workers possess techniques, experience and knowledge which enable them to carry out certain tasks more expertly than the average citizen, we don't feel that there is anything fundamentally mysterious about their abilities. As lay persons, we can read medical and law books from the library, make our own wills, conduct our own conveyancing, treat our own flu symptoms, study by correspondence, and buy tools and materials from a DIY store. We don't feel that one has to be a genius to be a teacher or a lawyer, but that you just need to have had some specialist training and a little more of a certain aptitude which, to some degree, is shared by everyone. Thus many people might feel that, for example, if they possessed just a little more patience they could have been a teacher. Now, there is plenty of evidence to suggest that patience is quite widely distributed in the general population: most people can exercise some restraint in the face of others' irritating behaviour. But imaginative verbal ability is also widely distributed: large numbers of people entertain their friends and colleagues with skilfully recounted anecdotes, invent bedtime stories for their children, get the timing and words just right in telling jokes, and rapidly solve ingeniously complicated crossword puzzles. Yet such people do not think of themselves as having 'almost enough' imagination and verbal skill to be a professional writer of fiction.

A point of clarification at this stage: the purpose of the argument is not to suggest that no valid judgement of relative skill or value may be made as between a novel written by Jane Austen and a story written by a member of a professional development reflective writing course (I write as a lifelong devotee of Jane Austen!). What I do wish to argue, however, is that in many very important respects what they have in common is just as significant as how they differ. An understanding of what they have in common is crucial for an understanding of the role of writing and sharing fiction in courses of professional reflection; whereas how they differ might be an important consideration for a course on literary appreciation.

This last comment brings us to the cultural barriers raised by the usual presentation of 'literature' in educational curricula, especially their tendency to emphasise 'the classics'. The presentation of a text and its author as 'classic' serves to remove them from the familiar scenario of people writing about their experience, and places them instead in a timeless realm, as people whom we have a duty to appreciate but cannot hope to emulate. Originally, of course, their apartness was indicated by the fact that they were written in Latin or Greek; in England, for the last hundred years or so, books written in English have become acceptable for 'serious study' but only on condition that their 'classic' status is held in mind. Hence the emphasis on the literature of the past and on analysing texts in such a way as to bring out their 'greatness'; so that 'potentially universal significance' is not seen to be a general quality inherent in all imaginative fiction (see previous section) but as part of the superiority of a very few texts, which mark them off from 'minor' or 'popular' work. Only 'the classics' are for education; popular texts are merely for 'entertainment'.

But 'entertainment' also is organised to preserve a strong sense of a literary hierarchy. The operation of the culture industry, like any other commercial operation, tends to provide those services which look as though they will yield a profit. Thus a small number of great works of the past and a small selection of contemporary works are heavily promoted and universally presented to our attention. Classic novels are serialised on TV and a handful of each year's published fiction becomes newsworthy as the 'shortlist' for literary prizes. As in the world of sport, the twin processes of competition and marketing serve to emphasise the activities of a relatively few 'stars'. A further point is that the great works of the past are out of copyright and thus very cheap to reproduce: imagine what money Vivaldi would currently be making if he earned a royalty every time a telephone answering system forces hapless callers to listen to the first few bars of *The Four Seasons* while they are shunted around an organisational switchboard!

Of course, one should not overstate the case. The media hype of super sports leagues and a handful of musical performers does not prevent widespread involvement in amateur music and amateur sport. And, by the same token, there is community theatre, and there are small-circulation magazines publishing poems and stories by people who do not make a living from it. But on the whole, the economic forces which shape the culture of modern societies tend to construct 'art' as something *provided*, by 'big names', to be consumed – not as something we all do for ourselves, with others, for conviviality and mutual enlightenment.

Let us, then, try to argue that the capacity for artistic creation is something we all possess, that professional reflection can therefore draw not only on our ability to appreciate established works of fiction, but also on our ability to create fictional structures which are intricate, complex, and successful, as a way of developing our understanding of our experience. Fortunately, the argument is already made, in John Dewey's book *Art as Experience* (1958) – which is nicely appropriate in view of Dewey's general influence on the reflective paradigm. Originally published in the 1930s, Dewey's ideas have recently been endorsed at length in Shusterman (1992), and even Adorno, who finds little comfort anywhere in his survey of modern culture and modern aesthetic theory, refers with respect to 'the one and only John Dewey, a truly emancipated thinker' (Adorno 1984: p. 450, see also p. 484). Dewey's main concern is, precisely, to argue that artistic creativity is an aspect of common human experience, in oppo-sition to the 'museum concept of art' (Dewey 1958: p. 6), in which works of art are separated off as remote and 'esoteric' (p. 10). Dewey is seeking 'the factors and forces which favor the normal development of common human activities into matters of artistic value' (p. 11). He thus describes the aesthetic structuring of experience in terms which emphasise its continuity with the general mental processes of 'making sense'. For example, it involves constructing out of the ceaseless and seamless flux of 'experience' *an experience* – with a beginning and an end (p. 40), grasping the unity of the different elements of an experience while retaining the distinct character of each element separately (p. 36), seeing the relationship between the different parts of an experience and how this relation-ship is developing (p. 40). It involves giving a form to experience which expresses its integration, its 'organisation ... growth ... development and fulfilment' (p. 55). Hence, the aesthetic awareness of experience is no more than 'the clari-fied and intensified development of traits that belong to every normally complete experience' (p. 46).

What Dewey is doing here is bringing together the two somewhat opposed aspects of 'imagination' and 'aesthetic' which we originally noted. He has been criticised for not distinguishing clearly enough how art is specific and different (Shusterman 1992: p. 55), but that is not the direction or purpose of Dewey's argument. On the contrary. Earlier in this chapter we noted the significance for the reflective paradigm of his argument that the basic methods of scientific inquiry are reproduced in the processes of 'careful thought' in everyday life (Dewey 1960: pp. 166–8); in *Art as Experience* (1958) he conducts a parallel argu-ment: that the basic processes we familiarly think of as 'artistic creation' also describe the construction and communication of human experience in general. In both cases he is concerned with political education in its broadest sense, i.e. education for citizenship: a democratic society needs its citizens to solve their practical problems like scientists and to grasp the meaning of their experience like artists.

One form of support for Dewey may be drawn from the argument of Terry Eagleton's book *Literary Theory* (1983). Eagleton begins and ends his examination of the various philosophical explanations which have been given of the nature of 'literature' by saying quite bluntly that literature (in itself) cannot be defined in terms of a special body of texts which are distinguishable from writing in general (pp. 11, 210). Literature is simply 'highly valued writing'; and what is highly valued varies according to the values of the person doing the valuing (p. 11), so that all attempts at defining the scope and limits of literature as a body of writing must end inconclusively. The sociological form of the argument is presented by Bourdieu:

> Questions of the meaning and value of the work of art ... can only find solutions in a social history of the field.
>
> (Bourdieu 1996: p. 290)

In psychological terms, corroboration for the general line of Dewey's argument comes from a number of writers who emphasise the narrative structure of human consciousness. Barbara Hardy (1974) for example, writes of narrative as 'a primary act of mind'. 'Narrative ... is not to be regarded as an aesthetic invention used by artists to control, manipulate, and order experience, but as a primary act of mind transferred to art from life' (p. 12). She describes 'the qualities which fictional narrative shares with that inner and outer storytelling that plays a major role in our sleeping and waking lives', and continues:

> We dream in narrative, daydream in narrative, remember, anticipate, hope, despair, believe, doubt, plan, revise, criticize, construct, gossip, learn, hate and love by narrative. In order really to live, we make up stories about ourselves and others.
>
> (Hardy 1974: p. 13)

Or, in the words of Anthony Paul Kerby:

> The self is generated and is given unity in and through its own narratives, in its own recounting and hence understanding of itself. The self ... is essentially a being of reflexivity, coming to itself in its own narrative acts.
>
> (Kerby 1991: p. 41)

Natalie Zemon Davis applies this approach to the writing of history in *Fiction in the Archives* (Zemon Davis 1987), as does Kathryn Hunter's account of medical practice and training, *Doctors' Stories* (1991).

So, if – along with Kerby – we can consider that our being has 'essentially' the structure of an author permanently weaving experience into a narrative pattern, then we ought be able to accept that we all (and not only geniuses or bestselling authors) have the capacity for writing fiction:

> The brain is a story-seeking, story-creating instrument.
>
> (Smith 1992: p. 63)

In other words, we don't store experience (as though it were 'information' or 'data'); we story it. Creating stories is, simply, one of the modes in which we comprehend our lives.

The multi-voiced text: collage, montage, patchwork

The notion of the 'storying imagination', however, has a weakness that we have not yet addressed, because the word 'story' itself contains a crucial ambiguity: on the one hand we say 'What's the story?' – meaning 'Give me your account of what actually happened'. On the other hand, we say (especially to children)

'Don't tell stories' – meaning, 'Don't tell lies' (there is a similar ambiguity both in the French word 'histoire' and the German 'Geschichte'). A story, then, being only one person's interpretation of events, is always open to the charge of being, for whatever reason, false. Similarly with the term 'fiction': we have emphasised frequently that 'fictional' means 'shaped and fashioned according to aesthetic judgements of value, significance and balance', but it does, actually, also mean, 'not true'. And for this reason Plato suggested that since poets and dramatists present only misleading illusions of truth, they should be excluded from his ideal republic (Plato, *The Republic*, ch. 10, part I). Clearly, in order to be taken seriously as an interpreter of reality, a writer of fiction needs to address the question, 'Why is this not "misleading", not a personal fantasy masquerading as truth?'.

The answer we have stressed so far is that a fiction presents itself as ambiguous, including various contrasting viewpoints and open to various inter-pretations. This answer corresponds to our current sense that any account of reality must inevitably be incomplete and/or ambiguous, since absolute truth is not available to us. But there is another, more powerful way in which art can answer the charge that it presents subjective interpretations as objective reality, and that is by explicitly showing us the subjective process of interpretation at work, by including in the text an account of its writing. This reflexive, self-analytical aspect of literature is already quite apparent in Romantic poetry (many of the poems of Wordsworth, Coleridge and Keats describe the poet having the experience that produces the poem) but it is particularly emphasised by writers concerned with 'modern' literature. 'Modern art does not hide the fact that it is something made and produced' (Adorno 1984: p. 39). The contem-porary work of literature, therefore, often includes a reference to its own 'constructedness' and thereby recognises that it is not so much a lamp shining out boldly and creating illumination, but a labyrinth of mirrors, creating a multi-tude of conflicting images (Kearney 1988: p. 17). Thus John Fowles plays with the possibility of different endings to his novel *The French Lieutenant's Woman*: 'The last few pages you have read are not what happened' (Fowles 1977: p. 295).

Kearney's analogy is particularly helpful in that it suggests one of the most frequent ways in which the modern fictional text makes explicit its constructed-ness, namely by showing the distinctiveness of the separate 'voices' of which it consists. It is presented not as a single interpretation of events unified by the author's mastery of the totality, but as a 'multi-voiced text' in which the author's voice is but one among many:

> The notion of a text which tells a (or the) truth as perceived by an indi-
> vidual subject (the author) whose insights are the source of the text's
> single authoritative meaning, is ... untenable.
>
> (Belsey 1980: p. 3)

To take some recent examples: Louis de Bernière's *Captain Corelli's Mandolin* (1994) and Rose Tremain's *Sacred Country* (1992) are both presented through the voices of many different characters, and Margaret Atwood's novel *Alias Grace* (1997) is an elaborate compilation of documents illustrating different perceptions of a series of events which remain mysterious to the end, even though they have a basis in historical 'fact'. Thus the modern work of fiction makes it clear that it embodies a reflective process of *trying* to understand events, and recognises that our means for understanding are such that our attempts can never be wholly successful: Arundhati Roy's novel *The God of Small Things* (1997) begins with a quotation from John Berger: 'Never again will a single story be told as though it's the only one.'

The modern work of art, then, recognises the need to combat the illusion that it is an authoritative representation of a single reality. Although we are concerned with the artistic medium of fiction, it is important to note that this basic worry (that the apparent 'realism' of the artwork is a potentially dangerous illusion) initially regained its current importance in the visual arts, around the beginning of the twentieth century. Awareness of the problem was initiated largely as a response of painting to the new media of photography and cinema. The age-old ambition of painting was to create an illusion of reality, to re-create on canvas the illusion of a 'real' landscape, individual person, flower arrangement, chair or pair of old boots. But in the mid-nineteenth century, along came photography and threatened to render that ambition irrelevant: achieving an exact illusion of reality became a trivial, effortless, routine, rather than an impressive achievement. Moreover, the photographed image was not only an apparently exact copy of reality but also an image which could be all too easily manipulated to create deception: events and scenes could be 'staged' for a photograph, while the photograph itself appeared to present them as occurring 'naturally'; and the printing process allowed images from quite different sources to be superimposed, creating an entirely illusory but apparently 'real' relationship between them. The camera thus combined the complete appearance of reality with unlimited possibilities for faking, and the traditional ambition of realism, as an artistic aim, was rendered worthless. The solution was to redefine the aim of art: instead of trying to reproduce reality (as though it had been 'objectively observed') it emphasised the explicitly subjective process of constructing new images by assembling and combining elements from a variety of different sources. The new emphasis was on making visible (and drawing attention to) the creative, interpretive process itself (Waldman 1992: pp. 10–11; Ades 1986: ch. 4).

This new approach was variously called 'collage', in which a work is composed by sticking together (French: 'coller', to paste) fragments from letters, scraps of newpaper, theatre programmes, wallpaper, etc. (e.g. the early paintings of Picasso, Braque, Gris – see Waldman 1992: pp. 17, 40, 48) or 'photomontage' (French: 'monter', to assemble) in which photographic images from different sources are combined into one overall image (e.g. the posters of George Grosz and John Heartfield – see Ades 1986: p. 23). One important aim of both 'collage' and 'montage' was to create a form which would break down the

barrier between the objects or documents of 'real life' and their artistic representation (Waldman 1992: p. 10). More importantly, from the point of view of the
relationship between art and reflection, the new approach provided a form in
which the artist could make a critical statement about reality by bringing
contrasting images together in new, surprising, even shocking combinations
(Ades 1986: ch. 2). The term 'montage' is also significant in that the word also
refers to the process of editing film (i.e. the basic process whereby a cinematic
narrative is constructed) and thus reminds us of the important influence of the
cinema on our current ways of presenting and understanding narrative.

The multi-voiced text, then, can be seen as the incorporation into fictional
narrative of this revolutionary re-focusing of the visual arts – painting, photography and cinema – with its radical implications for our thinking about how to
represent our interpretations of 'reality'. Thus it is significant that Rosalind
Krauss introduces her recent book on Picasso with an analysis of Andre Gide's
novel *The Counterfeiters*, published in 1925 (Krauss 1998: pp. 5ff.). Gide's novel
combines conventional story-telling, analytical essays, letters, and long extracts
from the journal of the central character, a novelist, describing his plans for his
next novel, to be called *The Counterfeiters*! Even more significantly, the whole work
focuses on the relationship between the counterfeit and the real, in human relationships, in ideas, and in the representation of events in writing. It thereby
exemplifies, both in its form and in its theme, the verbal collage and montage of
what we have called the 'patchwork text'.

In this way, modern forms of fiction, emphasising a diversity of voices and
the ironic relationship between them, and incorporating explicit reference to the
act of producing the text, address the key question posed at the outset of this
section: in what sense can a representation of reality be 'true'? No final answer
to such a question can be given. On the one hand the multiple/
patchwork/montage text does manage to 'disavow ... unity by stressing the
disparity of parts while at the same time reaffirming unity as a principle of
form' (Adorno 1984: p. 222). On the other hand, even the reflexive, obviously
fragile and incomplete unity of the patchwork construction may be accused of
making, implicitly, an unsustainable claim to 'understand' what it presents (p.
223). But at least the form of the patchwork text is a response to the seriousness
of the question, even if it only provides the beginnings of an answer: the patchwork text makes explicit its own ambiguity by reflexively recognising its own
status as 'not reality but a construct' and by presenting a disparate collection of
viewpoints. In this way, moreover, it is also a highly appropriate format for the
process of professional reflection. Professional reflection also needs to be tentative as well as incisive, a critique but never a simple condemnation, committed
but aware of alternatives, avoiding both grandiloquent claims to conclusive
objectivity and the narrow simplifications of merely technical problem-solving.
Such are the claims which might be made for the examples of patchwork texts
presented in Chapter 3.

Writing and sharing fiction: an emancipatory social practice for the storying imagination

So far, we have concentrated mainly on the educational and professional value of *writing* fiction. This section takes the argument further by focusing on the relationship between the writer and the reader of a work of fiction, as a process of communication which has it own specific educational value in that it requires a particular form of respect for the other. In this section, then, we examine how the literary imagination works as a social 'practice' (Eagleton 1983: p. 205) and in particular, how writing and sharing fiction may be thought of as complementary elements of a developmental social and educational process, i.e. as an emancipatory social interaction between writers and readers. In other words, the argument of this section will trace the link between the practice of writing and sharing fiction and the practice of critical reflection as what Mezirow terms 'communicative learning' (Mezirow *et al.* 1990: pp. 8–9).

The first point to note here is that any use of language needs to be understood as an act within a situation (Austin 1962). Even if someone makes what appears to be a 'statement of fact', we respond to it not only in terms of whether we accept its accuracy but in terms of its relevance and its purpose. If someone comes up and says 'It's hot today', we understand it as an invitation (to begin a conversation) and our response will depend more on whether or not we wish to accept the invitation than on whether or not we agree with the statement as such. In this sense, all language use can be understood as rhetorical – as attempted acts of persuasion within an interaction. 'Persuasion' here needs to be interpreted broadly, as an attempt to sustain the negotiation of a shared purpose between speaker and hearer, writer and reader, an attempt to remain in touch with 'the Other' of the interaction. And this is equally true of a greeting on the street, presenting a mathematical proof, putting forward an argument, describing a professional incident, telling a joke, and – of course – writing a story or a patchwork text.

So, let us consider a story as an attempt by a writer to 'remain in touch with' the imaginary reader, the Other for whom the story is written. Who is this imaginary reader? In part this is a conscious and carefully analysed decision, based on what one has to say, one's purpose (Sartre 1967: p. 12) and also one's understanding of the historical and cultural circumstances in which both writers and potential readers are situated (p. 50). The author thus constructs what Iser calls an 'implied reader' (Iser 1978). 'All works of the mind contain within themselves an image of the reader for whom they are intended' (Sartre 1967: p. 52) in the form of a set of historical allusions which, the author must assume, the reader will be able to recognise; otherwise every text would have to attempt to explain 'everything', which would be not only tedious but impossible (pp. 49–50). But although a writer starts out with a sense of having something worth saying to, and understandable by, a historically specific set of readers, the readership is never enterely limited in this way. A fiction, as we have seen, always has an implied generality, something worth saying in the light of general values (p. 13), so that, beyond the anticipated readers, it also aims to be persuasive for the widest possible readership. Hence, says Sartre, writing involves thinking 'What would happen if everybody read what I wrote?' (p. 14). Which is another way of suggesting that a fiction aims at including and integrating a diversity of elements (Welleck and Warren 1963: p. 243), in order to draw in a diversity of readers.

It is this process of drawing the reader into the story which, according to Kenneth Burke, creates its 'form':

> Form is the creation of an appetite in the mind of the auditor [audi-
> ence, readers] and the adequate satisfying of that appetite. This
> satisfaction ... at times involves a temporary set of frustrations, but in
> the end these frustrations prove to be simply a more involved kind of
> satisfaction.
>
> (Burke 1968: p. 31)

We are most familiar with this process as the creation of 'suspense'. For example, at the beginning of a story there may be a sequence of short scenes, apparently unconnected, creating for us an 'appetite' to know how, in the end, their connectedness will become clear (most contemporary films begin in this way and so do many novels – see the opening pages of Ben Elton's *Stark* [1989] or Michael Ondaatje's *The English Patient* [1992]). Burke's suggestion is that the form of a story is a structure designed to manage the 'psychology' of its readers, i.e. their desire to know how different elements will be linked, how mysterious events will become clear; and their satisfaction at the final integration or clarification. Simple though it is, Burke's argument brings out very clearly how writing a story can be understood as a social practice – a move in an interaction with the reader, an act of persuasion and negotiation.

Considering this interaction from the reader's perspective, Iser emphasises that 'reading' is always a complex and individual process of creating a meaning for a text (Iser 1978: p. 107), by making provisional (never final) selections of what is and what is not important (p. 126) and by filling in for oneself what seem to be its 'blanks' and 'inconsistencies' (p. 18). Iser's emphasis on the autonomy of the reader as a creative constructor of individualised meaning is a consequence of his and other writers' emphasis on the open, fragmentary quality of 'modern' literary forms and techniques (see previous section). This is partly due to the strong influence of the methods of cinema, where the creative work of the director consists mainly in editing skilfully between different material (Benjamin 1973a), but it is also a response to our contemporary sense that there can be no finally coherent or authoritative representations of reality (see references to the ideas of Lyotard and Rorty above). However, this complexity, ambiguity and discontinuity is not only a feature of contemporary fiction but of story-telling generally, and follows from general theories of sign systems, meanings and texts. Thus Barthes (1974) conducts a detailed analysis of an early nineteenth-century short story to indicate the many different dimensions (Barthes calls them 'codes') in which writers and readers must negotiate the meaning of the text.

This complex, interactive model of interpreting literary texts has been used as the basis for a method of understanding human behaviour in general, namely 'hermeneutics' ('the art or science of interpretation') (Dilthey 1976 [1900]: p. 112). The essence of the hermeneutic method is a process in which:

> The whole of a work must be understood from the individual words and their combinations, and yet the full comprehension of the details presupposes the understanding of the whole.
>
> (*ibid.*: p. 115)

Hence, as Gadamer (a recent exponent of hermeneutics) says, the structure of understanding 'is disclosed as the dialectic of question and answer' (Gadamer 1975: p. 340) – a virtual dialogue between writer and readers in which 'truth' is always sought but, given the 'circularity' of the process (p. 258), will never be final:

> The reconstruction of the question to which the text is presumed to be the answer takes place itself within a process of questioning through which we seek the answer to the question that the text asks us.
>
> (*ibid.*: p. 337).

Thus the 'truth' proposed by a story (or a patchwork text) has always, in the end, the uncertainty of a question: 'What does this sequence of events ultimately "mean"?' And the same is true of the reader's response: 'Here is my interpretation, but I know that there are others; what are they?'

This acceptance that understanding a text is an always incomplete process of interpretation (defined as such by the circularity of the hermeneutic questioning) leads Sartre to describe the relationship between writer and reader as one in which the writer must recognise the reader's freedom:

> Since the artist must entrust to another the job of carrying out what he [*sic*] has begun, since it is only through the consciousness of the reader that he can regard himself as essential to his work, all literary work is an appeal. … The writer appeals to the reader's freedom to collaborate in the production of his work. … The aesthetic object presents only the appearance of a finality and is limited to soliciting the free and ordered play of [the reader's] imagination.
>
> (Sartre 1967: pp. 32–3)

In writing a fiction, therefore, writers do not seek to render their readers 'passive', to 'overwhelm' them by proving a point; the writer writes in such a way as to allow the reader that 'aesthetic withdrawal' in which they can re-create the writer's story (*ibid.*: pp. 34–5).

Conversely, the act of reading must recognise the freedom of the writer (*ibid.*: p. 45). There are two ways in which we can elaborate this point. First, the hermeneutic 'rule' says that we must interpret details in the light of the whole text. So although as an individual reader I may find that a particular phrase or incident grabs my attention by, say, evoking a personal memory, I do not simply recreate the whole significance of the story in the light of that detail and claim it as 'the meaning'. The freedom of the reader to make a personal interpretation is limited by the respect due to the text as a whole, and this requires us to check our initial interpretations against the many other details of the text and to avoid claiming authority or finality for our own reading of it. Otherwise we impose ourselves on the author's text and thereby fail to learn from it. Second, the text stands separately. If we, the readers contribute so significantly to the meaning of the text, then we cannot claim to find, directly, in the text the experiences (the point of view, the values, the neuroses) of the author (Barthes 1977). The author's text creates the opportunity for us to exercise what Sartre calls the free and ordered play of our imagination (see above), and for that we are, as it were, grateful. But, thereafter, the author is free in the sense that they cannot be held responsible for what we, the readers, make of the text. Indeed, authors themselves can learn from the variety of readings that their texts provoke. The text is a terrain where interpretations meet, compete and mutually illuminate one another by virtue of the fact that all interpretations are put forward in a spirit of what Sartre calls 'generosity' (Sartre 1967: p. 44): 'The work of art is an act of confidence in the freedom of [hu]man[ity]' (p. 45).

Thus, in conceiving of the relationship between writer and readers of fiction as an interaction in which each respects the freedom of the other, we bring into view an emancipatory model of the operation of the literary imagination as a 'social practice'. Indeed, perhaps we have here a theoretical perspective on the testimony reported in Chapter 5, that the sharing of fictions in a regular workshop discussion group can create the very sense of 'trust' which it requires (see Chapter 5: p. 151). In other words, through writing and sharing fiction and reflecting on the significance of different readers' interpretations of our fictions, we can perhaps take part in a version of that community of free and explorative dialogue envisaged by Habermas and evoked within the reflective paradigm as 'communicative learning' – the developmental understanding of experience as both a personal and a collective endeavour. And it is the ambiguity of the aesthetic structure, the indirectness of the aesthetically shaped message and the elusiveness of the aesthetic judgement (its evasion of the directly ethical, the directly instrumental) which gives this model of emancipatory dialogue its plausibility and its strength.

Conclusion: writing and sharing fiction as an artistic practice for the reflective citizen

The general contention of this book is that the exercise of the literary imagination, in producing and sharing works of fiction, ought to be included as a key format in which to realise the creative examination of professional experience; it ought, therefore to be one of the methods envisaged within the reflective paradigm. Conversely, reflection on the meanings of work experience ought to be one of the practices in which the literary imagination can find a socially 'useful' function (Eagleton 1983: p. 208). That this contention is expressed as a series of 'ought's' is symptomatic of the equivocal social status of the arts in modern society. Even though we recognise that the imagination is a basic human capacity, we have inherited from the Romantic movement a notion of the artist as a rare and unusually 'gifted' or 'inspired' individual, and consequently a tendency to focus on 'great works of art', representing 'classics' from the past or a tiny proportion of the creative production of the present.

One can explain this state of affairs economically and culturally (see above) as an ideology which justifies various forms of exclusion and elitism. But we can also follow Dewey in refusing to accept this ideology, and emphasise instead that the concept of artistic creation is a model of the common human ability to express our experience in order to shape and realise its significance. One of the strategies for creating a better society , says Dewey, involves 'conferring aesthetic quality upon all modes of production' (Dewey 1958 [1934]: pp. 80–1).

This does not mean denying that there are indeed 'great' works of art, with a timeless capacity for inspiration and consolation, but it does mean avoiding the conclusion that most of us are incapable of producing artworks, only of 'consuming' them. Appreciating the brilliance and profundity of George Eliot's *Middlemarch* should not make us assume that we cannot write a short fiction of interest to our friends, ourselves and our colleagues, any more than the splendour of Salisbury cathedral should make us feel incapable of designing and building a perfectly serviceable greenhouse. Especially where the medium of language is concerned, general human ingenuity and capacity is as much in evidence as in DIY carpentry. We know how to tell anecdotes so that they are amusing – a test of verbal skill in many dimensions: choice of word, rhythm, balance, timing. Most newspapers carry crossword puzzles, appealing to the pleasure taken by an educated public in playing with the punning ambiguities of words and their ability to point simultaneously towards different forms of knowledge ('Awful woman novelist, with blue veins'? – 'Gorgonzola'; 'Place of retirement in France, but poorly illuminated'? – 'Unlit'; 'Stick; don't declare'? – 'Baton'). And we are deeply experienced and sophisticated in our grasp of the structures and methods of fictional narrative, having been immersed in them, from an infancy of fairy stories to an adulthood of novels, feature films and TV drama.

The point about the accessibility of the verbal medium of written fiction is that it is cheap, portable and universally available, as well as infinitely flexible. An argument might well be made for the widespread human capacity to express understanding in terms of improvised theatre or painting; and if possessing a camcorder ever becomes as widespread as possessing a pen and notepaper, then one might wish to argue strongly that the average educated citizen should not allow the achievements of Steven Spielberg, Alfred Hitchcock or Orson Welles to undermine their self-confidence as movie-makers, just as I am arguing that amateur fiction writers should not be disempowered by the example of George Eliot. But at the present stage of cultural and economic development, and with regard to the special function of language in developing one's understanding of experience, it is the general human capacity for verbal artistry which seems to present the strongest case for urgent recognition.

In the nineteenth century, when 'work' was very largely to do with the production of physical objects, William Morris argued that at one time all handicrafts, including the production of household goods, had expressed a sense of aesthetic value (Morris 1993 [1889]: p. 342) and, moreover, that all production *should* be imbued with aesthetic value (Morris 1994 [1884]: p. 18). It was to this belief that we owe his widely influential designs for wallpapers and fabrics. Morris's ideas were consciously derived from John Ruskin, especially Ruskin's vision of 'gothic architecture' (Ruskin 1985 [1853]) as a mode of production which fostered the imagination of the individual workman, and in which creative variety was more important than the imposition of a perfect regularity of form, which degraded the workman into a machine (Ruskin 1985: pp. 83–6). It is an indication that these ideas were perceived at the time to be of significance for the cause of adult education in general, that Ruskin was asked to publish his essay separately, so that it could be distributed to all workers attending courses at the newly opened Working Men's College in London (see p. 75).

However, unlike Ruskin and Morris, we live in a culture and an economy where the relative importance of material production has declined sharply, a culture of *mental* production and an economy where wealth is created by what management theorists have called 'knowledge workers' (Drucker 1974: p. 161; 1992: p. 81), whose value to their organisation lies in their capacity to be creative and to innovate (Senge 1990: p. 4; Peters 1989: p. 22). This is a new vision of the cultural role of professional work, reformulated for an age of unprecedentedly rapid change (Handy 1991); an age where the relationship between knowledge and practice is no longer one in which a body of authoritative scientific findings is directly applied to practice, but a relationship in which knowledge is always open to question and therefore must continually be re-negotiated for each practice context. Hence the recent rise to prominence of the reflective paradigm, as a model of professional knowledge for a culture of self-conscious change, doubt and uncertainty.

And indeed, Ruskin's emphasis on the aesthetic creativity of the individual worker against the imposition of a 'technical' regularity which left no room for individual interpretation, has interesting parallels with the rejection, by the writers of the reflective paradigm, of technical rationality and directly imposed theory in favour of individual interpretation and reflection on experience. We can elaborate the parallel as follows. Where production is predominantly the crafting of materials, the insistence by Ruskin and Morris that work should be artistic and not mechanical leads to the production of handicrafts as artworks. (In many respects this argument remains just as relevant for today as for the nineteenth century, but now a further stage to the argument can be added, as follows.) Where production is concerned with the crafting of knowledge, the suggestion that understanding experience must involve the creative imagination and not merely analytical rationality leads to the production of knowledge in the form of art – for example, through the creation and interpretation of fiction.

The parallel goes all the deeper, in that both Ruskin and Morris were responding to a sense of political disempowerment and spiritual alienation, from which, they argued, humanity could only be redeemed if 'work' could be redefined in such a way as to express the individual's creativity; otherwise we are doomed to permanent despair (Morris 1993: p. 367). Exactly the same hope might be said to inspire both the reflective paradigm of professional expertise and, even more explicitly, the argument of this book: that to fulfil its educational and political aspirations, the notion of the reflective practitioner (and indeed the notion of the reflective citizen in a democracy) needs to include the exercise of the artistic imagination.

For it is our general contention that, when it comes to understanding and representing experience, we can *all* be artists (perhaps a lot more readily and effectively than we can all be analysts). The realm of art is above all the realm of freedom and exploration, and it is the very elusiveness and ambiguity of art which means that even in a society where most of us experience alienation and oppression of one sort or another, where freedom for direct action is severely constrained, and where limiting ideologies are endlessly thrust upon us, the work of art can continue to express the spirit of independent critical inquiry, through the aesthetic shaping of the possibilities of our lives. Moreover, the power of the work of art (its emotional resonances, its capacity for generalisation, transformation and synthesis) means that in a community where fictions are widely created, shared and discussed, we may become more conscious of our own possibilities, of new understandings and even, in a small way perhaps, of strategies for developmental action.

EPILOGUE

The professional worker and the artist: two myths of betrayal

ur argument has been that complex understandings of professional experience can be explored through, and represented in, 'fiction', and that professional practitioners can do this effectively and with aplomb. It thus seems right and proper to allow the last word to a piece of fiction by a professional practitioner, Pat Wood, a social worker. Here, then, Pat Wood's story 'The listener?' is presented alongside Baudelaire's poem 'The albatross' to point up more sharply the parallels (referred to at various points in Chapter 7) between the cultural situation of the contemporary professional practitioner and that of the artist: both roles entail a critical engagement with personal and social experience, both are embattled and defensive, conscious of the importance of their role and the values it represents, and that in the society in which they live the role and its values are currently subjected to rejection and betrayal.

'The Albatross'

Often, for amusement, the men of the crew
Trap an albatross, that great bird of the seas,
As it follows the ship, gliding over the bitter waves
Like an indolent travelling companion.

Once deposited on the deck
This ruler of the heavens allows
Its great white wings to trail pitifully at its sides,
Clumsy and shameful, like oars.

How clumsy and drab he is, this winged voyager –
Once so beautiful, how comic now, and ugly.
One of the sailors pokes its beak with an old pipe,
Another mimics with a limp this cripple who once could fly.

The Poet himself is like this prince of the clouds:
He can ride the tempests and laugh at the archer's arrow,
But exiled on the earth and surrounded by mockery,
His giant wings prevent him from flying.

                    Charles Baudelaire, 1857 (free translation)

Baudelaire's famous poem presents the poet simply as a proud, misunderstood victim – the heroic myth of poetry; the poet betrayed and destroyed by the non-poetic citizens of an anti-poetic society. Whereas the irony of Pat Wood's story is that those who ignore and betray social work values have infiltrated the profession itself – as though a gang of tamed seagulls were to join in with the sailors in mocking the albatross.

'The listener?' by Pat Wood, social worker (reflective writing course, 1997)

She looked down at him, he looked so young and vulnerable, lying there. She leaned forward over the cot side to wipe away a small pool of saliva that lay glistening at the corner of his mouth. Tears filled her eyes, there was an ache of love in the pit of her stomach, and in her chest a pain of disbelief and anger.

* * *

He looked down at her, bending over the bed. He really was pushed for time today, however it shouldn't take too long, unless she wanted to talk of course. After all there was no way he could assess an unconscious patient. He glanced at the referral: 'Simon Jones, head injury'. I'll probably never see him again, he thought. He'll either die, or if he regains consciousness his behaviour will be too difficult for the ward to manage, and he'll be moved out of the hospital, to a specialist unit somewhere. His attention shifted to the woman. God what a mess she looks, he thought. I really haven't got time to stop today. She'll be upset, angry, looking for someone to blame, asking questions I can't answer. Another glance at the note from the nursing staff told him that the woman was Simon's mother. Still, he thought, she looks as if she's been around, and Simon's a big boy now. Took risks, that one, and one risk too many this time. He struggled unsuccessfully with the judgements he was making in his head. If he makes it, it'll cost someone's budget a bomb, he thought, remembering the overspend at the last Panel meeting.

Mostly he liked being a hospital social worker, it suited him. He didn't mind the paperwork, quite enjoyed the computer. Yes it suited him. Quick assessment, off to Panel with the package, he was difficult to refuse, they said, persuasive, and of course they couldn't block hospital beds, could they? But things like this, well pity the poor community social worker who picks this up, if he survives, and comes out of a rehab unit. One thing's for sure, he thought, glancing at the woman again, there's no money here, no litigation either. Let's get it over with.

* * *

She looked up at him, another stranger in this place full of strangers, all talking about things she didn't understand, asking her to sign forms, make decisions. ... Tears of sadness overflowed into the crying rage of grief. Listen to me, you bastard, rang in her head. 'I don't know who to turn to' whimpered out of her mouth.

Ten minutes later, and the stranger was gone. He'd asked questions, filled in another form, God knew what for, and told her his name. She'd forgotten it already. He'd said to ask the nurses if she thought he could be of any further help. Help? What help? Could he make Simon wake up? Her loving, mouthy son who would disappear for weeks and then come home to her with money, booze, hugs, kisses and promises. They were about the same age, she thought, her Simon and the stranger. But the young man with the steady job and posh voice didn't have her Simon's warmth, didn't put out a hand, didn't say as Simon would 'What you crying for, you silly old cow, come on tell me about it, I'll sort it'. The stranger would probably go far, as long as he didn't get involved with any of the poor sods he has to visit, she thought. What had Simon got? What had she got? They'd only really got each other. It felt like there was nothing now, how could she manage? She might as well jack it all in. That's what they said Simon had tried to do. She didn't believe that, he wouldn't. She needed to talk to Simon.

* * *

He got home at about six o'clock, sat down and poured himself a drink. The flat which usually felt peaceful and welcoming, felt unusually empty and lonely. Anyway, he reasoned, it had been a pretty good day really, loads of paperwork completed, and amazingly the computer records were almost up to date. No trouble from the Panel either. But he wished he'd not had to assess that bloke with the brain injury. Still what more could he have done? Polly will pick it up later, he thought, she's good at that sort of thing. Hopeless at the Panel though, faffs around, talks about the pain of the situation, can't she see the rest of us shuffling around on our chairs?

The phone rang, he jumped up, answered it quickly. He knew it would be his mother, she promised she'd phone this evening, she always kept a promise. There was so much he needed to talk to her about. Bloody good listener, my mum, he thought.

Final comment

Like Baudelaire's famous poem, Pat Wood's story presents a precise image with a general significance. By evoking a specific situation she provides a general analysis of fundamental issues: the relationship between power, emotions and values, between organisational and family roles, and between ideals and practical realities in a deeply flawed social order. Her story is a bitter critique, but it combines irony with compassion: we are not only shown the betrayal of moral values in favour of the narrow dictates of organisational budget management; we are also shown the suffering of the 'traitor', who urgently needs the caring reponse embodied in the professional values he has betrayed. The professional worker's betrayal of principles and the betrayal of others is essentially, and most damagingly, a self-betrayal.

Could this question be read back into Baudelaire's poem? Why is the poet/albatross so isolated, so vulnerable, so helpess? Is the isolation of the modern literary artist perhaps a form of *self*-isolation and thus also a form of self-betrayal, or at least a form of complicity with the structures of oppression (see Bourdieu 1996: pp. 60–8)? In contrast, Pat Wood's story presents not only betrayal but resistance: the social work profession does still contain figures who preserve its original inspiration.

The appeal of Baudelaire's poem lies in its implicit suggestion that the role of 'the poet' can be taken as a general symbol for the potential revolt of the critical individual (as a person, as a citizen) against the oppressiveness of social and political structures. But the force of his argument is limited by his self-pitying acceptance of the artist's cultural isolation, so that his revolt becomes merely a lament. We therefore need to recognise the importance of other, different examples of the emancipatory potential of artistic creativity, which, like this social worker's story, demonstrate that artistic creativity is part of our general capacity for critical reflection on our life experience and on our work with others. We need to emphasise, in other words, that there exists a widespread 'aesthetic competence' which is not merely the special skill of the 'lonely' artist (poet/author/writer) but a general characteristic of the reflective citizen. For all of us, one of our most important resources for finding and communicating our capacity for critical, reflective autonomy is our deep-seated grasp of the techniques of creative artistic expression. The educational task is to ensure that this widespread aesthetic competence is fostered, as a way of understanding ourselves (our capacities, our potential) in relation to the social world in which we live and work. Such is the thesis of this book.

BIBLIOGRAPHY

Abbs, P. (1974) *Autobiography in Education*, London: Heinemann.

Abrams, M. (1953) *The Mirror and the Lamp*, New York: Oxford University Press.

Ades, D. (1986) *Photomontage*, London: Thames and Hudson.

Adorno, T. (1984) *Aesthetic Theory*, London: Routledge and Kegan Paul.

Albo, G. (1994) '"Competitive austerity" and the impasse of capitalist employment policy', in Miliband, R. and Panitch, L. (eds) *Between Globalism and Nationalism*, London: Merlin Press.

Ashton, R. (1996) *George Eliot: A Life*, London: Hamish Hamilton.

Ashton-Warner, S. (1985a) *Spinster*, London: Virago Press.

——(1985b) *Teacher*, London: Virago Press.

Atkins, M., Beattie, J. and Dockrell, W. (1993) *Assessment Issues in Higher Education*, Sheffield: Department of Employment (UK Government).

Austin, J. (1962) *How To Do Things With Words*, Oxford: Oxford University Press.

Avis, J., Bloomer, M., Esland, G., Glesson, D. and Hodkinson, P. (1996) *Knowledge and Nationhood*, London: Cassell.

Bakhtin, M. (1984) *Problems of Dostoyevsky's Poetics*, Minneapolis, MN: University of Minnesota Press.

Barnes, J. (1990) *A History of the World in 10 ½ Chapters*, London: Picador.

Barthes, R. (1974) *S/Z*, New York: Hill and Wang.

——(1977) 'The death of the author', in *Image, Music, Text*, Glasgow: Collins/Fontana, pp. 142–8.

Belsey, C. (1980) *Critical Practice*, London: Methuen.

Benjamin, W. (1973a) 'The work of art in the age of mechanical reproduction', in *Illuminations*, Glasgow: Fontana/Collins, pp. 219–54.

——(1973b) 'The storyteller', in *Illuminations*, Glasgow: Fontana/Collins, pp. 83–110.

Benner, P. (1984) *From Novice To Expert: Excellence and Power in Clinical Nursing Practice*, Menlo Park, CA: Addison-Wesley.

Bernlef, J (1988) *Out of Mind*, London: Faber.

Bolton, G. (1994) 'Stories at work: fictional-critical writing as a means of professional development', *British Educational Research Journal*, 20, 1, pp. 55–68.

Boud, D., Keogh, R. and Walker, D. (eds) (1985) *Reflection: Turning Experience into Learning*, London: Kogan Page.

Bourdieu, P. (1996) *The Rules of Art: Genesis and Structure of the Literary Field*, Cambridge: Polity Press.

Bowie, A. (1997) 'Confessions of a New Aesthete', *New Left Review*, no. 225, pp. 105–26.

Boxer, P. (1985) 'Judging the quality of development', in Boud, D., Keogh, R. and Walker, D. (eds) *Reflection: Turning Experience into Learning*, London: Kogan Page, pp. 117–27.

Boyd, E. and Fales, A. (1983) 'Reflective learning: key to learning from experience', *Journal of Humanistic Psychology*, 23, 2, pp. 119–27.

Braverman, H. (1974) 'Scientific management', in *Labour And Monopoly Capitalism*, New York: Monthly Review Press, pp. 85–123.

Brecht, B. (1974) *Brecht on Theatre*, 2nd edn, London: Methuen.

Brookfield, S. (1990) 'Using critical incidents to expore learners' assumptions', in Mezirow, J. and Associates, *Fostering Critical Reflection in Adulthood*, San Francisco, CA: Jossey-Bass, pp. 177–93.

Bruner, J. (1990) *Acts of Meaning*, Cambridge, MA: Harvard University Press.

Bulman, C. (1994) 'Exemplars of reflection', in Palmer, A., Burns, S. and Bulman, C. (eds) *Reflective Practice in Nursing*, Oxford: Blackwell, pp. 131–54.

Burke, K. (1968) 'Psychology and form', in *Counterstatement*, 3rd edn, Berkeley, CA: University of California Press, pp. 29–44.

Cameron, B. and Mitchell, A. (1993) 'Reflective peer journals: developing authentic nurses', *Journal of Advanced Nursing*, 18, pp. 290–7.

Candy, P. (1990) 'Repertory grids: playing verbal chess', in Mezirow, J. and Associates, *Fostering Critical Reflection in Adulthood*, San Francisco, CA: Jossey-Bass, pp. 271–95.

Candy, P., Harri-Augustein, S. and Thomas, L. (1985) 'Reflection and the self-organised learner: a model of learning conversations' in Boud, D., Keogh, R. and Walker, D. (eds) *Reflection: Turning Experience into Learning*, London: Kogan Page, pp. 100–16.

Coleridge, S. T. (1960) [1817] *Biographia Literaria*, London: Dent.

Compton, B. and Galaway, B. (1979) *Social Work Processes*, Illinois: Dorsey Press.

Davis, D. and Boster, L. (1988) 'Multi-faceted therapeutic interventions with the violent psychiatric inpatient', *Hospital and Community Psychiatry*, 39, pp. 463–7.

Deshler, D. (1990) 'Metaphor analysis: exorcising social ghosts', in Mezirow, J. and Associates, *Fostering Critical Reflection in Adulthood*, San Francisco, CA: Jossey-Bass, pp. 296–313.

Dewey, J. (1958) [1934] *Art as Experience*, New York: Capricorn Books.

——(1960) [1933] *How We Think*, Lexington, MA: D. C. Heath.

——(1963) [1938] *Experience and Education*, London: Collier Macmillan.

——(1966) [1916] *Democracy and Education*, New York: Free Press.

Dilthey, W. (1976) [1900] 'The rise of hermeneutics', in Connerton, P. (ed.) *Critical Sociology*, Harmondsworth: Penguin, pp. 104–16.

Dreyfus, S. (1981) 'Formal models vs human situational understanding', Schloss Laxenburg, Austria: International Institute for Applied Systems Analysis.

Drucker, P. (1974) *Management*, Oxford: Butterworth-Heinemann.

——(1992) *Managing for the Future*, Oxford: Butterworth-Heinmann.

Eagleton, T. (1983) *Literary Theory*, Oxford: Blackwell.

——(1990) *The Ideology of the Aesthetic*, Oxford: Blackwell.

——(1996) *The Illusions of Postmodernism*, Oxford: Blackwell.

Egan, K. (1988) 'The origin of imagination and the curriculum', in Egan, K. and Nadaner, D. (eds) *Imagination and Education*, Milton Keynes: Open University Press.

Eisner, E. (1985) *The Art of Educational Evaluation*, Lewes: Falmer Press.

England, H. (1986) *Social Work as Art*, London: Allen and Unwin.

Faulk, M. (1994) *Basic Forensic Psychiatry*, London: Blackwell Scientific Publications.

Festinger, L. (1957) *The Theory of Cognitive Dissonance*, Evanston, IL: Row Peterson.

Field, J. (1991) 'Competency and the pedagogy of labour', *Studies in the Education of Adults*, 23, 1, pp. 41–52.

Forrest, D. (1989) 'The experience of caring', *Journal of Advanced Nursing*, 14, pp. 815–23.

Fowles, J. (1977) *The French Lieutenant's Woman*, London: Triad Granada.

Freire, P. (1972a) *Pedagogy of the Oppressed*, Harmondsworth: Penguin Books.

——(1972b) *Cultural Action for Freedom*, Harmondsworth: Penguin Books.

Freire, P. and Schor, I. (1991) *A Pedagogy for Liberation: Dialogues on Transforming Education*, London: Macmillan.

Frye, N. (1957) *The Anatomy of Criticism*, Princeton, NJ: Princeton University Press.

Gadamer, H-G. (1975) *Truth and Method*, London: Sheed and Ward.

Gardner, H. (1983) *Frames of Mind*, London: Heinemann.

Giddens, A. (1991) *Modernity and Self Identity*, Cambridge: Polity Press.

Goldberg, N. (1991) *Wild Mind*, London: Rider.

Goldman, A. (1995) *Aesthetic Value*, Oxford: Westview Press.

Gould, N. (1996) 'Using imagery in reflective learning', in Gould, N. and Taylor, I. (eds) *Reflective Learning For Social Work*, Aldershot: Arena/Gower, pp. 63–78.

Gould, N. and Taylor, I. (eds) (1996) *Reflective Learning For Social Work*, Aldershot: Arena/Gower.

Graves, D. (1983) *Writing: Teachers and Children at Work*, London: Heinemann.

——(1984) 'The writing process has growing pains', in McVitty, W. (ed.) *Children and Learning*, Rozelle, NSW: Primary English Teaching Association.

Greene, M. (1990) 'Realising literature's emancipatory potential', in Mezirow, J. and Associates, *Fostering Critical Reflection in Adulthood*, San Francisco, CA: Jossey-Bass, pp. 251–68.

Gregory, R. (1974) 'Ways forward for the psychologist: alternative fictions', in Meek, M. (ed.) *The Cool Web*, London: Bodley Head.

Griffin, A. (1983) 'A philosophical analysis of nursing', *Journal of Advanced Nursing*, 8, pp. 289–95.

Grumet, M. (1987) 'The politics of personal knowledge', *Curriculum Inquiry*, 17, 3, pp. 319–29.

——(1990) 'Retrospective: autobiography and the analysis of educational experience', *Cambridge Journal of Education*, 20, 3, pp. 321–5.

Habermas, J. (1970) 'Knowledge and interest', in Emmet, D. and MacIntyre, A. (eds) *Social Theory and Philosophical Analysis*, London: Macmillan.

——(1974) *Theory and Practice*, London: Heinemann.

—— (1976) *Legitimation Crisis*, London: Heinemann.

——(1978) *Knowledge and Human Interests*, 2nd edn, London: Heinemann.

Handy, C. (1991) *The Age of Unreason*, 2nd edn, London: Arrow Books.

Hannagan, V. (1991) 'Starting where we are: one way of warming up', in Sellers, S. (ed.) *Taking Reality by Surprise*, London: The Women's Press.

Haralambos, M. (1991) *Sociology: Themes and Perspectives*, 3rd edn, London: Harper Collins.

Hardy, B. (1974) 'Narrative as primary act of mind', in Meek, M., Warlow, A. and Barton, G. (eds) *The Cool Web*, London: Bodley Head.

Hardy, F. (1966) *Grierson on Documentary*, London: Faber.

Hart, S. (1996) *Beyond Special Needs*, London: Paul Chapman.

Heron, J. (1985) 'The role of reflection in co-operative inquiry', in Boud, D., Keogh, R. and Walker, D. (eds) *Reflection: Turning Experience into Learning*, London: Kogan Page, pp. 128–38.

Hirschhorn, L. (1991) 'Organising feelings toward authority: a case study of reflection-in-action', in Schön, D. (ed.) *The Reflective Turn*, New York: Teachers College Press.

Hixon, L. (1978) *Coming Home: The Experience of Enlightenment in Sacred Traditions*, New York: Larsen.

Hjelle, L. and Ziegler, D. (1981) *Personality Theories: Basic Assumptions, Research, and Applications*, 2nd edn, London: McGraw Hill.

Hunter, K. (1991) *Doctors' Stories*, Princeton, NJ: Princeton, University Press.

Iser, W. (1978) *The Act of Reading*, London: Routledge and Kegan Paul.

Jackson, V. (ed.) (1985) *The Complete Book of Patchwork and Quilting*, London: W. I. Books.

Jameson, F. (1998) 'Theories of the postmodern', in *The Cultural Turn: Selected Writings on the Postmodern, 1983–98*, London: Verso.

Jones, C. and Novak, T. (1993) 'Social work today', *British Journal of Social Work*, 23, pp. 195–212.

Joyce, J. (1956) [1916] *A Portrait of the Artist as a Young Man*, London: Jonathan Cape.

Kant, I. (1966) [1781–7] *Critique of Pure Reason*, New York: Anchor Books.

——(1987) [1790] *Critique of Judgment*, Indianapolis, IN: Hackett Publishing Co.

Kearney, R. (1988) *The Wake of Imagination*, London: Hutchinson.

Kelly, G. (1955) *The Psychology of Personal Constructs*, New York: Norton.

Kerby, A. P. (1991) *Narrative and the Self*, Bloomington, IN: Indiana University Press.

Knights, S. (1985) 'Reflection and learning: the importance of a listener', in Boud, D., Keogh, R. and Walker, D. (eds) *Reflection: Turning Experience into Learning*, London: Kogan Page, pp. 85–90.

Koestler, A. (1964) *The Act of Creation*, London: Penguin/Arkana.

Kolb, D. (1984) *Experiential Learning*, Englewood Cliffs, NJ: Prentice Hall.

Krauss, R. (1998) *The Picasso Papers*, London: Thames and Hudson.

Kubler-Ross, E. (1970) *On Death and Dying*, London: Tavistock.

Kuhn, T. (1962) *The Structure of Scientific Revolutions*, Chicago, IL: University of Chicago Press.

Levi, P. (1986) *The Periodic Table*, London: Abacus Books.

Lévi-Strauss, C. (1981) *The Naked Man*, London: Jonathan Cape.

Lively, P. (1997) 'A Christmas card to one and all', in *Beyond the Blue Mountains*, London: Viking/Penguin.

Lodge, D. (1990) *After Bakhtin*, London: Routledge.

Lukács, G. (1971) *The Theory of the Novel*, London: Merlin Press.

Lyotard, J.-F. (1984) *The Postmodern Condition: A Report on Knowledge*, Manchester: Manchester University Press.

Main, A. (1985) 'Reflection and the development of learning skills', in Boud, D., Keogh, R. and Walker, D. (eds) *Reflection: Turning Experience into Learning*, London: Kogan Page, pp. 91–9.

Maisch, M. and Winter, R. (eds) (1995 [undated]) *'Reflective Writing' by Essex Social Services Staff*, Chelmsford: Essex County Council Social Services and Anglia Polytechnic University.

Mattingly, C. (1991) 'Narrative reflections on practical actions: two learning experiments in reflective storytelling', in Schön, D. (ed.) *The Reflective Turn*, New York: Teachers College Press.

Mayeroff, M. (1971) *On Caring*, New York: Harper and Row.

Merton, R. K. (1957) *Social Theory and Social Structure*, New York: Free Press.

Mezirow, J. and Associates (1990) *Fostering Critical Reflection in Adulthood*, San Francisco, CA: Jossey-Bass.

Moffat, K. (1996) 'Teaching social work as a reflective process', in Gould, N. and Taylor, I. (eds) *Reflective Learning for Social Work*, Aldershot: Arena/Gower, pp. 47–62.

Morgan, G. (1993) *Imaginization: The Art of Creative Management*, Newbury Park, CA: Sage.

Morris, W. (1993) [1889] 'Gothic architecture', in *News from Nowhere and Other Writings*, London: Penguin, pp. 329–47.

——(1993) [1892] Preface to Ruskin's 'The nature of Gothic', in *News from Nowhere and Other Writings*, London: Penguin, pp. 329–47, 367–9.

——(1994) [1884] *A Factory as it Might Be*, Nottingham: Mushroom Bookshop.

Mouffe, C. (1993) *The Return of the Political*, London: Verso.

Naipaul, V. S. (1985) *Finding the Centre*, London: Penguin.

Norris, N. (1991) 'The trouble with competence', *Cambridge Journal of Education*, 21, 3, pp. 331–42.

Palmer, A. (1994) Introduction to Palmer, A., Burns, S. and Bulman, C. (eds) *Reflective Practice in Nursing*, Oxford: Blackwell, pp. 1–9.

Parker, F. (1991) *Victorian Patchwork*, London: Trafalgar Square Press.

Parsons, T. (1954) 'The professions and social structure', in *Essays in Sociological Theory*, New York: Collier Macmillan.

Paterson, B. (1995) 'Developing and maintaining reflection in clinical journals', *Nurse Education Today*, 15, pp. 211–20.

Peters, T. (1989) *Thriving on Chaos*, London: Pan Books.

Pierson, W. (1998) 'Reflection and nurse education', *Journal of Advanced Nursing*, 27, pp. 165–70.

Polanyi, M. (1962) *Personal Knowledge*, London: Routledge and Kegan Paul.

Powell, J. P. (1985) 'Autobiographical learning', in Boud, D., Keogh, R. and Walker, D. (eds) *Reflection: Turning Experience into Learning*, London: Kogan Page, pp. 41–51.

Propp, V. (1968) *Morphology of the Folktale*, 2nd edn, Austin, TX: University of Texas Press.

Raban, J. (1986) *Old Glory*, London: Picador.

Roche, M. (1992) *Rethinking Citizenship: Welfare, Ideology and Change in Modern Society*, Cambridge: Polity Press.

Rogers, C. (1983) *Freedom To Learn*, Columbus, OH: Bell and Howell.

Rorty, R. (1989) *Contingency, Irony, Solidarity*, Cambridge: Cambridge University Press.

Rotha, P. (1936) *Documentary Film*, London: Faber.

Rushdie, S. (1982) *Midnight's Children*, London: Picador.

Ruskin, J. (1985) [1853] 'The nature of gothic', in *Unto This Last and Other Writings*, London: Penguin, pp. 77–109.

Sangharakshita (1993) *A Survey of Buddhism*, 7th edn, Glasgow: Windhorse Publications.

Sartre, J.-P. (1967) *What Is Literature?*, London: Methuen.

——(1972) [1940] *The Psychology of the Imagination*, London: Routledge.

Schön, D. (1971) *Beyond the Stable State*, London: Temple Smith.

——(1983) *The Reflective Practitioner*, New York: Basic Books.

——(1987) *Educating the Reflective Practitioner*, San Francisco, CA: Jossey-Bass.

——(ed.) (1991) *The Reflective Turn*, New York: Teachers College Press.

Schopenhauer, A. (1995) [1819] *The World as Will and Idea*, London: Dent.

Senge, P. (1990) *The Fifth Discipline: The Art and Practice of the Learning Organization*, London: Century Business.

Shapin, S. (1994) *A Social History of Truth*, Chicago, IL: University of Chicago Press.

Shelley, P. (1988) [1821] 'A Defense of Poetry', in Selden, R. (ed.) *The Theory of Criticism*, Harlow: Longman, pp. 483–5.

Shusterman, R. (1992) *Pragmatist Aesthetics*, Oxford: Blackwell.

Smith, F. (1992) *To Think: In Language, Learning and Education*, London: Routledge.

Sobiechowska, P. (1998) 'A critical review and analysis of reflective writing for professional practitioners', unpublished M.A. dissertation, Chelmsford: Anglia Polytechnic University.

Taylor, I. (1996) 'Reflective learning and social work for the twenty-first century', in Gould, N. and Taylor, I. (eds) *Reflective Learning for Social Work*, Aldershot: Arena/Gower, pp. 153–61.

Tripp, D. (1993) *Critical Incidents in Teaching*, London: Routledge.

Tschudin, V. (1997) 'Nursing as a moral art', in Marks-Maran, D. and Rose, P. (eds) *Reconstructing Nursing: Beyond Art and Science*, London: Bailliere-Tindall.

Vygotsky, L. (1962) *Thought and Language*, New York: Wiley.

Waldman, D. (1992) *Collage, Assemblage and the Found Object*, London: Phaidon Press.

Walker, D. (1985) 'Writing and reflection', in Boud, D., Keogh, R. and Walker, D. (eds) *Reflection: Turning Experience into Learning*, London: Kogan Page, pp. 52–68.

Warnock, M. (1976) *Imagination*, London: Faber.

Welleck, R. and Warren, A. (1963) *Theory of Literature*, 3rd edn, Harmondsworth: Penguin.

Wertheimer, A. (1966) *Changing Days: Developing New Day Opportunities with People who have Learning Disabilities*, London: Kings Fund.

White, A. (1990) *The Language of Imagination*, Oxford: Blackwell.

Whitehead, M. (1980) 'Once upon a time?', *English in Education*, 14, 1.

Winter, R. (1986) 'Fictional-critical writing: an approach to case study research by practitioners', *Cambridge Journal of Education*, 16, 3, pp. 175–82.

——(1989) *Learning from Experience: Principles and Practice in Action Research*, Lewes: Falmer Press.

——(1991) 'Interviewers, interviewees and the exercise of power (fictional-critical writing as a method for educational research)', *British Educational Research Journal*, pp. 251–62.

Winter, R. and Maisch, M. (1996) *Professional Competence and Higher Education: The ASSET Programme*, London: Falmer Press.

Wittgenstein, L. (1967) *Philosophical Investigations*, Oxford: Blackwell.

Wolf, A. (1998) 'Two sides of A4 will not do the trick', *Times Higher Education Supplement*, 22 May, p. 11.

Wright, R. (1972) *Native Son*, Harmondsworth: Penguin.

Yelloly, M. and Henkel, M. (eds) (1995) *Teaching and Learning in Social Work: Towards Reflective Practice*, London: Jessica Kingsley.

Zemon Davis, N. (1987) *Fiction in the Archives*, Cambridge: Polity Press.

INDEX